D1442800

UNCOMMON SENSE

UNCOMMON SENSE

The Strangest Ideas from the Smartest Philosophers

Andrew Pessin

ROWMAN & LITTLEFIELD PUBLISHERS, INC.
Lanham • Boulder • New York • Toronto • Plymouth, UK

Published by Rowman & Littlefield Publishers, Inc.
A wholly owned subsidiary of The Rowman & Littlefield Publishing Group, Inc.
4501 Forbes Boulevard, Suite 200, Lanham, Maryland 20706
www.rowman.com

10 Thornbury Road, Plymouth PL6 7PP, United Kingdom

British Library Cataloguing in Publication Information Available

Library of Congress Cataloging-in-Publication Data

Pessin, Andrew, 1962-
  Uncommon sense : the strangest ideas from the smartest philosophers / Andrew Pessin.
    p. cm.
  ISBN 978-1-4422-1608-2 (cloth : alk. paper) — ISBN 978-1-4422-1610-5 (electronic)
  1. Philosophy—History. 2. Philosophers. I. Title.
  B74.P47 2012
  190—dc23

                                                                                    2012003460

∞™ The paper used in this publication meets the minimum requirements of American National Standard for Information Sciences—Permanence of Paper for Printed Library Materials, ANSI/NISO Z39.48-1992.

Printed in the United States of America

"For my fantastic wife GR, who makes every kind of sense,
and for my fantastic boys ERP, NRP, and NAP,
who make absolutely none and are
all the more fantastic for so doing ..."

Contents

Introduction:
"Stop Making Sense"

In my college days I discovered that nothing can be imagined which is too strange or incredible to have been said by some philosopher.

—René Descartes (1596–1650)

Not only is the world stranger than we imagine, it is stranger than we can imagine.

—Sir Arthur Eddington (1882–1944)

There's a famous anecdote related by the great ancient Greek philosopher Plato about the even more ancient (though slightly less great) Greek philosopher Thales. The latter was once walking about at night gazing upward at the starry sky, thinking profound and abstract thoughts about the heavens, when he tumbled into a well in front of him. A "witty and amusing" young girl nearby found this quite hilarious and observed that while Thales might be passionate about understanding nature, he was rather clueless when it came to seeing what was right before his eyes. As Plato then succinctly observes, the same joke applies equally well to all those "odd birds" who spend their lives in philosophy.

Except that the last laugh just might belong to the philosopher. For what if—just what if—seeing what's right before your eyes isn't all it's cracked up to be?

True, smarty-pants philosophers sometimes get lost in their own thoughts to the point where they fall into proverbial wells. They sometimes provide an inexpensive source of amusement and entertainment for the rest of us in their general lack of worldliness and their apparent disconnectedness to reality. But then again, when you think about it a little, if you want to get at a genuine understanding of the world, if you want to *really* get connected to "reality," who *do* you want to talk to exactly: a great philosopher such as Thales or Plato, or one of *us*—that is, the ordinary person making fun of them?

What *we* have going for us, of course, is our healthy abundance of good old-fashioned common sense. But what if the truth about things does not in the end *make* much sense—or at least make common sense?

Think about what common sense is, after all.

It's what we believe about things when we don't give them much thought. It's what we were taught in our childhood to believe about things by people who themselves believed them without much thought, and it's what we have continued to believe without much thought ever since. It's almost always simple and straightforward, the kind of thing that we can capture in a sentence or two: "What we see in front of us is really there," for example, or "Some things cause other things," or "Time flows," or "It's good to be a good person." It's what almost everyone believes about things, with near-universal consensus.

But now that we *are* actually beginning to think about it a little, what are the chances that common sense, so described, should actually be correct? Do we really imagine that the world is simple and straightforward? The world that exists on unimaginable scales of space and time, where space seems both to go on to infinity and be infinitely divisible, where time too seems to have neither beginning nor end? The world that requires advanced mathematics and not one but *two* theories of relativity to describe it? Simple and straightforward? Do we really imagine that the truths about the world might be adequately expressible in simple short sentences?

And then there's the fact that common sense is what almost everyone believes.

Well, the principles of democracy are splendid when it comes to choosing our political leaders and related matters, for all sorts of reasons. But it's not at all clear that their beneficial use extends much beyond that. There's a famous debate between Plato and his equally great student Aristotle, for example, on whether universals must be instantiated in particulars. (Don't ask!) There's another famous debate between influential Christian thinkers Anselm and Aquinas on whether the existence of God can be proved a priori. (Again, don't ask!) The seventeenth-century physicist Isaac Newton debated the philosopher G. W. Leibniz over whether space is "absolute" or "relational." (Don't even *think* about asking!)

When it comes to resolving such debates, to deciding which competing position is correct, no one believes that we should simply submit the question to a majority vote—or at least not to a majority vote of merely us card-carrying common sensers.

Indeed, as Descartes observes shortly after the passage quoted at the start,

[A] majority vote is worthless as a proof of truths that are at all difficult to discover; for a single [person] is much more likely to hit upon them than a group of people.

When it comes to determining subtle or unusual things—such as the truths about the world—we need more than our common sense.

We need philosophy.

Philosophy is what you get when you begin to actually think about things.

When you begin to think about what's right before your eyes and start to see questions where you previously assumed there were facts. When you begin to think about things in a new way, in a bigger way, beyond the here and now: when you begin to ask not merely how things really are but *why* they are, why there exists something rather than nothing at all, and how we are capable even of knowing *that* there exists something rather than nothing.

It's also what you get when you substitute, for your hunches and intuitions and common sense about things, something else: *arguments.* Not the kind of arguments we have with our friends and parents and partners, of course—the ones where voices get raised and mean things get said and everyone stops talking to everyone else, enjoyable as all that may be. Rather, *philosophical* arguments, chains of careful reasoning, from premises to conclusions, that we only occasionally need to bolster with a loud voice or a juicy insult. Good philosophical arguments only rarely end up changing your feelings about anyone, but they can sometimes do something far more profound.

They can change your mind.

They can get you to believe some pretty subtle and unusual and downright-strange things. Things that are about as far removed from common sense as they could possibly be. But when you *do* come to believe these things, you will believe them on the basis of good and solid reasoning, the kind of reasoning that is ultimately the foundation of making any sense at all.

Welcome, in other words, to the world of *un*common sense.

This book aims to be your initial guidebook to that world. Like any guidebook, it has its limits. Reading *Let's Go Europe* may be entertaining in its own right, but it just cannot substitute for actually going to Europe. Nevertheless, the primary goals of any travel book are, no doubt, both to whet your appetite toward actually making the trip and to prepare you well once you do.

This book's goals are the same.

It will take you through the history of Western philosophy, offering glimpses of some of the strangest ideas that some of the greatest minds of Western thought have come up with—or perhaps the greatest ideas that some of the strangest minds have come up with. We'll start at the beginning, with Plato, widely recognized as "the father of Western philosophy," and work toward the present day. Along the way, we shall visit with some representatives of the splendid medieval period, which can only correctly be called a "dark ages" of philosophy if, by the phrase "dark ages," you mean a period of profound insight, clarity, and inventiveness. We'll also spend time with some of the major early modern thinkers, beginning with the famous René "I think therefore I am" Descartes, himself generally recognized as "the father of modern philosophy" (which may or may not make Plato into a grandfather; I'm not sure). And we'll wrap up with a look at some of the most recent ideas of contemporary philosophers.

Selecting the contents for the volume was both easy and hard.

There were three major criteria for inclusion. First, the idea in question had to be very "strange," that is, far removed from ordinary common sense. Second, the philosopher proposing or defending the idea had to be very smart, even for a philosopher. Third, the philosopher had to offer very powerful arguments for the idea being proposed. The easy part of the selection process was that the twenty-five-hundred-year history of Western philosophy offers no shortage of ideas and philosophers meeting the three criteria. The hard part was limiting myself to eighteen, as a representative sample. But I console myself, for the sake of all those strange, smart, argumentative philosophers who had to be left behind, that if this book is successful, there could always be a sequel.

And if a guidebook aims to whet your appetite for the journey, its introduction, I suppose, should whet your appetite for the guidebook itself. So to that end, allow me to dangle before you a few of the things you will hear about—and maybe become persuaded of—by the time you're done with this book.

The world includes, it turns out, more than what meets the eye or than can be perceived by *any* human senses. Your actions are entirely caused by factors outside your control, but they may count as "free" anyway. You can prove that God exists just by thinking about it. And not merely that God exists but that God continuously creates you, or *re*-creates you, at every moment, and that He is the only true cause of anything that ever happens. Nonhuman animals, meanwhile, don't have minds at all: lacking thoughts, sensations, consciousness, they're just complicated mindless machines. Physical bodies don't actually have most of the properties they appear to have: colors, for example, exist not in bodies but only in the perceiver's mind. In fact, physical bodies *themselves* exist only in the perceivers' minds, as there is no physical world at all! Oh, and by the way, despite what I said a moment ago, there's no such thing as causation after all: things just happen, with nothing causing anything. Also, morality pretty much has things backward, as the things you think are good and evil are more or less reversed. But there may not be any rush in correcting your views here, because time doesn't actually flow; and anyway, your mental states (such as your beliefs) are not entirely up to you, as they are not entirely in your head or mind. And did I mention the idea that although animals lack minds, subatomic particles have them, even though the physical world doesn't exist?

You get the idea.

Or the ideas. Strange ideas, to be sure, and not at all what you'd ordinarily think about the world but what, perhaps, you *should* think. For if the world itself is a strange place, as Eddington suggests in the opening quotation, and if we seek the truth, then it is to the strange ideas that we must turn—especially when they are supported by such surprisingly powerful arguments.

So that young girl may have had a good laugh at Thales's expense, but Thales himself may have been the one who actually had things, all things, the true things, right. For if we seek the truth, the real truth, the *deep* truth about things, then maybe the bottom of the well is where we ought to be.

May this book help cushion your fall.

1

Plato

More Than What Meets the Eye

Strange Idea

There's more to the world than what you see—or even *could* see.

For, in addition to the ordinary objects that we may perceive around us, there also exist in a completely separate, nonphysical realm eternal, uncreated, unchanging—and unperceivable—objects called *Forms*.

Major Proponent

Plato (429 BCE–347 BCE)

Brief Biography

It has been said, and not inaccurately, that all of Western philosophy is one long footnote to Plato. Though Plato was, as a respected citizen of ancient Athens, deeply involved in the turbulent political events of his time, he eventually removed himself to become even more deeply involved in creating the art of philosophizing as we know it today. In about 387 BCE, on land dedicated to the demigod Academus, he founded a school correspondingly called the Academy, which endured as a model for "academics" until the Roman emperor Justinian finally shuttered it in 529 CE. Plato spent most of his own life teaching and writing, leaving to posterity a series of philosophical dialogues remarkable as much for their literary style as for their philosophical depth. The most famous of these is perhaps *Republic*, in which Plato not only outlines his model for the ideal political state but also shows how such a state must be grounded in an understanding of the human mind, and the soul, and morality, and knowledge, and pretty much everything else. He died in 347 BCE, leaving the Academy in the care of his nephew and philosophy itself in the care of millennias' worth of annotators.

The World's Most Famous Student

Most teachers are familiar with the following phenomenon. You give a beautiful lecture (in your humble opinion, anyway): clear, organized, methodical, and maybe even deep. Then your students write a paper about the material, and it comes back to you garbled, disorganized, haphazard, and shallow. You release a deep sigh of frustration until you realize that your own teachers probably felt the same about the papers *you* wrote as a student.

One hopes that Socrates felt differently about his own great student Plato, who was to capture Socrates's teachings and bequeath them to posterity.

Most of Plato's philosophical writings famously take the form of dialogues between various characters, and many of them feature his teacher Socrates (469 BCE–399 BCE). The question debated by scholars is to what degree, exactly, Socrates is *merely* a character: are these dialogues accurately reporting Socrates's views, or does Plato merely invoke Socrates to voice his own views? It doesn't help to resolve this problem that Socrates himself left no writings behind, so what we even know of his views is primarily what is expressed in Plato's dialogues.

Well, with little to go on here, I shall simply treat Plato as the one responsible for this chapter's strange idea. Whether or not his teacher deserves the credit—or discredit, as the case may be—shall have to remain unresolved.

Our first task, then, is to get clearer on what Plato's *Forms* are supposed to be.

What Exactly Are Forms?

Plato and his followers, as his own great student Aristotle (384 BCE–322 BCE) remarked, "separated universals from the particulars" and called them *Forms*.[1]

Got that?

Forms are *separated* universals.

Separated from what? From the "sensible order," that is, from the world as we can sense it with our eyes, our ears, and so on. Since Forms are not part of the sensible order, they are then taken to exist in some "separate" realm, distinct from that of the ordinary objects around us.

Moreover, they are separated *universals*.

Something is a *universal* insofar as it is or can be "repeatable," that is, occur in many particular things (or just *particulars*). For example, suppose that some grass, an unripe banana, and a certain automobile are all the same shade of green: the same greenness appears in each individual instance, or particular, so "Greenness" is a universal. Similarly, a ball, a boulder, and the sun may all be round: "Roundness" is then the universal occurring in each particular round thing. Or, of course, there are many electrons in existence: each individual electron is a particular, while "Electron" or "Electronhood" is a universal "repeating" itself in each particular.

In "separating Forms from the sensible order," then, Plato is suggesting that things such as Greenness, Roundness, and Electronhood are distinct from, or exist separately from, the individual things that *are* green, round, and electrons.

One Strange Idea Begets Others

Once you separate Forms in this way, you'll quickly move on to other strange ideas.

For one example, while individual green things, round things, or electrons—particulars—obviously exist in the world around us, if Greenness and the other Forms are separated from them, then they must exist "elsewhere" (whatever that means).

Similarly, the particulars typically *are* objects of our senses: we can see individual green things and round things and even observe (at least with fancy equipment) individual electrons. But if the Forms are separate from the particulars, then they themselves cannot be "seen" in the same way or sense.

Furthermore, while all the particulars around us are constantly in flux (coming into and going out of being, changing, etc.), the Forms, separate from them, may themselves be uncreated and unchanging: when a banana ripens, a particular individual thing may change from green to yellow, but Greenness itself, what it is to *be* green, never changes. Similarly, Socrates the human being may change over time in many ways: he may become more or less virtuous, taller, or shorter, and he may even, upon dying, lose his humanity altogether—but what Virtue itself is, as well as Height and Humanity, does not change.

Separating Forms from the sensible order, in other words, makes them into sorts of things very different from ordinary objects.

How Many Forms *Are* There?

The short answer is, a lot.

In his earlier dialogues, Plato was primarily concerned with Forms related to ethical concerns, such as Justice, Piety, and Goodness. To investigate these is to ask a question, such as, for example, "What is Goodness?" An answer might begin through a listing of various actions or things that are good, but that, of course, merely tells us where Goodness may be found, not what Goodness or the Good actually *is*. To determine *that* requires generating a definition of the Good, a definition such that every thing that fits the definition is good and every thing that doesn't, isn't.

And this process, the formulating of a definition, involves something other than our senses: we don't merely "look and see" what Goodness is but have to *think* about what it is that all good things might share. Plato writes,

> Do we say that there is such a thing as the Just itself, or not? We do say so, by Zeus. And the Beautiful, and the Good? Of course. And have you ever seen any of these things with your eyes? In no way, he said. Or have you ever grasped them with any of your bodily senses? I am speaking of all things such as Bigness, Health, Strength and, in a word, the reality of all other things, that which each of them essentially is. Is what is most true in them contemplated through the [senses], or is this the position: . . . he will [know] this most perfectly who approaches the object with thought [intellect] alone. (*Phaedo* 65d–66a, 57)[2]

Note here how this passage reflects the idea that the Form is separate from the particulars themselves, for those latter we surely do detect via our senses. Note, too, Plato's view that the Forms are "the reality" of things, "that which each of them essentially is": the Form of Goodness is what goodness essentially *is*, while particular good things merely reflect Goodness without capturing it completely. Furthermore, Plato adds elsewhere that the Forms are "perfect" and are what the particulars reflecting them strive, though not fully successfully, to be.

All these points are perhaps best illustrated by Plato's conception of mathematical Forms.

Consider the Form of the Triangle: the definition or essence of a triangle is to be a three-sided closed figure. But while every particular triangle we may encounter through our senses, every actual triangular thing, will reflect this essence, none will express it perfectly. For the line segments composing the sides of the Triangle are both perfectly straight and purely one-dimensional, lacking all breadth; but the sides of every actual particular triangle will be neither *perfectly* straight nor *entirely* lacking in breadth. We might say that every particular triangle is an "approximation" of the perfect Triangle, while "the Triangle" is the real deal. The same goes, naturally, for particular good things, beautiful things, and so on.

So far, then, Plato allows ethical Forms, mathematical Forms, and Forms such as Bigness, Health, Beauty, and Strength. But now that isn't all. In his late work, the *Timaeus*, Plato examines the creation of the universe. Here he suggests that, prior to creating, the Creator models what he creates on the Forms, much as a craftsperson might have a certain model or idea of a bed (say) in his head before building it. But, of course, one cannot impose Forms on nothing, any more than one could build a bed with no materials: there must be some matter or material with or on which to work. So just as a human craftsperson might take some wood and fashion it into a bed, so Plato's Creator took the matter of the universe and imposed Forms on it. He made humans and horses and stones by imposing Humanity, Horsehood, and Stoniness on the matter of the universe. This picture suggests that there are Forms corresponding to *every* natural kind of thing there is and, possibly, to every kind of artifact as well.

The analogy suggests one further question: if the Creator created all the particular things of the universe by imposing Forms on matter, then where did the Forms and matter *themselves* come from?

Answer: nowhere.

Unlike the particular things, which come and go and constantly change, Forms and matter simply always have been around, eternal, unchanging, and uncreated. As we'll explore in chapter 5, we have here the strange idea that the universe has, on the fundamental level, always existed.

Why Should We Believe in the Existence of Forms?

An excellent question and one, perhaps, you've been itching to ask.

Now Plato himself never sets down his arguments for the existence of Forms in any systematic way. But fortunately for us, his attentive student Aristotle summarizes several such arguments that are at least Platonic in nature.[3]

(1) The Meanings of General Terms

Every human being may be called "human"; every animal may be called "animal." Yet in no case is the name for some particular individual synonymous with the name for the general property or kind: when we say "Fred is human," what we mean by "Fred" is not what we mean by "human," obviously, for "Fred" applies only to that individual, while "human" applies to many others. Similarly, the name "Rover" is not synonymous with the general term "animal." Words such as "human" and "animal" therefore refer to something more general than any of the particulars around us, that is, a Form. So there must exist Forms, to serve as the meanings for our general terms.

Now this argument may invite the following objection.

Sure, "Fred" applies to only this one guy, while "human" applies to many others. But that may be only because "human" simply means "every human being," and while that meaning is more general than "Fred," that's not enough to make this "general" thing somehow *be* a "Form" existing separately from all particulars. Rather, the general thing is just the collection of all the particulars itself, of all the human beings—a collection as changing, transient, and this-worldly as the particular human beings themselves. So argument 1, the objection concludes, does not support belief in Plato's Forms.

The next three arguments are now responses to this objection.

(2) Destruction of Particulars

The word "human," the response now goes, cannot merely mean "the collection of all human beings," because what "human" means remains fixed even while that collection itself constantly changes. As we've seen, Socrates the human being may change, but what it is to *be* a human being never does; more generally, particular humans come and go, are born and die, but what it is to *be* human—what we mean by the general term "human"—does not. So there is more to the meaning of "human" than simply the collection of all particular human beings, and this additional thing is the Form, Humanity.

(3) Knowing What We Mean

To this point may be added another. We often know fully well what we mean when we use a general term even when we have no idea just which and how many particular individuals fit that term. In this case, we know fully well what we mean by "human" even when we haven't the faintest notion which and how many particular human beings there currently may be. Thus, what we mean by "human" is not merely "the collection of all humans," again, but rather something more general in nature: a Form.

(4) Sameness or Similarity

And indeed, there's a good *reason* we apply the same general word to distinct individual particulars. There's a reason that "human" applies to the many individual humans: it's that they are the same with respect to whatever we mean by "human." Imagine, to illustrate, that you are in the jungle looking for new species of animals. You come upon one animal and then another, and you determine that they belong to the same "species." How? Because they share certain key features: they are both mammals, they both have four legs and a certain striped pattern, and so on. They are both called "tiger," in other words, because they are both tigers: they are members of the same kind insofar as there is one thing they both are, namely *tiger*.

But that is to say that one thing—*Tigerhood*—is present in both of them. This particular tiger may be over here, that particular tiger may be over there, but Tigerhood is present in both places. Indeed, Tigerhood is *fully* present in both places because each animal is fully, completely, a tiger.

But think about what this means.

Sometimes we explain why two things are similar by saying they "share" a property. This is red and that is red; they share the property of Redness. But what does it mean to share something? Two people may share a condo, or a name, or (if they are conjoined) even a kidney: in each case, there is literally one thing to which both have access. So if this is a tiger and that is a tiger, there must literally be one thing—Tigerhood—to which both have access. But this one thing cannot literally be located in any one place. If it were located over *here*, the tiger over *there* couldn't access it; if it were over *there*, then the tiger over *here* couldn't access it. Indeed two tigers both have access to Tigerhood even if they are miles or continents apart. So whatever Tigerhood is, exactly, it is not literally located *anywhere*.

It is, in other words, a Form.

And like all Forms, the Form of the Tiger is separate from all the individuals who are themselves tigers.

That's why you should believe in the existence of Forms.

Philosophers and Cave Persons

So Forms are separate from the particulars of the world. Unlike particulars, they are uncreated and eternal and unchanging, and particular things are modeled after them and strive to be like them. As such, Forms are more perfect than, and ultimately more "real" than, the particulars of this world.

Just try telling all that to your friends.

For common sense tends toward precisely the opposite position.

What's "real," most people think, is what you can see and hear and touch. Anything else is just a fiction of some sort, a creation of the mind, an "idea." That's why many ordinary people look askance at the philosopher who incomprehensibly speaks of mysterious realms of separate beings!

The painful irony, from Plato's perspective, is that common sense has things entirely backward. It is the philosopher, grasping reality through careful reasoning and intellect, who has things right, while the ordinary individual, relying on what appears to his or her senses, gets things wrong.

Plato illustrates the situation in perhaps the most famous analogy in philosophy. In *Republic,* he writes,

> Imagine human beings living in an underground, cavelike dwelling, with an entrance a long way up. . . . They've been there since childhood, fixed in the same place, with their necks and legs fettered, able to see only in front of them.

... Light is provided by a fire burning far above and behind them. Also behind them, but on higher ground, there is a path stretching between them and the fire. Imagine that along this path a low wall has been built, like the screen in front of puppeteers above which they show their puppets. . . . Then also imagine that there are people along the wall, carrying all kinds of artifacts that project above it—statues of people and other animals. . . . Do you suppose . . . that these prisoners see anything . . . besides the shadows that the fire casts on the wall in front of them? (*Republic* VII, 514a–515b, 1132–33)

The cave people see not themselves or each other but only *shadows* of things projected on the wall in front of them, shadows of the things being carried by the people above and behind them. Since this is all they have ever seen, they believe that these shadows are what there is: reality consists in these "objects" and their motions.

But now consider

what being released from their bonds and cured of their ignorance would naturally be like. . . . When one of them was freed and suddenly compelled to stand up, turn his head, walk, and look up toward the light, he'd be pained and dazzled and unable to see the things whose shadows he'd seen before. (*Republic* VII, 515c–d, 1133)

Being used to seeing only shadows in dim light, a freed individual would initially have trouble seeing the actual carved objects themselves in front of the fire; and if you were to tell him that the carved objects were "more real" than the shadows he'd been accustomed to seeing, he would be very perplexed!

But now imagine further,

if someone dragged him away from there . . . up the rough, steep path . . . into the sunlight, wouldn't he be pained and irritated at being treated that way? And when he came into the light, with the sun filling his eyes, wouldn't he be unable to see a single one of the things now said to be true? (*Republic* VII, 515e–516a, 1133)

If seeing the carved objects before the fire was difficult, imagine how much more difficult it would be to look at the real objects, after which those carved objects were modeled, in the real sunlight! The freed individual would be disoriented, perhaps inclined to run back to the "reality" he previously knew. But in time, with some acclimation, he'd be able to see the trees, the animals, the objects here in the sunlight and come to recognize that the carved objects were themselves imitations of, imperfect copies of, those real objects; and then come to recognize that the shadows cast by those carved objects, which he initially took to be "reality," were about as far removed from true reality, outside the cave, as one could get.

Well, the overall analogy is clear.

The particular objects around us are like the shadows in the cave, while the Forms are the "real" objects outside the cave.

Those ordinary people who, by common sense, take the objects we perceive around us to be real are like the cave people who see only shadows and take these shadows for reality.

The philosopher is the one who has escaped from the cave and come into the sunlight, and who truly perceives reality, namely the Forms.

And now it is the philosopher who has the perhaps unenviable task of convincing those remaining in the cave, who have never seen the fire or the sunlight, that what they have been perceiving their entire lives is in fact far removed from what is truly, ultimately real.

And doing so without, hopefully, getting himself fettered into the chains of a psychiatric hospital while he's at it.

The Good Life of the Philosopher

Sign me up, Plato says!

For despite challenges such as these, he thinks, the life of the philosopher is the most worthwhile one.

For the normal person's life is devoted to the particular objects in the world, to perceiving them, loving them, acquiring them, and so on. The philosopher, to the contrary, shifts her attention from the particulars to the Forms, which are separate from this world. The nonphilosopher may be drawn to this or that beautiful object or person, but the philosopher is drawn to Beauty itself. The nonphilosopher attempts to acquire that which cannot permanently be acquired, the changing, transient particular objects of this world. But the philosopher aims to acquire, through reasoning and intellect, the eternal unchanging objects that are the Forms. The philosopher's life is occupied, in short, with objects far superior to those of the nonphilosopher's life.

But there's more.

Think, for a moment, about how the different Forms are all related to each other. The Form of a particular breed of cow (say, Holstein Cow) is an instance of the Form of Cow in general; but then Cow is itself an instance of the Form of Mammal, in turn an instance of Animal, in turn an instance of Living Thing, in turn an instance of Thing, or Being, and so on. All these biological Forms are closely related to each other in specific ways. Similarly, as soon as you reflect on the mathematical Form of Triangle, you can begin proving all sorts of things about triangles you may not have realized: that their angles add up to 180 degrees, the largest side is opposite the largest angle, and so on. All these mathematical Forms—Triangle, Angle, Side—are themselves related to each other in specific ways.

To study the Forms is ultimately to study their order and interrelations. It is to come to see how they all hang together, how despite their diversity there is a single system in which they all play specific roles. And—here's what's in it for you if you're thinking about signing up—when you study this order, Plato believes, *your soul itself becomes ordered.*

And a well-ordered soul is what we're all ultimately looking for, what's ultimately best for us, even if most of us don't realize it.

Indeed Plato extends the analogy of the cave to encompass this scenario as well. The freed individual first becomes accustomed to gazing at the carved objects in the fire, then to gazing at the "real" objects in the world outside the cave. But then, in due course, Plato writes,

> Finally . . . he'd be able to see the sun, not images of it . . . but the sun itself, in its own place, and be able to study it. (*Republic* VII, 516b, 1134)

The philosopher's gaze moves from the ordinary objects around us to the Forms but then, ultimately, to the very source of all illumination itself. In the analogy, it's the sun that makes all objects visible; but for the philosopher, Plato thinks, it is the very Form of the Good itself. Indeed, all Forms are particular instances of this higher goodness of which I've been speaking: the Form of the Good is the most perfect Goodness of which even all the particular Forms are mere imperfect reflections. And so, just as we are led from thinking of particular tigers to thinking of Tigerhood, we are led from thinking of individual Forms to thinking of Goodness itself: the Form that ultimately makes all other Forms graspable or "intelligible."

For the Form of the Good is what ultimately *in*forms the whole universe; all actual objects, in reflecting their corresponding Forms, ultimately reflect the Form of the Good. And the philosopher's soul, in coming to grasp the Good itself, therefore comes to grasp the fundamental ordering principle of all reality. In that moment, her soul achieves its highest possible state.

That is why the philosophical life is ultimately the best life—despite the nasty glances and occasional psychiatric fetterings. For you get, in the end, a pretty impressive payoff for endorsing that one small little strange idea about the Forms: a well-ordered soul in harmony with the overall Good of the universe.

May we sign you up, too?

Notes

1. See Aristotle's *Metaphysics* 1078b12–34, 356, in Ackrill (1987).
2. All Plato quotations are from Cooper (1997).
3. See Grube (1935/1980, 5ff.) for detailed discussion.

Primary Sources

Ackrill, J. L., ed. 1987. *A New Aristotle Reader.* Princeton, NJ: Princeton University Press.

Cooper, John, ed. 1997. *Plato: Complete Works.* Indianapolis, IN: Hackett.

Recommended Secondary Sources

Grube, G. M. A. 1935/1980. *Plato's Thought.* Indianapolis, IN: Hackett.

Kraut, Richard, ed. 1992. *The Cambridge Companion to Plato.* Cambridge, UK: Cambridge University Press.

———. 2011. "Plato." In *Stanford Encyclopedia of Philosophy*, edited by Edward N. Zalta. http://plato.stanford.edu/archives/fall2011/entries/plato/.

Silverman, Allan. 2008. "Plato's Middle Period Metaphysics and Epistemology." In *Stanford Encyclopedia of Philosophy*, edited by Edward N. Zalta. http://plato.stanford.edu/archives/win2008/entries/plato-metaphysics/.

2

Aristotle

NEITHER YOU WILL NOR YOU WON'T

STRANGE IDEA

Some ordinary statements about the future are neither true nor false.

You would think that simple statements such as "You will wear your blue shirt tomorrow" must be either true or false: you either will wear it or you won't, after all, since there are no other options.

But you'd be wrong.

MAJOR PROPONENT

Aristotle (384 BCE–322 BCE)

BRIEF BIOGRAPHY

Talk about a know-it-all! Plato's most famous student, Aristotle, didn't limit himself to philosophy but knew—in fact himself *discovered*—almost everything there was to know in his time. Born in northeastern Greece, Aristotle moved to Athens at about seventeen to enroll in Plato's Academy, where he then stayed two decades until Plato's death in 347 BCE. After moving around for a while, he got the ultimate gig, a job tutoring the Macedonian king's thirteen-year-old son Alexander, not quite yet known to the world as Alexander the Great. When, after a couple of years, the young Alexander had some conquering to go do, Aristotle returned to Athens and founded his own school, the Lyceum. Here, he and his students worked in the arts, astronomy, biology, botany, cosmology, and ethics, to list just some things at the start of the alphabet, not to mention philosophy. When the political situation got uncomfortable, Aristotle left Athens, not wanting to entice the city to do to him what it had done to Socrates (think: hemlock). He died quietly, not of hemlock, on the tiny island of Euboea.

Feeling Free

Consider some typical action: for example, putting on your blue shirt this morning.

Did you perform this action freely?

To many of us, it seems perfectly obvious that we did.

We typically *feel* free, to be sure, in many of our actions and choices. You were presumably not aware of any people or forces *compelling* you in your choice of the blue shirt over any other shirt (or dress, etc.), and whether you made the decision quickly or spent time deliberating, it no doubt felt like it was "up to you" what you ended up choosing to wear.

In fact, it probably felt as if you could do, or could have done, *otherwise* than what you did do: you could have gone with the black shirt or the green dress, although you happened not to this time. Indeed, you could even have chosen to wear nothing at all, strictly speaking; for even if that option—so frowned upon under the norms of our stuffy old culture—didn't occur to you consciously, it's hard not to think that it *was* open to you, genuinely available to you, the great social costs to you in exercising it notwithstanding.

That we typically act and choose freely is surely one of the basic tenets of common sense, something that nearly everybody believes, without reservation, without having to give it much thought.

It's also something that philosophers have seriously questioned, pretty much since they started philosophizing.

Two Attacks on Our Freedom

It turns out there are many strong reasons to think that everything that occurs—including our own actions and choices—is predetermined or predestined or inevitable in various ways that seem to rule out anything counting as "free."

Consider, for example, the views of some ancient Greek philosophers known as the *Stoics*, named after the porch (*stoa*, in Greek) on which they philosophized away the hours of the third century BCE. They believed that everything that occurs must be caused to occur, or *made* to occur, by whatever precedes it; otherwise, everything that occurred would be random, wouldn't make sense, and thus would be unintelligible. But then not only must any given event have a cause, they realized, but the cause *itself* must be caused by an even earlier cause and so on. But that means that the entire state of the universe, right now, was ultimately made to occur by everything that went before it, way back into the past, long before we were around. But then everything that has occurred, and everything occurring right now, and everything that will subsequently occur must have *had* to occur, or been *predestined* to occur—including our actions and choices.

Your choosing your blue shirt this morning? It was merely the necessary outcome of a long series of causes dating back to long before you were born.

So much for our freedom!

The situation only got worse when Christianity arrived in the first century CE. True, the new religion did insist on human freedom (against the Stoics) as part of its overall doctrine, but at the same time, it presented another serious problem for the *possibility* of that freedom. For God was said to be omniscient, or infallibly all knowing, and if God is all knowing, it would seem, He must know in advance everything that will occur. But if God knows now that you will choose to wear your blue shirt tomorrow, it doesn't seem that you could possibly do otherwise *than* to wear it—for if you were to do otherwise, you would directly cause God to have mistaken beliefs, which an infallibly all-knowing being simply cannot have.

Thus, God's knowing the future, His having *foreknowledge*, seems also to mean that everything we do is predestined and, again, to rule out our freedom.

The medieval period of philosophy was dominated by religious thinkers; not surprising, there is a large medieval literature on the problem of reconciling God's foreknowledge with human freedom. But since our freedom was itself such a central religious tenet, there is also a large medieval literature responding to the Stoics' "causation" challenge to human freedom as well. And, finally, there is an equally impressive literature responding to perhaps the simplest (yet broadest) challenge to human freedom of them all: the one raised by the featured thinker of our current chapter.

What makes Aristotle's argument against our freedom so compelling is that it presupposes very little.

You don't have to believe (with the Stoics) that everything has a cause, and you don't have to believe (with the religious thinkers) in the existence of God, either. You have to believe in only one thing: a very simple and very hard-to-deny law of logic—which means that *all* reasonable people, Stoic, religious, or not, have to grapple with it.

A Very Simple Law of Logic

"Every ordinary statement is either true or, if not true, false."

Some Slightly Technical Remarks, but Really It's Still Pretty Simple

Philosophers have a way of making simple things more complicated—you know, the whole "belaboring the obvious" thing. But the reason they do this is that what starts off seeming obvious often ends up being *not* so obvious.

That simple law of logic often gets a fancy name: the *Principle of Bivalence.* "Bivalence" means "two values" and refers here to the law's claim that every statement has one of the two possible "values," namely "true" or "false." The Principle of Bivalence should seem undeniably true, once you have stated it precisely. If a statement asserts something, how could what it asserts *not* be either true or false? If what it asserts is in fact the case about the world, the statement is true; if what it asserts is not the case about the world, the statement is false. Since those two possibilities appear to exhaust the options, then every statement must indeed be either true or false.

With respect to statements about the past and present, in fact, Aristotle begins by agreeing that the Principle of Bivalence applies. In fancier language, he writes,

> With regard to what is and what has been it is necessary for the affirmation or the negation to be true or false.[1]

"What is" refers to statements about the present; "what has been" refers to statements about the past; and Aristotle is here agreeing both that affirming (i.e., asserting) any such statements must result in something either true or false, and that negating (i.e., denying) any such statements must result in something either true or false. Take a statement about the past: "Lincoln lived in the nineteenth century." To assert this would be to assert something either true or false (in this case, true); to negate it, by uttering "Lincoln did *not* live in the nineteenth century," would also be to assert something either true or false (in this case, false).

So far, so good.

But let's now turn our attention from "what is" and "what has been" to "what will be," that is, to statements about the future.

To Begin with the End

Just so we know where he's heading, Aristotle next states the *conclusion* toward which his argument is aiming. With respect to statements about the future, he writes,

> If every affirmation or negation is true or false it is necessary for everything either to be the case or not to be the case.

Focusing just on affirmations, the conclusion in question is this: if we say that every statement about the future is either true or false—that is, if we accept the Principle of Bivalence for future statements—then it will follow that everything that occurs in the future will necessarily occur, will *have to* occur, and thus raise the problems for human freedom that I mentioned earlier.

But why should the Principle of Bivalence lead to this dire consequence?

How a Simple Law of Logic Threatens Our Freedom

Aristotle now enters his main argument:

> For if one person says that something will be and another denies this same thing, it is clearly necessary for one of them to be saying what is true—if every affirmation is true or false; for both will not be the case together under such circumstances.

Suppose Fred asserts that "the reader will put on his blue shirt tomorrow" and Wilma denies it. Since they contradict each other, they cannot both be right. But "if every affirmation is true or false"—if the Principle of Bivalence applies here—it must be the case that one of these two people *is* right. We might say, for any particular statement, it is necessary that the statement either be true or false, for there simply are no other options.

But now,

> if [something] is white now it was true to say earlier that it would be white; so that it was always true to say of anything that has happened that it would be so.

Suppose that tomorrow comes and you do put on your blue shirt. Should that happen, then it would seem that Fred, who had asserted *today* that "you *will* put on your blue shirt tomorrow," was right, that is, was speaking truly. Indeed, had Fred asserted that statement at *any* time in the past, even millions of years ago—changing the word "tomorrow" for the specific calendar date, of course—he would have spoken truly: given that you do put on your shirt on that calendar date, it has *always* been true to say that you *would* put it on on that date.

But then comes the crucial move.

For, as Aristotle observes,

> if it was always true to say that it was so, or would be so, [then] it could not not be so, or not be going to be so.

If it was always true, always has been true, that you would put on your blue shirt tomorrow, then it could not be the case that you do *not* put on that shirt tomorrow. You *have* to put on that shirt tomorrow: you cannot *not* put it on.

Why would that be?

Well, suppose for a moment that, in fact, it really is true right now that you will put on that shirt tomorrow. If so, then there's nothing you could do *not* to put it on tomorrow; for were you to actually do any such thing, it wouldn't in fact be true, right now, that you *will* put it on, which contradicts our starting supposition. So on the supposition that this statement about the future, "You will put on your blue shirt," is true right now, there's nothing you can do *not* to put on that shirt.

But wait, you might object, who's to say that we're working with the correct supposition?

You're right: of course, it might *not* be true right now that you will put it on. So suppose that it's *not* true right now that you will put the blue shirt on tomorrow. Then, given the Principle of Bivalence, it must be false right now that you will put on that shirt tomorrow. But then similar reasoning will apply: if it is false right now that you will put it on, then there's nothing you can do *to* in fact put it on; for were you actually to do any such thing, it wouldn't in fact be false, right now, that you will put it on, which contradicts our current supposition. So if this statement about the future, "You will put on your blue shirt," is false right now, there's nothing you can do that would result in your putting on that shirt.

Or, as Aristotle puts it,

> but if something cannot not happen it is impossible for it not to happen; and if it is impossible for something not to happen it is necessary for it to happen. Everything that will be, therefore, happens necessarily.

If it's true right now that you will put it on, then you *have* to put it on: it's necessary that you will and impossible for you not to. Or, on the flip side, if it's false right now that you will put it on, then you *cannot* put it on; it's impossible for you to put it on. Of course, we do not know, right now, whether it's true or false that you will put on that shirt; even *you* cannot know for sure, since no matter what your current intentions might be, the future is not perfectly known to you. But we don't need to actually know whether the statement is true or false, because *whichever* it is, whether it's true *or* false, whatever in fact happens *has* to happen, and it happens necessarily. And since, by the Principle of Bivalence, every statement about the future must be either true or false, it follows that "everything that will be happens necessarily."

And if it happens necessarily—it has to happen, it's impossible for it not to happen—then it's hard to accept that it happens freely.

That's how the Principle of Bivalence seems to rule out human freedom.

So we started with the obvious, with our feelings of freedom and our simple assertion that statements have to be either true or false. But what wasn't so obvious was that we were going to end up having to choose between them.

A Consequence of the Main Argument

Upon reaching this conclusion that "everything happens necessarily," Aristotle next observes that if this were true,

> there would be no need to deliberate or to take trouble (thinking that if we do this, this will happen, but if we do not, it will not).

Once you realize that something *has* to occur, that it cannot *not* occur, it seems pointless to attempt resisting it. Why bother deliberating about what to do when it's already determined, in advance, what you will end up doing? And how could the ultimate outcome end up depending on what we choose when, in fact, it has always been determined long in advance what the ultimate outcome of everything is?

The Principle of Bivalence seems, in short, to make our deliberations both pointless and ineffective.

The Other Hands Begin to Stir

Aristotle no sooner draws this consequence than he begins, rather surprisingly, to use it as an objection to his own original argument! He writes,

> But what if this [consequence] is impossible? For we see that what will be has an origin both in deliberation and in action, and that, in general, in things that are not always actual there is the possibility of being and of not being; here both possibilities are open, both being and not being, and consequently, both coming to be and not coming to be.

He first points out here that deliberation in fact often does play an important role in bringing things about. You, for example, might think long and hard about what shirt to wear before finally deciding on that blue shirt. So if the main argument somehow leads to denying a role for deliberation in our actions, Aristotle is suggesting, then something must be wrong with the main argument. *If you deliberate u must deliberate whether it*

Now this objection isn't actually a very good one. *makes a diff, or not.*

That you will deliberate is true or false, even tho you believe your choice is predetermined.— So also is your choice of deliberating. Paradox!!!

The main argument isn't claiming that we never do in fact deliberate or that deliberation doesn't often produce our actions; it can happily accept that we do, and it does. Rather, the main argument can simply be applied to the deliberating process itself: for, by its reasoning, if everything that occurs does so necessarily, then so, too, would our deliberating! If it has always been true that you will put on that blue shirt tomorrow, then it has equally always been true that you would go through precisely that deliberative process in deciding to put on that shirt. So the fact that we often do deliberate has no bearing, ultimately, on how persuasive the main argument is, since the argument is overall perfectly consistent with our actual activity of deliberating.

But Aristotle has other tricks, and other hands, up his sleeve.

The second point in the passage just quoted is more interesting. Here Aristotle is claiming that the main argument's conclusion—that everything happens necessarily—can't actually be right, because we see in many things that "there is the possibility of being and of not being," that "both possibilities are open." Aristotle illustrates the claim as follows:

> For example, it is possible for this cloak to be cut up, and yet it will not be cut up but will wear out first. But equally, its not being cut up is also possible, for it would not be the case that it wore out first unless its not being cut up were possible.

So suppose it's true right now that the cloak will wear out (say) tomorrow. If this is true, then it's obviously "possible" for the cloak *not* to be cut up, since "wearing out" is one manner of going out of existence without being cut up. But more important, now, Aristotle insists, even if it's true that the cloak *will* wear out and not be cut up, it remains *possible* for it to be cut up instead of wearing out. And if so, then its wearing out can't in fact be "necessary," can't *have* to happen, since it is at least possible for it not to happen.

We'll return in a moment to two curious facts here: Aristotle doesn't quite explain what he means when he insists that it remains "possible" for the cloak to be cut up even when it *will* in fact wear out (and thus not be cut up), nor does he provide any actual argument to support his insistence. But first let's note that if, indeed, his insistence is correct, then it follows after all, as he writes, that "not everything is or happens of necessity."

If not everything happens of necessity, then the main argument—which attempted to prove that everything *does* happen of necessity—must go wrong somewhere.

But where?

Aristotle's Own Conclusion

Very simply, in the assumption of the Principle of Bivalence.

The main argument began by suggesting that every statement must be either true or false—in particular, that statements about the future must be either true or false. It then showed that, for any such statement, if the statement is true, then it's necessarily true; if the statement is false, then it's necessarily false; so either way, whatever happens, happens of necessity.

Aristotle's way out of accepting this conclusion then: simply to deny that the Principle of Bivalence applies to these statements about the future.

Thus, he writes,

> Clearly, then, it is not necessary that of every affirmation and opposite negation one should be true and the other false. For what holds for things that are does not hold for things that are not but may possibly be or not be; with these it is as we have said.

The first sentence is denying the Principle of Bivalence: not every statement must be either true or false. Bivalence does hold "for things that are," that is, statements about the present: these must be either true or false. But it "does not hold for things that are not but may possibly be or not be": that is, statements about the future with respect to which of the relevant events may possibly come about and *also* may possibly *not* come about, as in the cloak example. So, he says, the Principle of Bivalence does not apply to these sorts of statements about the future.

What, then, of the statement that "you will put on your blue shirt tomorrow"?

Aristotle's answer: it is neither true *nor* false. For were it either, the main argument would go through, and your choice of attire would be necessary. So it must be neither. And your freedom in behaving is thereby preserved.

But wait a minute.

If Aristotle, in the end, disarms the "logical" attack on human freedom and so *defends* our freedom, thus agreeing with common sense that we are free, then why exactly have we been accusing him in this chapter of propounding a "strange" idea?

But Wait a Minute Indeed

Not only will you put on your blue shirt tomorrow, but you will also notice two important things here and now.

First, as we mentioned, when Aristotle presents his cloak example, he *offers no actual argument for his position*. He merely insists that although the cloak *will* wear out (i.e., will not be cut up), it remains "possible" for the cloak not to wear out but to be cut up instead. But merely insisting on this possibility is no demonstration of this possibility, and in light of the main argument, the one that demonstrates how the Principle of Bivalence entails that everything happens of necessity, it is hard to see why we should side with Aristotle here. (It's even hard to understand why, given his lack of argument, *Aristotle* sided with Aristotle here!)

Second, though Aristotle quite smoothly concludes that the Principle of Bivalence does not apply to these statements about the future, *he also offers no actual reply to the key argument*, the one that he himself presented, supporting the application of the Principle of Bivalence to these statements in the first place!

Recall, earlier, that he had written,

> if [something] is white now it was true to say earlier that it would be white; so that it was always true to say of anything that has happened that it would be so.

That sounds pretty compelling. If you do end up putting on that blue shirt tomorrow, then wasn't it true, at all earlier times, that you were going to put it on? And if you do end up putting it on tomorrow, then isn't it true, right now, that you *will* put it on? Aristotle offers no actual reasons to reject these claims. But this is the key argument supporting the Principle of Bivalence itself: for either you will or will not put on your shirt, so it must be either true or false, right now, that you will put on the shirt.

How could it be otherwise?

Something is fishy here.

Either This Idea Is Strange or That Idea Is Strange

Why, then, are we labeling Aristotle as the supporter of a strange idea?

Well, yes, he is, in the end, defending human freedom, and insofar as that fits common sense, it may not be particularly "strange."

But it's also clear that his heart is not quite in this defense. As we just noted, he doesn't actually provide the two arguments that he ought to have provided were he really to be taking on the main argument. Instead, he just insists on human freedom without giving us any good reason to believe in it. And from the philosopher's perspective, to insist on something you don't have any good reason to believe is, well, pretty strange.

But second and more important, even if we take Aristotle at his word—he really does reject the main argument and perhaps has some good reasons for so doing (which for some less good reason he isn't sharing with us)—think about at what cost: by rejecting the Principle of Bivalence for future statements. It's neither true nor false, right now, that you will put on that shirt tomorrow. But how, exactly, could that be? It must be either true or false because those are the only options, no?

To suggest otherwise seems, well, pretty strange.

So there's at least one strange idea in here somewhere.

Either Aristotle truly endorses the main argument despite appearing half-heartedly to reject it, in which case he gives up on human freedom. Or else, in the end, he truly rejects the main argument, in which case he gives up on the Principle of Bivalence.

For the purposes of this chapter, I went with the latter. But feel free—even if in fact you aren't—to take your pick.

Notes

1. All quotations are from *De Interpretatione*, chapter 9, in Ackrill (1987, 17–19).

Primary Source

Ackrill, J. L., ed. 1987. *A New Aristotle Reader*. Princeton, NJ: Princeton University Press.

Recommended Secondary Sources

Barnes, Jonathan, ed. 1995. *The Cambridge Companion to Aristotle*. Cambridge, UK: Cambridge University Press.
Shields, Christopher. 2008. "Aristotle." In *Stanford Encyclopedia of Philosophy*, edited by Edward N. Zalta. http://plato.stanford.edu/archives/fall2011/entries/aristotle/.

3

Augustine

FORCED TO BE FREE

STRANGE IDEA

You act freely despite the fact that you are caused to do perhaps everything you do, by events ultimately out of your control.

MAJOR PROPONENT

Augustine (354 CE–430 CE)

BRIEF BIOGRAPHY

Aurelius Augustinus, more commonly "St. Augustine," often simply "Augustine," was born in what is today known as Algeria, and he spent most of his life in Northern Africa. He experienced many things in his life, not least of which was perhaps the most famous conversion to Christianity in all of history, which he recounted in his widely read autobiographical work, *Confessions*. In brief, in about 386 CE, he thought he heard a child's voice singing, "Pick it up and read it . . . . " Opening a Bible at random, to Romans 13:13–14, he read, "Let us behave decently . . . not in carousing and drunkenness, not in sexual immorality and debauchery. . . . Rather, clothe yourselves with the Lord Jesus Christ" (New International Version). Since he had in fact devoted much of his life to that point to drunken carousing, sexual immorality, and debauchery, this seemed to be speaking directly to him. Augustine promptly converted to Christianity, then went on to become a bishop, a saint, and eventually a doctor of the church, composing along the way an enormous body of philosophical and theological work. He died in a place called Hippo, as the Vandals were besieging the gates of the city.

Plenty of Problems for Freedom

In the previous chapter, we examined a "logic" argument against our acting freely, namely that the law of logic known as the Principle of Bivalence entails that all our future actions and choices are entirely unavoidable and necessary and thus not free. At the beginning of that chapter, though, I mentioned two other arguments for the same troubling conclusion, one grounded in the idea of causation and the other in God's infallible omniscience. And in a moment, we'll look at an argument made by the great Roman orator Cicero (106 BCE–43 BCE), which combines both.

It's worth noting, first, though, that if Cicero's combination argument is persuasive, then it actually allows two different conclusions, strictly speaking. For the core of his argument is the claim that God's knowledge of the future (or *foreknowledge*) is inconsistent with human freedom, which means that we cannot believe in both: if we believe that God has foreknowledge, then we must give up belief in our freedom; or, if we believe in our freedom, then we must give up belief in God's foreknowledge. But that claim on its own is neutral as to which belief to accept and which to reject.

Cicero himself—committed to the importance of human freedom—ends up giving up belief in God's foreknowledge. For a pre-Christian pagan, this wasn't perhaps all that difficult for him to do.

But this option was quite unacceptable to the early Christian thinker Augustine (*Saint* Augustine to you, by the way). Yet Augustine found it equally unacceptable to give up belief in human freedom, since human freedom is itself an indispensable tenet of Christianity. Thus, Augustine wanted to defend both God's foreknowledge *and* our freedom without giving up either. What he needed to do, then, was not merely reject Cicero's final conclusion but reject the very argument that leads to the conflict between foreknowledge and freedom in the first place.

To see how he does this—and thus comes to endorse the strange idea that our freedom is compatible with, well, *everything* being predetermined—we shall begin with a look at Cicero's argument, at least as it is seen through Augustine's eyes.

Cicero's "Execrable" Argument

Augustine begins his summary of Cicero's argument in a way that doesn't exactly hide his opinion of it:

> Now what was it that Cicero so dreaded in [God's foreknowledge], that he struggled to demolish the idea by so execrable a line of argument?[1] (V.9, 191)

Augustine then presents Cicero's argument as follows:

> [Cicero] reasoned that if all events are foreknown, they will happen in the precise order of that foreknowledge; if so, the order is determined in the [foreknowledge] of God. If the order of events is determined, so is the causal order; for nothing can happen unless preceded by an efficient cause. If the causal order is fixed, determining all events, then all events, he concludes, are ordered by destiny. If this is true, nothing depends on us and there is no such thing as free will. "Once we allow this," he says, "all human life is overthrown. There is no point in making laws, no purpose in expressing reprimand or approbation, censure or encouragement; there is no justice in establishing rewards for the good and penalties for the evil." (V.9, 191)

Let's now work through this argument carefully.

Cicero in Smaller, More Digestible Chunks

Suppose, to begin, that God does have foreknowledge and thus completely and correctly knows all events in advance of their occurrence.

Since an infallible God could never make a mistake, then everything that He believes will occur, clearly *has* to occur. But the only events that have to occur, which *must* occur, are those events that are unavoidably caused to occur by events preceding them. Since God foreknows all events, then all events are unavoidably caused to occur by earlier events preceding them.

And what about these earlier events themselves? Since God foreknows their occurrence, too, the same reasoning applies, and they in turn must be caused by even earlier events, and so on.

But now, human actions and choices are foreknown in just the same way as all other events. So they too must be unavoidably caused by events preceding them and thus out of our ultimate control. And if so, then it seems, finally, that "nothing depends on us and there is no such thing as free will."

Note, first, how Cicero links the two lines of argument mentioned earlier, the ones grounded in the causal order and God's foreknowledge, respectively: that God can never make an error means that the events He foreknows *have to* happen, and for events to have to happen in turn requires that there be a causal order in the world.

Then note, next, how problematic the apparent conclusion is.

For if our actions and choices really are unavoidably caused by preceding events, then "all human life is overthrown." Should you choose to do something morally good, you should receive no credit for it, since your choice was caused by earlier events not in your control. Nor could we blame bad people for doing bad things, for the same reason: they were caused to make their bad choices by earlier events out of their control. Overall, Cicero concludes, if we accept the existence of this complete causal order in which our actions are mere mechanical cogs, then "there is no point in making laws, no purpose in expressing reprimand or approbation," and "no justice in establishing rewards for the good and penalties for the evil": for none of our actions are ultimately up to us.

To make this point vividly, in a more contemporary way: to suppose there is such a causal order might be like imagining that the universe began with a Big Bang, which then established a long sequence of events causing each other, eventually resulting in your choosing (tomorrow, say) to put on that darn blue shirt again. That you were going to put on that shirt tomorrow was entirely determined by the state of the universe at the moment of the Big Bang, long before you even existed. But then it's hard to see how you or your choices are genuinely responsible for your behaviors.

It particularly seems wrong to *condemn* you for wearing that awful shirt, since your wearing it was determined not by you but by the laws of physics.

The Pagan and the Christian Agree

Cicero and Augustine may disagree on many things—including that bit about a God sending His son as a savior—but they do at least share their distaste for this conclusion so far. Augustine writes,

> It is to avoid these consequences . . . that Cicero refuses to allow any foreknowledge. And he constrains the religious soul to this dilemma, forcing it to choose between those propositions: either there is some scope for our will, or there is foreknowledge. He thinks that both cannot be true; to affirm one is to deny the other. If we choose foreknowledge, free will is annihilated; if we choose free will, [foreknowledge] is abolished. And so . . . Cicero chooses free will. (V.9, 191)

Neither Cicero nor Augustine will give up belief in our freedom, given those disastrous consequences just mentioned. Cicero, believing freedom to be incompatible with foreknowledge, preserves the former by giving up the latter.

But it is to escape from the horns of this very *dilemma*—a situation where you are confronted by only two options, both of which are bad—that Augustine begins to mount his response.

What's at Stake?

Only Christianity itself.

The other major Western monotheisms, Judaism and Islam, too, of course, but Augustine's concerns are understandably rather more with Christianity. He writes,

To acknowledge the existence of God, while denying him any [foreknowledge] of events, is the most obvious madness. Cicero himself realized this, and almost ventured on the denial referred to in Scripture, "The fool has said in his heart: God does not exist" [Ps. 14.1]. (V.9, 190)

Western monotheists believe not merely that God exists but specifically that an *omniscient* God exists, with complete foreknowledge. To deny God's foreknowledge would then amount to denying God's very existence. So Augustine sees himself not merely as responding to some small philosophical argument but as defending the faith in the most fundamental of ways.

Thus, he writes,

In seeking to make men free, [Cicero] makes them irreverent. . . . Against such profane and irreverent impudence we assert both that God knows all things before they happen and that we do by our free will everything that we feel and know would not happen without our volition. (V.9, 191–92)

So God's foreknowledge is to be reconciled with our freedom.
The key question is how.

Yes, Please, How?

Surprisingly simply, in a way. But appreciating the force of Augustine's maneuver will take a little work.

Augustine's entire response to Cicero is more or less captured here:

Now if there is for God a fixed order of all causes, it does not follow that nothing depends on our free choice. Our wills themselves are in the order of causes, which is, for God, fixed, and is contained in his foreknowledge, since human acts of will are the causes of human activities. Therefore he who had [foreknowledge] of the causes of all events certainly could not be ignorant of our decisions, which he foreknows as the causes of our actions. (V.9, 192)

So Augustine *grants* Cicero one of the key premises, namely that there is "a fixed order of all causes." He's granting, in other words, that everything that happens has to happen, since it is caused to happen by events preceding it. He's also granting, specifically, that our very wills, our very efforts, or endeavors— or *volitions*, as philosophers like to say—belong to that causal order and are thus themselves caused to occur by preceding events.

But for Cicero, this meant that our actions and choices are not ultimately in our control and thus undermine our freedom. Yet for Augustine, somehow, this shall be the key move that ultimately *supports* our freedom.

How so?

The crucial observation is this: once you grant that our wills are "in the order of causes," you are granting not merely that they are themselves caused by earlier events but also that *they are themselves causes of subsequent events*, such as our actions.

But then, Augustine holds, that latter fact secures our freedom, for it makes our actions dependent on our will:

> How then does the order of causes, which is fixed in the [foreknowledge] of God, result in the withdrawal of everything from dependence on our will, when our acts of will play an important part in that causal order? (V.9, 193)

So the debate comes down to this.

Both parties agree that God's foreknowledge requires that there be a causal order of events whereby each event is caused by earlier events and then causes subsequent events, and both parties agree that our "wills" are members of this causal order.

But Cicero then looks backward in time. In seeing how our will depends on earlier events, he concludes that our will would not be in our control and, thus, we lose our freedom. Augustine, to the contrary, looks forward in time, and in seeing how our various actions are caused by our preceding will, he concludes that our actions *would be* in our control and thus count as free. In this way Augustine reconciles God's foreknowledge, which encompasses the whole causal order, including our wills, with our freedom.

But, of course, whether this reconciliation is successful depends on the plausibility of preferring the "forward" look to the "backward" look.

And that's where matters get more subtle.

Freedom, Necessity, and Our Quest for Control

Augustine raises this question in a slightly different form. He asks, "Are men's wills under the sway of necessity?"

> Now if, in our case, "necessity" is to be used of what is not in our control, of what achieves its purposes whether we will or no—the "necessity" of death, for example—then it is obvious that our wills, by the exercise of which we lead a good life or a bad, are not subject to a necessity of this kind. (V.10, 194)

So we would say that our actions are "necessary," or have to happen, here, only if they would occur "whether we will or no." Thus, it is necessary, or unavoidable, that we die, for our deaths will occur even if we don't want or will them to.

But of course, most of our ordinary actions are not like this. We often do various things *because* we want or will to, and we typically don't do them if we don't:

> We do a great many things which we should not have done if we had not wished to. In the first place, our willing belongs to this class of acts. If we so wish, it exists; if we do not so wish, it does not; for we should not will, if we did not so wish. (V.10, 194)

Indeed, granting that something is not done from necessity if we "do it because we want to, and wouldn't if we didn't," then the very act of willing itself is by definition not done from necessity: for obviously we only will if we will, and we don't will if we don't will!

The language here concerns "necessity," but that is intimately related to other language. Earlier, I framed the question as that of whether our actions are "in our control." Well, what does it mean for something to be "in our control," if not that the thing will occur if we want it or will it to and won't if we don't? To say that something is *not* in our control, as in the death example, typically means that it will occur whether we want or will it to or not. But, then, the only time that we truly act in a way *not* in our control is when we are compelled to act, when we're forced to do something *against* our will. And most of what we do is not like that.

And, of course, it's a short step from here to speaking about acting freely.

Freedom and Two Different Senses of "In Our Control"

For what do we mean when we say that we do something freely, if not that the action was "in our control": that we did it because we wanted to and wouldn't have done it if we hadn't wanted to?

Here is Augustine's most subtle move.

For Augustine's conception of freedom here *is completely neutral on the question of whether our wills themselves might have causes or be caused*. It just doesn't matter that something (an earlier event, the laws of physics, your brain cells firing) may cause you to want or will to do a certain thing. As long as you do that thing "willingly," *because* you willed to, then the action is "in your control," and it counts as free. Our actions often flow from our wills even if our wills are themselves caused, and that's all we need for freedom—at least according to Augustine.

Of course, it remains easy to understand why Cicero felt that the chain of causes leading up to our willing might take away our freedom: given that sequence of causes, our actions are in some sense "not in our control," since they were causally predetermined to happen by past events themselves not in our control. And so Augustine is willing to admit that there is a *sense* in which our actions do occur "of necessity": given this sequence of causes and given God's foreknowledge of that sequence, whatever you do has to occur, precisely when it occurs.

But this sense of necessity, this *other* sense according to which our actions are not in our control, does not remove the sense in which they *are* in our control and thus in which we are free.

To see why not, Augustine offers another example:

> We do not subject the life and the foreknowledge of God to necessity, if we say that it is "necessary" for God to be eternal and to have complete foreknowledge; nor is his power diminished by saying that he cannot die or make a mistake. The reason why he cannot is that, if he could, his power would certainly be less; and he is rightly called "all-powerful," although he has not the power to die, or to be mistaken. "All-powerful" means that he does what he wills, and does not suffer what he does not will. . . . It is just because he is all-powerful that there are some things he cannot do. (V.10, 194–95)

Here we have another case where we might say that something is necessary, but where we would not think that saying that involves any limit or constraint on the being. God cannot die or make an error: it is *necessary* that He always exist and always have true beliefs. But we hardly think that this sense of necessity limits God in any way. Indeed, it's just the opposite: it is because God is *unlimited* in power and knowledge that He cannot die or err.

Similar considerations now apply to our case.

It may be necessary (in one sense) that we do a certain action at a certain time, given the sequence of causes leading up to our willing it and then doing it. But given what it means to say that something is in our control or that we act freely—namely, that we do it because we want to and wouldn't if we didn't—then all this means, in effect, is that it is necessary that we do the action freely! For, if it is necessary that we will to do the thing, it is also necessary, by definition, that whatever we do because we will to do it, we do freely. It is only when something happens to us against our will, when something occurs despite our *not* willing it, that we lose our freedom. Thus, the sense of necessity stressed by Cicero—that we have to do whatever we do, due to the long chain of causes—does not in fact limit or constrain our freedom.

To the contrary, it guarantees it.

Augustine thus concludes,

> It does not follow, then, that there is nothing in our will because God foreknew what was going to be in our will; for if he foreknew this, it was not nothing that he foreknew. . . . Hence we are in no way compelled either to preserve God's [fore-

knowledge] by abolishing our free will, or to safeguard our free will by denying (blasphemously) the divine foreknowledge. We embrace both truths. (V.10, 195)

If God foreknows all and so foreknows what we will will and do, then indeed we are doing the thing because we will to do it—and thus, by definition, we are doing it freely. Foreknowledge and freedom are compatible.

Must All Human Life Now Be Overthrown?

Suppose for a moment that Augustine's clever move here works—that is, defining freedom in a way that fits with the existence of the causal order. We must still ask whether Cicero's deepest concerns have been met.

As we saw earlier, if Augustine grants the causal order—that all our wills are caused by preceding events—then it still seems that we ought not give people credit or blame for doing morally good or evil things, for all their actions are ultimately the product of earlier causes. Nor is it clear what the point of "making laws" would be or "expressing reprimand or approbation": people will do whatever the preceding sequence of causes makes them do, regardless of what we do afterward.

So wouldn't human life be "overthrown" here after all, as Cicero worried? Not so fast, responds Augustine.

By dint of reasoning similar to the earlier, he writes,

It is not true that reprimands, exhortations, praise and blame are useless, because God has knowledge of them before; they are of the greatest efficacy in so far as he has foreknown that they would be effective. (V.10, 195)

It is precisely because our wills are subject to the causal order that there is a point to these practices—for these then become factors that subsequently influence our wills! Often, we do good things precisely *because* of the praise and reward that we know will follow upon them, and we forgo doing bad things *because* of the ensuing blame and punishment. That these are causes of our wills doesn't take away from the fact that we often behave as we do, good or bad, because we want to behave that way.

And that, again, is the essence of free action: doing what you want to and not being forced to do what you don't want to. God's foreknowledge of our actions does not remove either their freedom *or* our moral responsibility for doing them.

Indeed, Augustine continues,

The fact that God foreknew that man would sin does not make a man sin; on the contrary, it cannot be doubted that it is the man himself who sins just because he whose [foreknowledge] cannot be mistaken has foreseen that the man himself would sin. A man does not sin unless he wills to sin; and if he had willed not to sin, then God would have foreseen that refusal. (V.10, 195)

The fact that God foreknew you would do something does not itself make you do that thing, after all. It's rather the other way around: He foreknew it because you in fact were going to do it. And if He foreknew that you would do it, He also foreknew that you would *want* to do it, and your doing it because you want to do it is precisely what makes it a free action.

The devil may have made you do that terrible thing, then, but if he also made you want to do it, then you did it freely, and it is you who will rightly take the rap.

Or so says Augustine.

The Having of the Cake and the Eating of It, Too

According to Augustine, then, God's having foreknowledge is not merely compatible with our acting freely. Rather, further, since locating our wills in the causal order plays such a crucial role in establishing our freedom—we act freely insofar as our wills cause our actions—God's foreknowledge (of the causal order, including our wills) actively *supports* our freedom.

Still, admittedly, it's hard to fully accept the claim that we act freely even when everything we do is made to happen by earlier events in the causal order. It's one thing to define freedom as "doing what you want," but it's another altogether to ignore the fact that our wants are often themselves not in our control. If in fact the devil does make me *want* to do it, too, then shouldn't he take at least some of the rap?

Reconciling freedom and the causal order may still require a little more than what Augustine has given us.

Perhaps a few crumbs of the cake remain on the plate.

Note

1. All Augustine quotations are from St. Augustine (1984), *The City of God*, translated by Henry Bettenson.

Primary Sources

St. Augustine. 1984. *The City of God*. Translated by Henry Bettenson. London: Penguin.
Yonge, C. D., trans. 1911. *M. Tullius Cicero: On the Nature of the Gods; On Divination; On Fate; On the Republic; On the Laws; On Standing for the Consulship*. London: Bell.

Recommended Secondary Sources

Mendelson, Michael. 2010. "Saint Augustine." In *Stanford Encyclopedia of Philosophy*, edited by Edward N. Zalta. http://plato.stanford.edu/archives/win2010/entries/augustine/.

Stump, Eleonore, and Norman Kretzmann, eds. 2001. *The Cambridge Companion to Augustine*. Cambridge, UK: Cambridge University Press.

4

Anselm

GOD IS NOT JUST A GOOD IDEA

STRANGE IDEA

You can prove the existence of God merely by thinking about God.

MAJOR PROPONENT

Anselm (1033–1109)

BRIEF BIOGRAPHY

Anselm was born in what is today northwestern Italy, and little is known of his earliest years, except that he eventually arrived in northwestern France, at the age of 26, in 1059. There, he entered the Benedictine abbey at Bec as a novice; he rose quickly to prior and, then, by 1078, to abbot. Under his leadership, Bec's intellectual reputation grew, aided by Anselm's prolific writings and voluminous correspondence with rulers, nobles, and clerics all over Europe. In 1093, Anselm became archbishop of Canterbury, where much of his time was spent in conflict with the English king William II, who was apparently not very fond of anyone other than himself having any authority over anything. Indeed, by 1097, Anselm found himself exiled in Rome, where he stayed until William got himself killed in 1100. William's successor, Henry I, let Anselm back into England, only to promptly resume the same power struggle, resulting in Anselm's being exiled yet again from 1103 to 1107. This instability didn't deter Anselm from his tireless writing up to his death, however, and as a result of this work, Anselm was canonized in 1494 and named a doctor of the church in 1720.

Strange or Common Sense?

Belief in the existence of God, that is.

It is a little hard to tell these days.

Theism—belief in the existence of God—was certainly widespread for at least two thousand years across the broad reaches of Western civilization. And while religious-oriented philosophers were engaged nearly continuously during that whole time in evaluating whether God's existence can be proved by rational argument, probably few ordinary people felt that to be a burning question: God's existence was perhaps seen as rather obvious, or at least as obvious as the existence of an invisible, nonphysical being *could* be. Belief in God was indeed, for a long time, the commonsense position.

But then came the European Enlightenment, the Age of Reason. With the eighteenth and nineteenth centuries came the ideas that religious belief was merely ungrounded superstition and foolishness and that scientific inquiry, the very epitome of reason, should be the guide to the truth about the universe. These ideas made it possible to reject belief in God openly, publicly, even scornfully, and many people began to do just that, at all levels of society.

And today?

Well, there is certainly no shortage of religious believers across all areas of the West, broadly construed. But religious belief has now splintered into many forms, not all of which count as "belief in God" as construed for the many previous centuries. It also seems hard to deny that, with some lip service to the contrary aside, the main cultures of Western nations are staunchly secular. So it isn't easy to decide, these days, whether common sense supports the belief in God or denies it.

But fortunately we don't have to.

Because the strange idea of the current chapter isn't simply the idea that God exists.

It's the idea, rather, that God's existence can be proved merely by thinking about the very idea of God.

A Brief History of the Ontological Argument

Religious philosophers have attempted to prove God's existence in many ways.

Some of these arguments are based on various features of the universe. They claim, for example, that for there to exist any motion in the universe, or causation, there must exist some "First Mover" or "First Cause," who is naturally understood to be the God of Western monotheism. Some of these arguments observe that the universe shows evidence of purpose or design and claim that for this to be so, there must be (or have been) an "Intelligent Designer," who again would be that God. Some arguments have also claimed that the very possibility of genuine morality, of a real difference between right and wrong, presupposes the existence of a divine lawgiver: God again, as you no doubt guessed.

But none of these arguments are as famous, or perhaps as infamous, as the *ontological argument* for the existence of God.

Why is it called the "ontological" argument?

Ontology is a fancy word derived from Greek meaning "the study of what exists." You might think, then, that an "ontological argument" would be any argument proving the existence of something, except that you'd be wrong. For philosophers *love* to make arguments proving the existence of various other things (such as minds, morality, mathematical objects), and no one ever refers to those arguments as "ontological" ones.

In fact, it seems that no real reason can be given for the name, other than that the great eighteenth-century German thinker Immanuel Kant (1724–1804) apparently christened it as such. And what seems particularly salient about it, about *the* ontological argument, is not that it proves the existence of something but rather that it has a unique *strategy* in doing so: unlike those other arguments for theism, which begin by looking at features of the universe, the ontological argument claims that the very concept or *idea* of God itself is sufficient to prove God's existence. Who needs to waste time and effort looking at and studying the universe to prove God's existence when you can merely think about it for a few minutes?

For such an allegedly simple strategy, however, the ontological argument has had a rather complicated history.

Credit is usually given to the subject of our current chapter—the great medieval Christian thinker Anselm—for providing its first clear and explicit formulation. But the ink on Anselm's parchment was not even dry when his argument received a blistering critique by a contemporary monk named Gaunilo, whose ink *also* hadn't dried before Anselm himself offered a prompt (if slippery) response. Their exchange was then studied, and debated, and elaborated on for the next six centuries, at which time the famous seventeenth-century French thinker René Descartes (1596–1650), of "I think therefore I am" fame, offered his own version of an ontological argument. This one in turn received its own blistering critique (not to mention its name) a century later by the aforementioned Kant, which many philosophers took to be one of those rare events in philosophy: a universally persuasive "knockdown" argument that served as the clear death knell of the whole "just think about it" manner of proving God's existence. And, indeed, it was just that, at least for a couple of centuries.

But then, in the twentieth century, something remarkable happened. Something even rarer than a knockdown argument.

Something knocked down got back up.

Informed by important advances in contemporary metaphysics and at the hands of some smart and influential thinkers (such as Cornell University philosopher Norman Malcolm, 1911–1990, and the University of Notre Dame's Alvin Plantinga, b. 1932), the ontological argument was resurrected in new and subtle ways. The work was so powerful that the ontological argument is now, once again, in this century, an active subject of philosophical investigation.

A dead argument came back to life.

Let's have a look.

In the Beginning

"Well then, Lord," Anselm writes,

> You who give understanding to faith, grant me that I may understand, as much as You see fit, that You exist as we believe You to exist, and that You are what we believe You to be.[1]

There are a couple of interesting points to make from the start.

First, Anselm addresses his proof to God, whom he says "gives understanding to faith." This reflects the fact that Anselm's faith precedes the proof itself: he believes in God whether or not he will be able to prove, rationally, that God exists. This serves to remind us that it's an open question whether a theist, a believer, even requires or *ought* to require rational argument for her theism. Many theists have held, in fact, that no genuine proof of God's existence is possible or even desirable, as they think that belief in God must be a matter of faith. So while the philosopher Anselm seeks to supplement his faith with "understanding," not all his fellow believers feel the same need.

Second, note that there are *two* things that Anselm seeks: not merely proof (or "understanding") *that* God exists but also that God is *what* Anselm believes God to be. This reflects an extremely important point that many people—believers and disbelievers alike—often fail to recognize: you can't have a meaningful debate about God's existence until you have some agreement on just what God is supposed to be. And, in fact, most philosophical thinking about God has focused, through the centuries, not on whether God exists but rather on exactly which properties or attributes God is supposed to have and their precise nature. What exactly is the attribute of *omnipotence* (being all powerful) all about, in other words, and must God possess it? What about *omniscience* (being all knowing)? And what about more obscure attributes, such as *eternality,* or *immutability,* or (believe it or not) *simplicity*?

What's particularly important about Anselm's strategy, as we'll next see, is that his definition or conception of *what* God is, of what God's essence or nature is, is going to do all the heavy lifting in his proof *that* God is.

So what does Anselm "believe God to be"?

The Greatest Conceivable Being

Anselm next writes,

> Now we believe that You are something than which nothing greater can be thought.

There it is, in effect, the first step or premise in the ontological argument: God is "something than which nothing greater can be thought." Now this expression is quite a mouthful, particularly if you are going to repeat it a number of times in the course of discussing the argument. So it's not uncommon for people to phrase it a little differently: "God is the greatest thing we can think of" or "God is the greatest conceivable being."

This difference in phrasing seems quite small, but it is actually rather significant, and Anselm himself chose his original phrasing with great care. For our alternative phrasing may imply, in a way that Anselm's does not, that God is in fact "conceivable," that is, that we can indeed think or conceive of God in some reasonably complete way, with a full grasp of His nature. But, of course, few thinkers believe this to be so: God is understood to be infinite in nature, while our minds are both quite finite and very fallible, so we should never presume to say we have fully grasped God's nature. Anselm's phrasing nicely avoids implying that we *can* fully grasp God's nature; it states merely that nothing *greater* than God can be thought or conceived by us. But still, given the mouthful problem, we'll feel free to use "greatest conceivable being" to express this idea of God as long as we keep in mind that no one here believes that God is actually fully conceivable.

Nor should one make the opposite mistake, that God is *not at all* conceivable.

For while we may not have a "full" or "perfect" idea of God, we do have at least some idea of God, however inadequate or incomplete. Anselm, in any case, requires that we have one, since his argument obviously depends on it. And which idea is that? The idea of a, or perhaps the, greatest conceivable being. This tells us very little about God, of course. It says nothing about any of God's specific attributes, for example. On its own, it's neutral on the question of whether this God, the greatest conceivable God, is the same God that Western monotheists believe in, the one who is the First Mover and the First Cause and the Intelligent Designer. But it's enough, at least, to get the conversation started.

Even more important, it's an idea of God that even the atheist, the disbeliever, can and generally does accept.

After all, even the atheist must have *some* idea of God to reject God's existence! When he insists that "God does not exist," he does not mean that unicorns don't exist or that utopias don't exist: he means that *God* doesn't exist. But he can only mean that God doesn't exist if he means something by the word "God." And whatever it is he means by the word "God" will just be his idea of God, whatever that may be. And "greatest conceivable being" is as good an idea as any of God, from the atheist's perspective.

So the theist and the atheist can agree on *what* God is or is supposed to be: the greatest conceivable being. They have to agree, as mentioned earlier, if their disagreement is even to be meaningful, if they are not to be talking past each other. What their disagreement is, then, is not about what God is or about God's nature. To the contrary, as Anselm puts it, it's about this:

> Or can it be that a thing of such a nature does not exist, since "the Fool has said in his heart, there is no God"?[2]

The "Fool" here, of course, is the atheist (from Anselm's perspective), and what the theist and the atheist disagree about is not what God's nature is, as the greatest conceivable being, but about whether something *of* that nature, something that fits that description, exists in reality.

God Existing in the Mind

Anselm now continues,

> But surely, when this same Fool hears what I am speaking about, namely, "something-than-which-nothing-greater-can-be-thought", he understands what he hears, and what he understands is in his mind, even if he does not understand that it actually exists.

Here comes a crucial move. To put it simply, Anselm is claiming here that, at the least, God exists *in the mind* of the atheist, even if the atheist doesn't understand that God also really exists outside his mind. In particular, the claim is that "whatever you understand exists in your mind"—so, insofar as the atheist understands the definition (and thus has the idea) of God, as the greatest conceivable being, then this thing, the greatest conceivable being, exists in his mind.

This shall be the second step or premise of the argument.

Now this premise may sound a little strange to our twenty-first-century ears. These days, we do sometimes speak of things being "in" our minds, perhaps, but when we do, we are usually speaking loosely or figuratively. When we're more precise, we might say not that the thing itself is in the mind but merely that we have an *idea* of the thing in our minds. So you might be thinking about your beautiful new car, or beautiful new boyfriend, or that hideous old tree in the courtyard, but you wouldn't be tempted to say that those objects themselves are literally "in" your mind: what's in your mind are just your ideas of those objects, which are quite distinct entities from the things of which they are ideas.

Yet it seems that Anselm is taking this quite literally: when someone has or understands the idea of the greatest conceivable being, then that very being *itself* is existing in the person's mind.

In fact, Anselm is merely expressing here a view that was prevalent throughout the medieval period of philosophy. Objects, it was held, can exist in different modes or forms: the same object could exist "really," in the world, as well as "mentally," in a mind. And while this strange idea might itself be a good candidate for its own chapter in this book, it's worth defending it a bit here since the ontological argument makes use of it.

Let's consider two ways to defend it.

First, suppose that we side with our more modern view: we say that what is in our minds are only "ideas" and that ideas are always completely distinct entities from the things in the world they are ideas "of." If we say this, then it turns out that we enter into one of the thorniest problems in the history of philosophy, one that remains unsolved to this day, namely, how are we able to think about things *in the world* at all? To try to think about that gnarly old tree in the courtyard, after all, the mind can do nothing other than reflect on the idea of the tree that it finds within itself. But if that idea is utterly distinct from the tree itself, what makes it the case that it's *the tree* we are thinking of as we do our thinking—and not merely our own idea? The very difficult worry, in short, is that once you distinguish ideas from the things of which they are ideas, then your mind shall have no way, ever, of actually engaging with the world outside!

Second, the things that are in our minds must have *some* kind of being or reality. After all, when we think about a thing, it's not nothing we're thinking about; even when you're thinking about something that you don't think really exists out there in the world (such as a unicorn), it's not a *nothing* you're thinking about but a *something*: a unicorn. Moreover, when you think first about a unicorn and then (say) about that repulsive diseased tree, there are two different things that you are thinking about in turn. But if the things in our minds were nothings, had no reality or being, then there could not be two of them—since all nothings are the same. So if you can think about two different things in turn, there must be, there must exist, in some form, two different things in your mind. But now suppose that you are thinking about that abomination in your courtyard, and then you go look at it in all its repulsive glory. Is the thing that you were thinking about the same thing you are now looking at? Of course! It was *that tree* you were thinking about, not something else, and it is *that tree* you are now looking at. Since what you were thinking about is the same thing as the thing in the courtyard you're now looking at, then we should say that the thing in your mind is the *same thing* as the thing in the courtyard.

But if so, then the very same thing—the tree, your beautiful car, your lovely boyfriend, and, of course, God—can exist both "in" the mind and "in" reality.

Now Anselm feels your pain here. He recognizes that this is a subtle and strange claim, and so he attempts to illustrate it as follows:

> For it is one thing for an object to exist in the mind, and another thing to understand that an object actually exists. Thus, when a painter plans beforehand what he is going to execute, he has [the picture] in his mind, but he does not yet think that it actually exists because he has not yet executed it. However, when he has actually painted it, then he both has it in his mind and understands that it exists because he has now made it. Even the Fool, then, is forced to agree that something-than-which-nothing-greater-can-be-thought exists in the mind, since he understands this when he hears it, and whatever is understood is in the mind.

So the painting first exists in the mind of the painter when he is planning it, and then it comes to exist in reality after it is painted. In a similar way, the second premise of the ontological argument shall be that God, the greatest conceivable being, exists at least in the mind even of the atheist.

The key question is now whether the greatest conceivable being also must be said to exist in reality.

God Existing Outside the Mind

Anselm next asserts his eventual conclusion:

> And surely that-than-which-a-greater-cannot-be-thought cannot exist in the mind alone.

But to get from his two premises so far—that God is the greatest conceivable being and that God exists at least in the mind—to this conclusion, Anselm undertakes an interesting style of argument known, in fancy Latin terms, as a *reductio ad absurdum*, or "reduction to absurdity." A *reductio* (for short) makes use of the widely accepted fact that a contradiction, or contradictory statement, can never be true. To both assert something and deny it is always to speak falsely, in other words, since the assertion and the denial of the same proposition cannot both be true. It follows, then, that if you can show that a particular claim leads, logically, *to* a contradiction, then that original claim itself must be false. For if the claim *were* true and it leads logically to something else, that other thing would also have to be true, which a contradiction can never be.

A *reductio* then works like this. First, assume that the proposition that you are examining is true. Then show that if it were true, it would lead to a contradiction. Then conclude that the original proposition must in fact be false.

Thus, Anselm next turns to constructing a *reductio* with the proposition "God exists in the mind alone." If he can show that that proposition leads to a contradiction, he will have shown that that proposition is false.

Here's how he does it:

> For if it exists solely in the mind . . . it can be thought to exist in reality also, which is greater. If then that-than-which-a-greater-cannot-be-thought exists in the mind alone, this same that-than-which-a-greater-*cannot*-be-thought is that-than-which-a-greater-*can*-be-thought. But this is obviously impossible.

Trying saying *that* ten times fast! This is the mouthful that I was talking about earlier, so let's tease it apart.

Assume, for a moment, that God, the greatest conceivable being, exists only in your mind.

You could then quite easily think of that same being as *also* existing in reality as well, just as the painter can think of the painting as existing only in his mind and then as coming to exist in reality as well.

But to think of this being as existing in reality as well, Anselm holds, is to think of it as being greater than it would be if it existed only in your mind: for surely a really existing being is greater than one that exists only in someone's mind, even someone of your impressive stature! But then the "greatest conceivable being," this thing that we said was in your mind, would be a being than which a greater *can* be conceived. So this thing in your mind would simultaneously be both "the greatest conceivable being" and "not the greatest conceivable being" (since you could conceive of a greater one existing in reality), which is clearly a contradiction.

And contradictions, as we noted, must always be rejected—as well as any propositions that logically lead to them.

But what led to this contradiction?

The starting assumption that God exists in your mind alone. By a *reductio*, whatever leads to a contradiction must itself be rejected. We must therefore reject the assumption that the greatest conceivable being exists only in the mind.

If it does not exist only in the mind, then what?

It must also exist in reality.

Or as Anselm puts it,

therefore there is absolutely no doubt that something-than-which-a-greater-cannot-be-thought exists both in the mind and in reality.

Thus, God exists, really exists, outside the mind.

As simple as that.

To Tie It All Together

To put it all in one place, then, Anselm's ontological argument looks like this:

God is the greatest conceivable being.

God exists at least in the mind.

Assume for a moment that God exists only in the mind.

Then the greatest conceivable being would be one than which a greater *can* be conceived.

But that is a contradiction, so the assumption leading to it must be false.

Therefore God does not exist only in the mind.

Therefore God exists in reality too.

The foolish atheist is therefore contradicting himself when he denies the existence of God: for denying the existence of God amounts to asserting that the greatest conceivable being is not the greatest conceivable being.

And so you—who, no doubt, are no logical fool and thus know better than to contradict yourself—can now prove that God exists, merely by thinking about your idea of God.

As simple as that.

Notes

1. All quotations are from Anselm's *Proslogion*, chapter 2, translated by M. J. Charlesworth (1965).

2. Anselm is here quoting Psalms xiii.I, lii.I.

Primary Source

M. J. Charlesworth, trans. 1965. *St Anselm's Proslogion with a Reply on Behalf of the Fool by Gaunilo and the Author's Reply to Gaunilo.* Oxford, UK: Clarendon Press.

Recommended Secondary Sources

Davies, Brian, and Brian Leftow, eds. 2005. *Cambridge Companion to Anselm.* Cambridge, UK: Cambridge University Press.
Williams, Thomas. 2011. "Saint Anselm." In *Stanford Encyclopedia of Philosophy, edited by* Edward N. Zalta. http://plato.stanford.edu/archives/spr2011/entries/anselm/.

5

Maimonides

KEEPS GOING, AND GOING, AND GOING . . . OR NOT?

STRANGE IDEA

The universe has either always existed, infinitely far back in time, or else had a first moment of creation—take your pick.

MAJOR PROPONENT

Maimonides (1138–1204)

BRIEF BIOGRAPHY

Moses ben Maimon, or Maimonides, was the greatest Jewish philosopher and rabbinic scholar of the medieval period and perhaps of all time. Born in Cordova, Spain, under relatively tolerant Muslim rule, things got much less tolerable when the Almohads arrived in 1148 along with their generous offer to all non-Muslims of the choice among conversion, exile, or death. Maimonides's family chose the second, moving first to Morocco and then, in 1166, to Egypt. There Maimonides achieved great fame working long days as a physician, seeing countless patients (including the Sultan), while working even longer evenings achieving great fame as a religious scholar and greater infamy as a philosopher. Indeed, his massive compendium of Jewish Law assured his reputation among orthodox Jewry as the leading rabbinic thinker of the day just as his great philosophical masterpiece, *The Guide for the Perplexed*, got itself banned and occasionally burned by the very same communities. Maimonides died in Fostat, now part of Old Cairo, in 1204.

A Rock and a Hard Place

That's what we're between in this chapter.

The rock is the idea that the universe has always existed. By the *universe* here we mean everything other than God Himself, which might include physical matter and anything nonphysical or spiritual, such as minds, souls, angels, and so on. In saying that it has always existed, we don't imply that any particular thing or kind of thing has always existed: only that things *of some sort* or another always have—something, in short, rather than nothing. And to say that it has *always* existed is to say that no matter how far back in time you go, *something* was always there. Think about the past, then think further back, and then further back still: there is always *something*.

The universe has just always sort of been there.

The hard place is the idea that the universe did have a beginning, a "first moment" of creation.

That may sound appealing until you think about what was going on before that first moment. Could the universe, the something, have been brought into being literally from or out of nothing? Does that even make sense? And mustn't there have been something, at least time itself, for there to have been a "before" that moment? But if there was time before the "first moment," then it wasn't a *first* moment after all! So there was no beginning, and the universe, to the contrary, has always existed. . . .

One of these must be right, it seems.

But both are pretty strange.

Reason, Maimonides will tell us, leaves us stuck between them.

The Guide for the Perplexed

That is the title for Maimonides's great philosophical masterpiece. And while you are likely to feel pretty perplexed *after* reading it, that's nothing, he thinks, compared to how perplexed we all are before we read his work.

Especially because we don't realize it.

For most people don't know enough even to realize how perplexing deep and important matters are. His book was therefore composed for that relative minority of individuals who are thoughtful enough to have already begun thinking about the deepest things and who have gotten just far enough to glimpse how far removed, sometimes, the truth of things might be from ordinary common sense. It was composed for people who have already begun to see how strange it all is.

It was composed for people like you.

Or at least people like you who are also drawn toward leading a religiously observant life and who have had just enough exposure to philosophy to begin questioning that life but not quite enough to begin answering those questions. What such people desperately need, Maimonides thinks, is a wide-ranging, systematic, and coherent theology and, most of all, an honest one: namely, one that recognizes the very real limits that we human beings must confront in our effort to understand the universe.

It's in that context that we now enter that narrow space between the rock and the hard place.

"In the Beginning . . . "

"God created the heavens and the earth."

So it says in the beginning of many common translations of the Hebrew Bible. But what it doesn't say is what that all means.

Fortunately, the philosophers had already had fifteen centuries, by Maimonides's time, to think about the "beginning," so Maimonides begins his own investigation with a look at what some of his august predecessors had to say on the subject.

Three Theories of the Beginning

"Among those who believe in the existence of God," Maimonides writes, "there are found three different theories as regards the question whether the [universe] is eternal or not" (II.XIII, 171).[1]

The first theory is that the universe was brought into existence by God out of nonexistence or nothingness. This theory is of course widely held by many religious believers. We'll refer to it by the Latin expression *creation ex nihilo*, or "creation out of nothing."

The second theory belongs to "all philosophers whose opinions and works are known to us" (II.XIII, 172). By these, he seems to mean most philosophers of his time, including major Christian and Islamic philosophers in addition to Plato. According to this theory, "a certain substance has coexisted with God from eternity" (II.XIII, 172). There never was absolutely nothing, in other words, but rather there has always been *something*. This is not to deny that God played some important causal role with respect to the universe. But it was not the work of creating something out of nothing.

So what was it?

A common idea from Plato's time onward was that, just as a proper understanding of a sculpture requires reference to its shape or form and to the material of which it is composed, so too must *all* created things be understood as a
combination of both "matter" and "form." And just as a sculptor can do nothing without some material to work with, the theory here is that God may well
have shaped our universe into its current form, but even He needed some matter to work with. This matter "has coexisted with God from eternity" and stands

> in the same relation to God as the clay [does] to the potter. . . . God can do with
> it what He pleases; at one time He forms of it heaven and earth, at another time
> He forms some other thing. (II.XIII, 172)

On this second theory, then, matter itself has always existed, while God's
role was (merely) to shape or form it into the universe as we now see it—rec-
ognizing that the particular form of the universe may well undergo various
sorts of changes over time.

Finally, the third theory is one Maimonides attributes to "Aristotle, his
followers, and commentators" (II.XIII, 173). This theory agrees with the second that the universe as a whole is eternal but disagrees that it has taken on
different forms over time. For the universe, it holds, "in its totality has never
been different, nor will it ever change" (II.XIII, 173). Not only is basic matter eternal, then, but so are even the specific forms that matter has taken on.

Three theories, then.

To choose among them, we'll need some arguments.

First Make the Job a Little Easier

Maimonides doesn't usually care about making our intellectual burdens any
lighter, but here for once he is good enough to do so.

For he first maintains that he needn't bother to address the second and
third theories separately. What matters to him is only whether the universe
was created *ex nihilo*, as religion teaches, or whether it has always existed, and
despite their differences of detail, the second and third theories agree that
something has always existed, from eternity. They may therefore be treated as
a single competitor to *creation ex nihilo*.

So why exactly do their proponents believe that the universe has always
existed?

Two Arguments for Eternity

Maimonides quickly returns to making our lives more difficult again. For he
next takes us through no fewer than eight Aristotelian arguments for the eter-

nity of the universe, pausing only to throw in some Aristotelian objections to the *creation ex nihilo* theory along the way. But since our mere human lives—possibly unlike the universe—are sadly finite, we'll just look at a couple here.

(1) Aristotle's "First Method" for proving eternity, according to Maimonides, goes like this:

> According to Aristotle, motion . . . is eternal. For if the motion had a beginning, there must already have been some motion when it came into existence, for transition from . . . non-existence into existence, always implies motion; then that previous motion, the cause of the motion which follows, must be eternal, or else the series would have to be carried back *ad infinitum*. (II.XIV, 174)

Wherever there is change or motion, that change or motion either has always been in process or had a beginning. If it has always been in process, then it is eternal, and we have made our point. But if it had a beginning, then there must have been something to *cause* that change or motion. But then the thing causing the change or motion must itself be changing or moving, to transition from being in a state of not causing to a state of causing. But then that *new* change or motion is itself either eternal (and we've made our point) or had a beginning, and if the latter, then there must have been an even *earlier* cause of that change, and so on, all the way back to infinity—in which case, too, the universe has existed from eternity.

So either way, the universe is eternal.

(2) And then there's Aristotle's "Sixth Method":

> An agent is active at one time and inactive at another, according as favourable or unfavourable circumstances arise. . . . As, however, God is not subject to . . . [changes] in His will, and is not affected by obstacles and hindrances that might appear or disappear, it is impossible . . . to imagine that God is active at one time and inactive at another. He is, on the contrary, always active in the same manner as He is always in actual existence. (II.XIV, 175)

If God did create the universe *ex nihilo*, then He must have moved from a state of not acting (before creating) to one of acting (in creating). But God, in being unlimited in power, could not be constrained by transient external obstacles, nor, in being perfect and eternal Himself, could He ever be moved to act by transient external "favourable" circumstances. It follows then that whatever God does, in His eternal and unchanging state, He always has been doing and always will do. If God creates the universe at all, then, He has always been creating it (and always will).

In which case, the universe is as eternal as God.

And then if these two arguments aren't enough for you—if you were still leaning toward *creation ex nihilo*—you've got to deal with some difficult problems first.

Two Problems for *Creation Ex Nihilo*

(1) For one, you'll need to develop a theory of time.

For time is not an object or a thing in the way that a material object is. Time doesn't just sit there, occupying space, as material objects do; time itself has no causal properties. If time is real, then, it is not itself a thing but rather must be the *property* of some thing or things. Indeed, one plausible idea is that time is really just the measure of motion: a year, say, is what measures the return of the physical earth to the same location relative to the sun, as a day is what measures a complete rotation of the earth. But if time is the measure of motion, there can be no time where there is no motion. And since there can be no motion where there are no things moving, there could be no time before there were any things in the universe.

But *creation ex nihilo* requires that there *was* time before there were things: for it says that first there was nothing, *and then*, later, there was something. So *creation ex nihilo* requires something which simply cannot be.

(2) And then there is the inconvenient fact that *creation ex nihilo* seems to be rather inconceivable, as the philosophers might say. It is certainly hard to imagine how one might bring something into being out of absolutely nothing. But it may even be a *contradiction* and thus quite impossible.

Why?

Objects consist (it was held, recall) of both matter and form; causal activity then consists of imparting varying forms into matter, matter that must already exist to receive the causal activity. To cause an object consisting of matter and form to come into existence *ex nihilo* seems to require, then, that the matter be absent (the *nihilo* part) and simultaneously present, to receive the causal activity. But that is a clear contradiction and therefore impossible.

So much the worse for *creation ex nihilo*.

Reason Strikes Back—Against the Arguments for Eternity

But Maimonides is not about to let Aristotle and his ilk have the last word.

First, the two arguments for eternity.

(1) Eternal motion?

Very nice, except for one thing: the argument presumes that how things were for God "at the beginning" are exactly as things are right now, for us. All the motion we currently observe does require a causal explanation, which in turn requires an earlier motion, and so on. But on what basis may we assume that how things are right now must be how they always have been, in particular when we are talking about God?

Every fully developed thing, Maimonides observes, has different properties from those it had when it first came into being. The human embryo in the womb (for example) has little in common with the adult human being. If you project the adult's properties backward in time, onto that embryo, you are almost certain to go wrong: if you see the adult eat and drink through her mouth and then conclude that the embryo in the womb must have done the same, then you will surely deserve the failing grade you receive on your biology exam.

But then it follows that just because motion *now* has certain characteristics and requires certain causal explanations, there is no reason to demand that earlier motion, original motion, as it were, has the same. And once we relinquish that demand, there is no reason to hold that motion ultimately goes back to eternity: there might well have been an initial, original motion that constituted the creation of the universe.

(2) God's changing states?

The argument is plausible enough, Maimonides observes, when applied to finite, physical beings dealing with external factors: when external conditions get cold, we human beings are moved to seek shelter, and when the conditions get warm, we move back outside. Our wills are, indeed, transient, changeable, and constantly affected by external conditions.

But it's precisely this that does *not* apply to God. When an "action has no other purpose whatever than to fulfil the will, then the will does not depend on . . . [external] circumstances" (II.XVIII, 182): God's will is not, therefore, motivated by anything external and transient.

But then, the Aristotelian objects, "is not change imputed [merely] in the fact that the will of the being exists at one time and not at another?" (II.XVIII, 183). Aren't we projecting a change in God's will, in other words, when we imagine that first He is not creating and then, subsequently, He creates?

No, Maimonides replies, you are again wrongly projecting truths about finite physical human beings onto God. We "first" will something and "then" will something else; our wills change. But the

> will of an absolutely spiritual being [like God] which does not depend on external causes is unchangeable, and the fact that the being desires one thing one day and another thing another day, does not imply a change in the essence of that being. (II.XVIII, 183)

It's not that God first wills for the thing to occur on day one and *then* wills for it not to occur on day two but, rather, that God eternally, unchangingly, wills both that it occur on day one and that it not occur on day two. God's will does not therefore change over time; it's rather that God unchangingly wills that the *world* change over time. Thus, Maimonides concludes, we need not hold "that the Creation, after a period of inaction, is due to a change in the Creator Himself" (II.XVIII, 182).

So much for the arguments for eternity.

Reason Strikes Back—Against the Two Problems for *Creation Ex Nihilo*

(1) The theory of time?

Everything is correct about this objection, Maimonides suggests, except its conclusion.

True, there could exist no time unless there were things moving. But rather than conclude that there has always been motion, one should conclude that, in the beginning, *God created time along with the moving things.* There never was a moment "before" creation, in other words, because there was no time before creation. There was just creation, of the first things along with the first moment, and the universe has been on its way ever since. And that, ultimately, is what *creation ex nihilo* is all about: that creation occurs from nothing, from nothing prior, in some initial moment.

(2) Yes, but what about the inconceivability, the contradiction?

Yes, Maimonides grants, there would perhaps be a contradiction were we to imagine finite beings such as ourselves creating something out of nothing. But that's our problem, not God's. For you only get the contradiction mentioned earlier when you assume that matter must previously be present for creation to occur. But it is precisely that assumption that is challenged when it is *divine* creation in question. Before God created the world, there need not have been any preexisting matter. And that is just to say that there is no contradiction in allowing *creation ex nihilo.*

So much for the two problems for *creation ex nihilo.*

So have we now proved that the first theory of the universe, *creation ex nihilo*, is correct?

One Argument for *Creation Ex Nihilo*

Not yet.

We've only shown that *creation ex nihilo* is not *impossible* and not obviously false. To prove that it's actually *true*, Maimonides would need to find explicit arguments directly supporting it. And, fortunately, there were plenty of such arguments available to him. For there was a prominent school of medieval Islamic philosophers known as the *Kalām*, who generated many such arguments, some of which might even strike us today as pretty compelling.

Here's one small example of such an argument, as presented a century later by "the Christian Maimonides," as some refer to Thomas Aquinas (1225–1274):

> If the world always was, the consequence is that infinite days preceded this present day. But it is impossible to pass through an infinite medium. Therefore we should never have arrived at this present day; which is manifestly false.[2]

This argument points out a deep problem in holding that the universe has existed eternally. To say that the universe has always existed is to say that its duration stretches infinitely far back into the past. But if so, then to have arrived at this present day, the universe must in fact have completed an infinite journey, from way back then to now. But surely one could never complete an infinite journey! It must therefore be *false* that the universe stretches back infinitely far in time. There must then have been a first moment: the moment of creation.

Pretty convincing, yes?

Striking Back at Reason Itself

No, unfortunately.

Maimonides, in a moment of perhaps uncharacteristic humility, admits that he cannot *prove* the doctrine of *creation ex nihilo*. In a further moment of his in fact quite characteristic intellectual integrity, he notes that

> another person may perhaps be able to establish by proof what appears doubtful to me. It is on account of my great love of truth that I have shown my embarrassment in these matters, and I have not heard, nor do I know that any of these theories have been established by proof. (II.XXIV, 198–99)

It's not that Maimonides doesn't know the many *Kalām* arguments attempting to prove *creation ex nihilo*. It's just that he doesn't find any of them convincing. Moreover, he thinks it very dangerous (from the perspective of religious people) to accept such important doctrines as *creation ex nihilo* on the basis of faulty proofs: for if you do so, then you risk people's promptly rejecting the doctrine as soon as the flaws in the proofs are exposed. Far better, he suggests, "that a proposition which cannot be [proved] be received as an [unproved] axiom, or that . . . [it] be accepted [merely] on [religious] authority" (II.XVI, 178).

In short, it's far better for people to believe in *creation ex nihilo* as a mere article of faith and so go on to develop the right religious beliefs and practices than to risk their rejecting that belief and, consequently, their religious beliefs and practices, by falsely advertising *creation ex nihilo* as rationally proven.

Aquinas agreed with his Jewish predecessor here and so was as concerned as the latter in determining just where the limits of reason lie, that is, which religious doctrines can actually be proven and which must be accepted merely on the basis of revelation or religious authority. And, indeed, Aquinas agreed that the particular argument just presented for *creation ex nihilo* was not convincing:

> Passage is always understood as being from term to term. Whatever bygone day we choose, from it to the present day there is a finite number of days which can be passed through. The [argument] is founded on the idea that, given two extremes, there is an infinite number of mean terms.[3]

The point is subtle but quite lovely. Aquinas agrees that one could never complete a journey of infinite length, but he denies that the eternity of the universe entails that one has actually done that. After all, he says, pick any day in the past you like and compute the length of time between that day and the present day, and you will always generate a finite number! The temporal distance from a week ago to today is seven days; from a billion years ago to today is a billion years, very large but finite; and so on. You can *never* find a day, no matter how long back you look, from which an infinite number of days has been traversed to the present day, even *if* the universe has no first moment.

The small conclusion: this argument for *creation ex nihilo* fails.

The medium conclusion: reason on its own cannot prove *creation ex nihilo*, nor can it prove, as we've seen, the competing idea that the universe is eternal.

From the perspective of reason, then, equally strong arguments can be made for both our strange ideas—eternity and *creation ex nihilo*—but reason cannot ultimately determine which arguments prevail.

The big conclusion, then: the debate is a draw.

Reason Isn't Everything

Or at least it's a draw from the perspective of reason, according to which, as Maimonides puts it, "either of the two theories . . . [is] admissible" (II.XVI, 178). But sometimes—and this is a philosopher speaking—we have reasons *beyond* reason to believe certain things.

If you are a religious person, then you may have religious reasons to believe certain things. After acknowledging that both theories are "admissible," for example, Maimonides continues, "I accept [Creation] on the authority of Prophecy, which can teach things beyond the reach of philosophical speculation" (II.XVI, 178).

But it needn't just be "prophecy" if that response doesn't satisfy you.

Maimonides goes on to argue that accepting *creation ex nihilo* allows you to make sense of a number of other important religious doctrines as well. That the universe is intentionally designed by God, that it has an ultimate purpose, that miracles sometimes occur, that there's room for people to exercise genuine free will, and so on, he argues, all fit better with *creation ex nihilo* than they do with the doctrine of eternity. This fit is not quite an argument for the former's truth, of course, but it does show the numerous theoretical advantages that accrue once you accept the doctrine "as an axiom," or on authority.

And then there may be rather profound practical considerations.

The best human life, Maimonides thinks, requires living as a member of a community. Religious devotion, he further thinks, provides the glue that keeps communities together and thus makes the best human lives possible. If you accept the eternity of the universe, you will lose those other important religious doctrines: the eternity doctrine is "apt to corrupt the notions concerning God" (II.XXII, 194). If you had genuine proofs of eternity, fine: intellectual integrity would require affirming it. But in the absence of such proofs, in the absence of certain proofs either way, then you should affirm the doctrine that will better support religion, and thus community, and thus the possibility of the best human lives.

That is not itself, again, an argument for the truth of *creation ex nihilo*. But it's an argument for believing it anyway.

Notes

1. All Maimonides quotations are from M. Friedländer (1904/1956).
2. St. Thomas Aquinas (Fathers of the English Dominican Province 1920, 1.Q46. A2, 242–43).
3. St. Thomas Aquinas (Fathers of the English Dominican Province 1920, 244).

Primary Sources

Fathers of the English Dominican Province, trans. 1920. *St. Thomas Aquinas: Summa Theologica.* Allen, TX: Christian Classics.
Friedländer, M., trans. 1904/1956. *The Guide for the Perplexed by Moses Maimonides.* New York: Dover.

Recommended Secondary Sources

Seeskin, Kenneth, ed. 2005. *The Cambridge Companion to Maimonides*. Cambridge, UK: Cambridge University Press.

———. 2010. "Maimonides." In *Stanford Encyclopedia of Philosophy*, edited by Edward N. Zalta. http://plato.stanford.edu/archives/spr2010/entries/maimonides/.

6

Thomas Aquinas

GOD HAS *NOT* BEEN ON VACATION SINCE THE ORIGINAL CREATION

STRANGE IDEA

God didn't merely create the universe at the beginning but continuously re-creates it at every moment.

MAJOR PROPONENT

Thomas Aquinas (1225–1274)

BRIEF BIOGRAPHY

Born in a town midway between Rome and Naples, Aquinas was already studying at the local Benedictine abbey by the age of five. In 1239, he moved to the University of Naples, where at nineteen, he decided to join the Dominican Order. His parents, apparently strongly preferring the Benedictine Order, promptly had him kidnapped and detained for two years. Eventually, his mother let him escape through a window to go join the Dominicans, with whom Aquinas traveled to Cologne to study with Albertus Magnus, then on to the University of Paris, where he assumed a prestigious chair of theology. Over the next decade, he moved around often, studying, teaching, and writing all over Italy, before returning to Paris. But then during a mass in December of 1273, he suddenly had a mystical experience so profound that he stopped working altogether thereafter. When queried, he said only that all that he had written seemed like "mere straw" to him. A few months later, he was dead. Though some of his voluminous writings were initially controversial—three years after his death many of his ideas were officially condemned—they soon became officially required reading, in effect, and he went on to be canonized in 1323 and made doctor of the church in 1568.

Back to the Beginning

"In the beginning God created the heavens and the earth."

The dramatic beginning of the Hebrew Bible needs no further introduction, particularly in light of our discussion in the previous chapter. But philosophers are especially fond of extending things—such as the beginning of the universe backward, to infinity—so no matter how extended our discussion of the universe has been so far, you can be sure it can always be further extended.

So there's no conclusive proof about whether the universe had a beginning; that, at any rate, was the conclusion of the previous chapter. But if we are to take the scriptures at all seriously, then we must admit that despite this lack of "proof," the opening expression seems clear enough: God created the universe *in the beginning.* And what that surely suggests is that His act of creation occurred at a specific time, namely the "beginning," the very first moment, whenever exactly that was, long ago. But that in turn now suggests something else: that the act of creation was just that, a "creating," an act that would cease as soon as the thing being created was finished being created, in this case the very instant after the universe came into being: the *second* moment, as it were (or the "seventh day," if you want to be nitpicky about the scriptures).

Clear enough—unless you are a philosopher.

The Second Moment

But the universe didn't stop there.

For no sooner did it come into being than it began to change in various ways. Indeed, even Aristotle admits as much, the same Aristotle who argued in the last chapter that the universe was eternally *unchanging:* for he meant that only in a general sense, with respect to the *kinds* of things there are, and he was perfectly happy to admit that all the details, the particulars, of the universe are continuously in flux. Details, for example, about just which individual creatures there are: at one moment the population of the universe is one particular set of individuals, but check back in a hundred years, or a million, and chances are that a whole host of new individuals have taken over. Your great grandparents only came into being at their births, for example, or maybe their conceptions. But it's a pretty safe bet that they are no longer around, having been replaced on this planet first by your grandparents, then by your parents, and then most recently by you.

It's too depressing to continue this thought any further forward in time, so let's not. You get the point: since the "beginning," a lot of new things have come into being and then been replaced by even more new things.

So, now, who is responsible for all that creating?

A Couple of Lousy Options

Well, God created "in the beginning." If that means what it says, then it seems to follow that by the second moment, He was done. So whoever was responsible for creating all the beings that weren't present in the beginning was not God. That would all be very well and good except for the fact that many religious thinkers don't like this idea. It sounds like saying that God is not in fact responsible for the existence of everything, since there are things, gazillions of things, that He did not Himself create. It would be far preferable, most such thinkers hold, were *everything*, every thing, to depend on God for its existence, were God to be the creator of all.

That suggests a very tempting second option perhaps: to say that God does all the creating after the beginning too. Now *that* would be very well and good except for one other thing: it seems to make every thing that exists quite literally count as a miracle. After all, the initial creation of the universe out of nothing, its *creation ex nihilo*, is generally deemed to be the first and greatest of all the miracles that God has performed. To then add to this miracle the claim that God has also created all the subsequent beings, too, would seem to elevate the value of those latter at the cost of devaluing the original creation. Part of the great miracle of *creation ex nihilo* is precisely that it's not the sort of thing that happens every day. It loses that cachet if it *is* the kind of thing that does happen every day.

So, two options so far but two lousy ones.

Perhaps we can do better.

A Third, Medieval Option?

When in doubt in philosophy, one goes medieval.

Medieval philosophers love to make distinctions, and one such might be helpful in fixing the second option here. The basic idea is to distinguish between two kinds or manners of creating and then suggest that the kind of creating God does "in the beginning" is different from, and more impressive than, the kind of creating He does at every moment thereafter. If that works, then we can say that God does indeed create every thing, from the first moment to the current moment, without elevating each creation after the beginning to the same status of the creation at the beginning.

Let us distinguish, then, between *creation ex nihilo* and, to use a bit more Latin, *creation ex materia*.

The former is old hat for us. It is creation "out of nothing," and I shall now use the term exclusively to refer to what God did at the beginning and to what only God is *ever* capable of doing: creating some thing where the instant before there was literally nothing at all (other than God Himself, of course). Most philosophers appreciate how hard it is to make sense of this idea, as we saw, since it seems impossible to understand how something could be brought into being out of absolutely nothing, and that's why most philosophical theists restrict this ability to God and count it as a miracle beyond the ken of our reason.

But now *creation ex materia* is far less mysterious and not particularly miraculous: it means creation "out of matter," and it's what occurs when something new is merely fashioned out of matter or materials that themselves are already preexisting. When a sculptor sculpts a sculpture out of clay, when an auto manufacturer assembles an auto, when nuclear fusion creates a lovely horrible massive explosion: all of these are instances of *creation ex materia*. As our examples show, this manner of creation need not be the exclusive domain of God, as even we mere mortals do it all the time. Nothing miraculous here; nothing particularly impressive: *creation ex materia* thus nicely fits the bill of being less significant in rank than *creation ex nihilo*.

And that point indicates how we may use the distinction to create a third option to supplement our previous lousy two. We may now say that the miraculous act of creation described in the Hebrew Bible was God's creating the world *ex nihilo*. That act ceased when the "heavens and earth"—all physical matter throughout the cosmos, perhaps all nonphysical things too—came into being, in that first moment. Subsequently, many new individuals have arisen by ever-changing new combinations of physical matter (and perhaps nonphysical too), but there is nothing miraculous about this: it is only an ongoing process of *creation ex materia*. If we must insist that God is directly causally responsible for the creation of all subsequent beings, then we may say that He creates all these later beings by *creation ex materia*.

But wait a moment—must we insist on God's direct causal responsibility for the creation of every thing?

A Fourth Option

Perhaps not.

Perhaps it isn't absolutely necessary to insist on God's *direct* causal responsibility, for the preceding remarks now suggest another possibility: given the distinction between *creation ex nihilo* and *creation ex materia*, we might allow that created things themselves, or *creatures*, have direct responsibility for creating some things on their own.

By "creature," I don't mean merely animals, as the word is generally used today: I mean any created thing, which is presumably everything other than God Himself. This would include animals but also all other living things, and inanimate things, and anything else (if those categories aren't exhaustive!). In the case at hand, then, we might say this: perhaps God originally created the universe *ex nihilo*, but then, subsequently, other beings have arisen by means of *creation ex materia*—performed not necessarily by God but, perhaps, by the various creatures themselves, or maybe even the laws of nature.

On this view, God maintains *indirect* causal responsibility for every thing, for He creates *ex nihilo* the beings that, with their natures and by means of the laws of nature, then create *ex materia* the subsequent beings. Indeed, this view fits nicely with what we observe every day: creatures in the world, including ourselves, bring other creatures into being, either by very pleasant biological processes or by mechanical processes such as the construction of artifacts. God started the whole ball rolling and then equipped the ball to continue rolling, so He gets ultimate causal credit; but His creatures can share in the process too.

So our third option in fact has split into two: once we distinguish *creation ex nihilo* from *creation ex materia*, we can decide whether creatures are responsible for the latter or whether it is God alone who is responsible for all.

But Never Mind: They're Both Lousy Too

In chapter 9, we'll look at one philosopher's arguments that God alone does pretty much everything. But fortunately we can spare ourselves, here, the work of choosing between the third and fourth options. Neither will actually solve our problem.

For we have a deeper problem.

Suppose we do invoke *creation ex materia* to solve our initial problem, the one about giving God causal responsibility for creating new individuals without our having to admit continuous miracles.

The deeper problem is this: even if all subsequent creation involves merely new beings being fashioned from preexisting matter, what is it, exactly, that keeps all that matter, out of which the new individuals are created, in existence from moment to moment? After all, the sculptor will only successfully fashion a new sculpture if her clay remains in existence throughout the process. A similar problem arises for spiritual things such as souls and minds, and although it's not thought that new individuals are formed from or "out of" these, we still must wonder what keeps a soul or mind in existence once it is created. It's only after we have a satisfactory answer to *this* problem that we can even think about invoking *creation ex materia* to solve our first problem.

Since God's initial act of creation seems, by the Hebrew Bible, to be limited to the first moment, it might be tempting to believe that matter, or creatures more generally, is, once created, such that it is able to persist in being all on its own, without divine assistance.

Tempting unless, of course, you are Thomas Aquinas.

Continuous Creation

Most philosophers in Aquinas's thirteenth century agreed that God created the universe in the first place. But then opinions began to diverge with respect to the precise relationship that God has had with the universe since then. Some believed that God has indeed left it alone, the occasional miracle aside, that just as a builder builds a house that then persists on its own, so too, God's universe now persists on its own, matter in general and minds and souls in particular.

But this tempting doctrine, Aquinas believed, is false: God didn't merely create the universe but must also continuously act to *keep* all things in existence. Creation was not a one-time activity but ongoing.

God *continuously* creates the world, to put it dramatically.

But now why *in* the world should one believe that?

Being and Becoming (and the Causing Thereof)

Did we mention that medieval philosophers love to make distinctions?

Here is another one: the distinction between the *becoming* of a thing and the *being* of the thing. The "becoming" of the thing refers to the process of its coming *into* being; the "being" of the thing refers to its basic nature, to what it fundamentally is (on which I will elaborate shortly).

And then here is another one: if there is a distinction between becoming and being, then there must also be a distinction between the *causing* of becoming and the *causing* of being with respect to a given thing.

As Aquinas describes it, to cause the becoming of a thing is, basically, to cause it *ex materia*. The builder causes the becoming of the house just as a cook causes the becoming of the meal: in both cases, the agent, the one doing the causing, arranges preexisting materials (bricks and cement or meat and spices, respectively) in various new ways to bring about a new entity, an "effect." The agent is responsible here for the process by which the effect comes into being, or "becomes."

In so doing, however, the agent does not cause the *being* of his effects.

For the being of a thing concerns not the process whereby it comes into existence but rather its basic nature and properties. The fact that bricks have or can have certain properties (such as hardness, weight, and shape), the fact that cement has or can have certain properties (such as hardness and strength), the fact that bricks with their various properties can be combined with cement, with its various properties, in various ways—these are due to the very nature (or "being") of bricks and cement. So, too, with respect to the being of the house that gets built with these bricks and cement: the fact that it has its various properties (size, shape, heat insulation, etc.) in turn depends on the nature and properties of the materials that constitute it, along with the ways that these materials are arranged. The builder is not himself responsible for any of these; he arranges the materials, but he doesn't give them their properties or nature.

The builder is responsible for causing the *becoming* of the house, in other words, for the process of arranging the materials, but he is not responsible for causing its *being*, for the fact that materials with those properties *can* be arranged to produce a house with those properties.

In a similar way, the cook creates neither the meat nor the spices, *nor* the fact that when they are so arranged and processed, the result is that delicious spicy meat dish; she is responsible merely for the fact that something with this being, this nature, has now "come" into being, or "become."

But now wait a minute. If the builder and the cook are causally responsible only for becoming but not for being—who is?

No One?

But why must anyone or anything be responsible at all? Couldn't being just be what it is, on its own, without having been caused?

Those are good questions. The kinds of questions philosophers love. Because they get right to the heart of some very deep things.

In this case, the deep thing is this: is the universe even intelligible? Does it, must it, make *sense* to us? Or might it just consist of a random collection of disordered things and events, with perhaps a little rhyme but definitely no reason?

Well, if you're a philosopher, you'll certainly at least hope for the former. Or at least you'll have to work on the assumption that the universe does, as a whole, make sense—perhaps not common sense (clearly) but *some* sense. And if it is to make any sense at all then, it seems, whenever things happen or whenever things exist, there must be a cause or explanation for their happening and existing.

So if being is a real thing, a real phenomenon, then someone or something must be causally responsible for it.

Although we'll revisit the point in chapter 9, there is no particular controversy for our current concerns over who or what causes the becoming of various things: individual creatures (such as builders and cooks) can cause *ex materia*. But who, then, could be responsible for the *being* of things? For the fact that there even exist certain kinds of basic materials and the fact that these materials will, when variously arranged, result in various things with various properties or features?

For the most basic, fundamental properties of the universe?

When you put it that way, it's pretty easy to appreciate Aquinas's answer: not the builder or the cook, obviously, but God.

But What Does That Have to Do with Continuous Creation?

Only everything.

Let's get back to the whole intelligibility thing.

Whatever is real must have some cause.

But now there's a general principle about causation that Aquinas endorses: a particular effect only obtains while the cause is actively causing. Otherwise (if you think about it), the effect would be in existence without a cause, and it would be unintelligible to us why the effect exists. This causal principle quite readily applies to the causing of becoming: the becoming of an effect (the process of building, in our example) only occurs while the agent, the builder, is actively doing his thing. When he goes on his lunch break, so does the process of building.

But now, Aquinas argues, this causal principle must also apply to the being of an effect as well. As he puts it,

> as the becoming of a thing cannot continue when that action of the agent ceases which causes the *becoming* of the effect: so neither can the *being* of a thing continue after that action of the agent has ceased, which is the cause of the effect . . . in *being*.[1]

The facts that its materials continue to exist, that they have their properties, that when so arranged they result in a house: these very basic facts, too, will only persist as long as their cause keeps doing *its* thing.

So yes, then, when the builder finishes his activity of building, the process of becoming ceases, but the house continues to persist in existence (at least if he is competent!). But this does not mean that the house is continuing to persist in existence *on its own*. For as long as the house persists in being, as long as those basic facts about its nature and properties continue to obtain, then the cause of that being must be continuing *its* activity, of causing being.

And, of course, it's not just things like buildings that persist in being. It is the universe as a whole, with its own basic nature and properties. If the universe as a whole persists in being, then its cause of being must persist in its causal activity.

So God didn't merely cause the creation of the universe in the beginning, concludes Aquinas. He continuously causes its being at every moment in which it persists.

God continuously creates everything and every thing.

But Wait, There's More!

If you accept this conclusion, it turns out, you get an additional theological bonus at no extra charge.

Aquinas, along with many others, believes that it's antithetical to God's nature for Him to actively destroy anything. Truly pure goodness or *infinite* goodness, the thought goes, must produce only being and not produce non-being or destruction, for only the former is genuinely good. Yet creatures quite obviously go out of existence sometimes. So if we are to avoid saying that things occur without God being involved, we must say that God is responsible for those creatures going out of existence. Yet how could He be if His nature rules out the ability to actively destroy?

With continuous creation in the arsenal, we've got our answer.

For God is indeed actively responsible for the existence of all the beings in the universe, by virtue of His continuously creating being, by continuously willing that various creatures exist. But, if so, then He may remove a creature from being without ever directly or actively willing that that creature be destroyed: He need simply *cease to will its existence.* Or as Aquinas puts it,

> if God were to annihilate anything, this would not imply an action on God's part; but a mere cessation of His action.[2]

All God does, then, is create existence or being, as His purely good nature requires; creatures stop existing only when God—for good reasons, we assume—*stops creating* them.

So God continuously creates except, sometimes, when He doesn't.

Then poof!

It's a Miracle!

Of course it is.

The creation of being, as described, pretty much just is *creation ex nihilo*, and we have just learned that this process was not confined to the beginning after all but is ongoing and continuous. We are more or less back in the category of the aforementioned "second option."

Except that there are resources available to us now that perhaps mitigate the earlier concern about the multiplicity of miracles. In particular, we've got the distinction between being and becoming and the causing thereof. So we can now deal with the fact that new creatures are constantly coming into existence by attributing it to the causing of becoming, which isn't particularly miraculous, especially if we also choose to assign that causing to the creatures themselves.

Of course, it's true that the ongoing existence of being remains miraculous, an ongoing *creation ex nihilo*, but that, perhaps, is just as it should be. For we can now see that every individual thing, the arising of each creature, may be understood as an appealing combination of the miraculous and the ordinary.

The builder builds; a house comes into being.

That there should exist this particular thing, this particular house, here and now, rather than some other particular thing; that bricks and cement have been combined this way to produce a house, rather than other materials having been combined to produce an ice cream cone or an apple tree—that isn't itself any particular miracle but attributable to ordinary causal processes involving creatures and the laws of nature. The fact that a house now exists here (rather than something else) may thus be assigned to the builder, which would perhaps justify the extraordinarily large bill he just gave us.

But that there exists *anything at all*—at any time or in any place, including here and now where our new house is—rather than nothing; that there is being and not complete nothingness; that the whole package persists and doesn't just evaporate into a void: well, that *is* rather miraculous, in the end, and justifiably attributable to God.

Now let's just hope it doesn't go *poof!* for a while.

Notes

1. St. Thomas Aquinas (Fathers of the English Dominican Province 1920, 1.Q104. A1, 512).

2. St. Thomas Aquinas (Fathers of the English Dominican Province 1920, 1.Q104. A3, 514).

Primary Sources

Bourke, Vernon J., trans. 1975. "That God Preserves Things in Being." In *Thomas Aquinas: Summa Contra Gentiles*, III.65. South Bend, IN: University of Notre Dame Press.

Fathers of the English Dominican Province, trans. 1920. *St. Thomas Aquinas: Summa Theologica*. Allen, TX: Christian Classics.

Recommended Secondary Sources

Kretzmann, Norman, and Eleonore Stump, eds. 1993. *The Cambridge Companion to Aquinas*. Cambridge: Cambridge University Press.

McInerny, Ralph, and John O'Callaghan. 2010. "Saint Thomas Aquinas." In *Stanford Encyclopedia of Philosophy*, edited by Edward N. Zalta. http://plato.stanford.edu/archives/win2010/entries/aquinas/.

7

René Descartes

"A Monstrous Thesis"

STRANGE IDEA

Animals entirely lack thoughts, feelings, and sensations and instead are merely mindless automatons.

MAJOR PROPONENT

René Descartes (1596–1650)

BRIEF BIOGRAPHY

Born in northern France, "the father of modern philosophy" was sent at age ten to the prestigious Jesuit school at La Flèche, where he developed reputations for being good both at math and at sleeping late. After completing his education, he joined the army, as doing so was a good way to get free travel and board and, since he was a volunteer, he wouldn't actually have to fight anyone. In November of 1619, when his regiment was wintering in Germany, he had the profound contemplative experience that would result, years later, in the world's most famous philosophical slogan, "I think therefore I am." After some years in Paris establishing his reputation as the world's greatest mathematician, he moved to Holland in 1628, where he would spend two decades cementing an additional reputation as the world's greatest natural philosopher (or "scientist"). Along the way, he became embroiled in many intellectual controversies, but this further reputation for cantankerousness didn't prevent him from being invited, in 1649, to become personal tutor to Queen Christina of Sweden. What Her Highness didn't mention, however, was that she wanted her lessons at five in the morning, which didn't fit well with his sleeping habits mentioned earlier. Soon after arriving in Stockholm, Descartes developed pneumonia and died.

Truth in Fiction?

There's a famous (and hopefully made-up) story about the hero of this chapter.[1] Never marrying, Descartes preferred instead, it seems, to spend time with a life-sized mechanical doll, so much so that he carried it (or "her"?) with him wherever he traveled, in a specially designed case. One night, while he was traveling on a ship, the captain and the crew got curious. Restraining the philosopher, they grabbed his oversized piece of luggage and opened it. Horrified, they promptly tossed the creature overboard, though not, for some reason, fortunately, Descartes himself.

This story is perhaps at least exaggerated. Nevertheless, it may contain a grain of truth, at least in reflecting Descartes's sincere and deep commitment to the scientific theory of the world that he himself developed. Indeed, it is his scientific theory, known as *the mechanical philosophy*, that ultimately earned Descartes the title of "father of modern philosophy" by which he is widely known today.

Before we can appreciate how Descartes came to his very strange idea about animals, then, we'll need to look at his science.

The Mechanical Philosophy

This theory consists of two major components.

(1) *Dualism.* This is the doctrine that the world contains two fundamentally different kinds of substances or things: mental and physical. "Mental" things are minds or souls, concepts used more or less interchangeably by Descartes. "Physical" things are everything else, everything made of matter, including the stars and planets and the earth and, most important, the bodies of animals, including humans. Minds and their states are nonphysical or immaterial; matter, in itself, is entirely devoid of all mental properties and lacks all capacity for thought or awareness.

(2) *Mechanism.* This is the doctrine that, apart from the possible causal influences of minds, physical matter itself operates purely "mechanically," or like a machine. Matter, being devoid of all thought, is characterized only by such passive properties as having a size or shape and is thus incapable of moving itself; thus, Descartes holds, God, upon creation, must Himself have originally set matter in motion, and all motions since creation are subsequently governed by the "laws of motion" discovered by physicists.

And that is all.

What Does the Mechanical Philosophy Explain?

Everything, more or less.

Or so thought Descartes, who was known for many great things, though humility was not among them.

Descartes in fact had plenty of evidence supporting the mechanical philosophy, which was one reason why the theory was extremely influential throughout the seventeenth century. Indeed, he himself did more than perhaps anyone in showing just how much one could explain about the world in purely mechanical terms. He even wrote works called *The World* and *Treatise on Man,* in which he explained almost *everything* about the world and man, respectively: the origin of the cosmos, the nature of the sun and stars and light, and planets, comets, and the earth; how mountains, seas, and rivers are formed, how metals arise in mines, and how plants grow; fire and heat; the nature of animals and, in particular, of human beings, and so on.

Most important for us, he writes that in his quest to understand how various functions in our bodies work,

> I supposed . . . that in the beginning God did not place in this body any rational soul [i.e., mind]. . . . And when I looked to see what functions would occur in such a body I found precisely those which may occur in us without our thinking of them, and hence without any contribution from our [mind]. . . . These functions are just the ones in which animals without reason may be said to resemble us. (*Discourse* V, 134)

And which bodily functions are these, whose operations don't require minds? After an account of human anatomy, Descartes writes,

> I showed what structure the nerves and muscles of the human body must have in order to make the [fluids] inside them strong enough to move its limbs . . . what changes must occur in the brain in order to cause waking, sleep and dreams; how light, sounds, smells, tastes, heat and the other qualities of external objects can imprint various ideas on the brain through the mediation of the senses; and how hunger, thirst, and the other internal passions can also send their ideas there . . . memory . . . imagination. (*Discourse* V, 139)

Descartes's claims here are quite astounding, if you think about them. Waking, sleep, and dreams; sensations, hunger, and thirst; memory and imagination; many of the movements of ours limbs: all these can be explained purely mechanically, that is, on the assumption that our body is a purely physical object governed only by the laws of physics. Or, as he puts it in his *Treatise on Man,*

> these functions follow from the mere arrangement of the machine's organs every bit as naturally as the movements of a clock or other automaton follow from the arrangement of its counter-weights and wheels. (*Treatise,* 108)

And lest someone think this idea impossible to believe, he develops the automaton analogy by promptly adding the following to his description of all the functions he claims to be able to explain:

> This will not seem at all strange to those who know how many kinds of automatons, or moving machines, the skill of man can construct with the use of very few parts, in comparison with the great multitude of bones, muscles, nerves, arteries, veins and all the other parts that are in the body of any animal. For they will regard this body as a machine which, having been made by the hands of God, is incomparably better ordered than any machine that can be devised by man, and contains in itself movements more wonderful than those in any such machine. (*Discourse* V, 139)

This claim, that much of what our bodies do can be explained purely mechanically, is at the heart of that strange story of Descartes's mechanical doll. For if Descartes did possess such a thing, it was probably not for the reasons you were thinking—shame on you!—but for *scientific* reasons, as a demonstration of the wonders of the mechanical philosophy.

And you thought science was all laboratories and equations!

The "Monstrous Thesis"

So now if Descartes believes that so much of *human* behavior may be explained mechanically, it is perhaps not so surprising that he holds that all the behavior of nonhuman animals (henceforth, just "animals") may be explained purely mechanically.

To say this, of course, is just to say that animals (or their bodies) are merely *automatons*: literally, from the Greek, "self-movers," the idea being that all the motions of an animal body may be explained by the laws of physics governing the body, without invoking the external impetus of any mind or anything mental.

And *that* amounts to saying that there is no need to think of animals as having minds or souls or any "inner" conscious sensations or awareness at all, since everything about their behavior can be explained without those. To paraphrase Descartes's famous disciple Nicolas Malebranche (1638–1715), animals eat without pleasure and cry without pain, and they desire, fear, and know absolutely nothing. Or as it has been summarized even more recently, animals don't actually feel any pain (for example) but merely behave "*as if* they feel pain when they are, say, kicked or stabbed" (Regan and Singer 1976, 4).

The lights are on, so to speak, but there's nobody home in there.

Strong Reactions

Descartes's doctrine invited criticism, ranging from mild to outraged, almost as soon as he penned it. His own contemporary, the British philosopher Henry More (1614–1687), called it "an internecine and murderous opinion,"[2] while some twentieth-century writers have called it a "grim foretaste of a mechanically minded age" that "brutally violates the old kindly fellowship of living things,"[3] or just simply a "monstrous thesis."[4]

But why exactly does Descartes's doctrine invoke such strong reactions?

One reason might be what appears to be the simple absurdity of the doctrine: it seems just obvious to many people that many animals enjoy some sort of mental life, at least some form of conscious awareness. That's probably why Descartes's idea sounds so strange, on first blush.

But another reason for the strong reaction might be what seems to be its immediate moral implications: if there is no mentality, no consciousness, within animals, then perhaps it doesn't really matter how we treat them, any more than it matters how we treat inanimate objects like rocks. Not only may we be justified in exploiting them for our purposes, but we also needn't worry *how* we exploit them: if they don't really feel pain, then it can hardly matter if we beat them or starve them or how we slaughter them, if it suits our interests.

In the twenty-first century, as public sentiment for "animal rights" grows, it's easy to understand why Descartes's doctrine may appear not merely strange but downright abhorrent.

If we're to believe it, then, we'd better have some pretty good arguments. (Not to mention something to say about the moral implications, but that we'll save for another time.)

Descartes's Theory of Knowledge

Perhaps the best way to approach Descartes's "monstrous thesis" is to follow his own train of thought toward it.

That train surely begins with his *epistemology*: his theory of what true knowledge consists of his method of how to obtain it. And that method is, quite famously, the "method of doubt," so vividly illustrated in his most well-known work, *Meditations on First Philosophy*. That text begins with these lines:

> Some years ago I was struck by the large number of falsehoods that I had accepted as true in my childhood, and by the highly doubtful nature of the whole edifice [of knowledge] that I had subsequently based on them. I realized that it was necessary . . . to demolish everything completely and start again right from the foundations if I wanted to establish any [knowledge] at all. (12)

To obtain reliable knowledge, Descartes continues, it is necessary first to call everything you believe into doubt and see, in effect, if any of your beliefs somehow are impossible to doubt. Any such beliefs would quite literally be indubitable or absolutely certain, and could then serve as the foundation for your knowledge of the world.

But now if these indubitable beliefs are to serve that function, Descartes thinks, you need to be cautious in just how you build on them. Indeed, it is advisable to keep any potential new belief in doubt unless you can discover very compelling reasons to accept it.

We must keep this in mind as we turn to animal minds.

The Default Position on Animals

With that epistemology, then, all Descartes really needs to do to support his thesis is *not* to prove directly that animals don't have minds but merely argue that there are no truly compelling arguments that they *do* have minds.

And so he proceeds. In one letter he writes,

> I do not think it can be proved that there is [no thought in animals], since the human mind does not reach into their hearts. (To More, 2/5/1649, CSM III, 365)

We can't prove directly that animals lack minds. But then,

> We know of absolutely no [source] of movement in animals apart from the disposition of their organs. (*Fourth Replies*, 161–62)

> [Animal behavior] is not at all a sufficient basis to prove that [they have minds]. (To Reneri, April or May 1638, CSM III, 100)

So there's the claim, at any rate, that there are no good reasons to think animals have minds.

The task thus becomes this: to look at the reasons why people think that animals have minds and challenge those reasons.

So Why Do You *Think* Animals Have Minds?

Again, you might think it's just obvious. But remember, the job of philosophy is to question the obvious.

And when you do, Descartes suggests, you may discover that your opinion that animals have minds isn't so much "obvious" as merely one of those opinions we simply inherit from our childhood, when we tend automatically to adopt the views of those around us without attending to them. Indeed, these opinions constitute much of ordinary common sense—and are precisely the sort of opinions that his epistemology urges are most important to question:

> Those who want to discover truth must above all distrust opinions rashly acquired in childhood. (To Reneri, April or May 1638, CSM III, 99)

To help us undo our childhood bias, Descartes next offers a little thought experiment.

How to Disarm Your Inner Child

> Suppose that a man had been brought up all his life in some place where he had never seen any animals except [human beings]; and suppose that he was very devoted to the study of mechanics, and had made . . . various automatons shaped like a [person], a horse, a dog . . . and so on, which walked and ate, and breathed, and so far as possible imitated all the other actions of the animals they resembled, including the signs we use to express our [emotions], like crying when struck and running away when subjected to a loud noise. Suppose that sometimes he found it impossible to tell the difference between the real [people] and those which had only the shape of [people]. . . . Now, I say, you must consider what would be the judgement of such a man when he saw the animals we have; especially if he were filled with the knowledge of God, or at least had noticed how inferior is the best skill shown by [people] in their artefacts when compared with that shown by nature in the composition of plants. . . . There is no doubt that he would not come to the conclusion that there was any real feeling or emotion in them, but would think they were automatons, which, being made by nature, were incomparably more accomplished than any of those he had previously made himself. (To Reneri, April or May 1638, CSM III, 99–100)

Were you *not* inflicted with your rash childhood opinions but instead simply looked at animal behavior in a clear, unprejudiced light, you would *not* think it so obvious that they have minds. This would especially be true if you'd had experience constructing machines that could imitate animal behavior, and all the more so when you recognized that nature (and of course God) can construct far better automatons than any human being. If anything, your default opinion in this case would rather be the opposite, that animals *were* mindless automatons.

So you can't just insist that animal minds are "obvious." If you are to believe that they do have minds, then you've got to ask specifically what reasons or evidence you have for so believing.

When you do, you'll probably come up with something like this:

But They're Just Like Us!

Aren't they? Like us, in relevant ways? In their bodies and in their behavior? So if we have minds, then isn't it at least reasonable to believe that they do?

Descartes naturally has anticipated this argument:

> I see no argument for animals having thoughts except this one: since they have eyes, ears, tongues and other sense-organs like ours, it seems likely that they have sensation like us. (To More, 2/5/1649, CSM III, 365)

And similarly,

> Most of the actions of animals resemble ours, and . . . this has given us many occasions to judge that they act by an interior principle like the one within ourselves, that is to say, by means of a [mind] which has feelings and passions like ours. (To Reneri, April or May 1638, CSM III, 99)

They look like us in relevant respects (sensory organs) and often behave like us (eating, moving, running from danger), and that leads us to believe, by analogy, that they have minds like ours.

So is this convincing?

Throwing Out the Baby with the Bathwater

To see why it isn't, let's return to that thought experiment a moment ago.

For on further reflection, that thought experiment might be just a little *too* powerful. For might it not also compel us to reject more than just animal minds—but also the belief that other *people* have minds too?

If seventeenth-century engineers could make automatons mimic animal behavior quite well, that's nothing compared to what twenty-first-century engineers can do, what with their fancy robots and computers and technology, with *human* behavior. So if that thought experiment shows that animal behavior does not give us good reason to think that animals have minds, shouldn't it also show that we lack good reason to think that other humans have minds—since all their behavior could just be mimicked by a well-programmed automaton, especially if God Himself might be the programmer?

Descartes was well aware of this problem. (Don't forget his traveling companion!) Speaking of various grottos and fountains in the royal gardens of his time, he writes that

> one may compare the nerves of the [human body] . . . with the pipes in the works of these fountains, its muscles and tendons with the various devices and springs which serve to set them in motion, its [blood] with the water which drives them [and so on]. . . . External objects, which by their mere presence stimulate [the body's] sense organs and thereby cause them to move in many different ways . . . are like visitors who enter the grottos of these fountains and unwittingly cause the movements which take place before their eyes. For they cannot enter without stepping on certain tiles which are so arranged that if, for example, they approach a Diana who is bathing they will cause her to hide in the reeds, and if they move forward to pursue her they will cause a Neptune to advance and threaten them with his trident. (*Treatise*, 100–101)

It's primitive but clear: if all animal behavior may be explained purely mechanically, then how can we be so sure that the same isn't true of other human beings?

Fortunately, Descartes has an answer.

They're Not *Quite* Just Like Us

The one argument for thinking that animals have minds invokes the resemblance of their sensory organs and behavior to ours. But, Descartes writes,

> There are other arguments, stronger and more numerous . . . which strongly urge the opposite. (To More, 2/5/1649, CSM III, 365–66)

The first such argument is that there are also important *differences* between animals and humans, differences that require us to ascribe minds to the latter but not the former. Speaking precisely of the possibility that someone might build machines which imitated human behavior, Descartes writes,

> If any such machines bore a resemblance to our bodies and imitated our actions as closely as possible . . . we should still have two very certain means of recognizing that they were not real [people, i.e., with minds]. The first is

that they could never use words . . . as we do in order to declare our thoughts to others . . . [or] produce different arrangements of words so as to give an appropriately meaningful answer to whatever is said in [their] presence, as the dullest of [human beings] can do. Secondly, even though such machines might do some things as well as we do them, or perhaps even better, they would inevitably fail in others, which would reveal that they were acting not through understanding but only from the disposition of their organs. For whereas reason is a universal instrument which can be used in all kinds of situations, these organs need some particular disposition for each particular action. (*Discourse* V, 139–40)

Thus, there are two criteria by which we can distinguish real human beings with minds from mere automatons: the proper use of language and the general use of reason as a "universal instrument." Much more could be said here, but lest you think Descartes's view is scientifically dated, note that his observations here have actually proved quite prescient. For while twenty-first-century researchers have made great strides in getting computers and robots to imitate human behavior in many respects, it is precisely in the mastery of language and in the general use of reason that they have struggled. These may well be the final frontiers, so to speak: the definitive limit to the purely mechanical, and the defining mark of the mental.

But now, if these two criteria distinguish genuinely minded human beings from mere machines, they also distinguish human beings from animals.

Again there's much that could be said, but Descartes argues at some length that no animals display the linguistic or reasoning capacities displayed by humans—and once again proves quite prescient, as to this date no animal has yet been discovered to match the range of our linguistic and reasoning abilities.[5]

But then the conclusion becomes clear.

We must attribute minds to human beings because no purely mechanical process could generate or explain our linguistic and rational behavior. But animals, despite some resemblance to us, simply do not resemble us in those two ways. Instead, everything about them *can* be explained purely mechanically, in terms of physical bodies moving by the laws of physics.

So not only is there no compelling reason to think that animals do have minds, but there's even some reason to think they do not!

The Immortal Souls of Oysters and Sponges

But there's a little bit more, at least for the religious crowd.

If you, with your indefatigable common sense, continue to insist that animals have minds, Descartes writes,

To this I . . . reply . . . that if [animals] thought as we do, they would have an immortal soul like us. This is unlikely, because there is no reason to believe it of some animals without believing it of all, and many of them such as oysters and sponges are too imperfect for this to be credible. (To the Marquess of Newcastle, 11/23/1646, CSM III, 304)

Or as he says elsewhere,

it is more probable that worms, flies, caterpillars and other animals move like machines than that they all have immortal souls. (To More, 2/5/1649, CSM III, 366)

Note the two distinct components to Descartes's argument here. The first is that if any animal is said to have a mind, then all must be. And the second is that anything that has a mind must be said to have an immortal soul.

Now the first is rather surprising, in light of the clear differences between such primitive animals as "worms, flies, and sponges" and higher animals such as dogs, cats, or chimpanzees. But even if we reject the first component, by ascribing minds only to higher animals, we must still contend with the second.

And here Descartes's point is simple: given *dualism*, the doctrine that the mental and the physical are distinct, then any creature with a mind will have, in effect, an "immortal soul."

There are two reasons for this.

First, if the mind is distinct from the body, then the destruction of the body does not entail the destruction of the mind.

Second, minds, in being nonphysical, are not the sorts of things that are composed of smaller pieces; as such, they cannot be built up or decomposed piecemeal. But that means they exist "all or nothing": they must be created from scratch at the start and destroyed into nothingness at the end, the kinds of processes of which, for religious thinkers, only God is capable.

If animals have minds, then there is something nonphysical to them—in which case, they will enjoy the same immortality as human beings do.

This conclusion might provide some consolation to those people inclined to include their pets in their wills. But it would provide only consternation to anyone committed to the Christian faith in the seventeenth century and beyond, according to which only we humans get the eternal benefit (or punishment) of an immortal afterlife. Denying that animals have minds might bring you commitment to the crazy house in our current century, but affirming that they do might violate your commitment to *God's house*, if you are a believer.

Use the mind that you (as a human being) do have, Descartes might advise, to figure out which commitment matters more.

Notes

1. See Gaukroger (1995, 1ff.).
2. More to Descartes, 12/11/1648 (AT V, 243).
3. Gibson (1932, 214).
4. Smith (1952, 136).
5. See *Discourse V* (140–41).

Primary Sources

Discourse = *Discourse on the Method*, CSM I
Fourth Replies = *Fourth Set of Replies, Objections and Replies to Meditations*, CSM II
Meditations = *Meditations on First Philosophy*, CSM II
Treatise = *Treatise on Man*, CSM I
The World, CSM I
AT = Adam, Charles, and Paul Tannery. *Oeuvres de Descartes*. Vols. 1–11. Paris: Librairie Philosophique J. Vrin, 1996.
CSM = Cottingham, John, Robert Stoothoff, and Dugald Murdoch. *The Philosophical Writings of Descartes*. Vols. 1–2. Cambridge: Cambridge University Press, 1985/1984.
CSMK = Cottingham, John, Robert Stoothoff, Dugald Murdoch, and Anthony Kenny. *The Philosophical Writings of Descartes*. Vol. 3. Cambridge: Cambridge University Press, 1991.

Recommended Secondary Sources

Cottingham, John. 1978. "'A Brute to the Brutes?': Descartes' Treatment of Animals." *Philosophy* 53:551–59.
———, ed. 1992. *The Cambridge Companion to Descartes*. Cambridge: Cambridge University Press.
Gaukroger, Stephen. 1995. *Descartes: An Intellectual Biography*. Oxford: Oxford University Press.
Gibson, A. Boyce. 1932. *The Philosophy of Descartes*. London: Methuen.
Harrison, Peter. 1992. "Descartes on Animals." *The Philosophical Quarterly* 42:219–27.
Hatfield, Gary. 2011. "René Descartes." In *Stanford Encyclopedia of Philosophy*, edited by Edward N. Zalta. http://plato.stanford.edu/archives/sum2011/entries/descartes/.
Regan, Thomas, and Peter Singer, eds. 1976. *Animal Rights and Human Obligations*. Englewood Cliffs, NJ: Prentice Hall.
Smith, N. Kemp. 1952. *New Studies in the Philosophy of Descartes*. London: Macmillan.

8

John Locke

TRUE COLORS

STRANGE IDEA

Physical objects, such as bodies, are not really colored. Rather, colors exist only in the minds of the perceivers.

MAJOR PROPONENT

John Locke (1632–1704)

BRIEF BIOGRAPHY

Enjoying the patronage of the local member of parliament, British philosopher John Locke received an excellent early education, ending up first at the prestigious Westminster School in London at fifteen and then at the even more prestigious Christ Church College at Oxford. There he remained many years, receiving a BA and an MA and becoming a lecturer in Greek, in 1660, and then of rhetoric in 1663. By various turns, this led him to a career in medicine, which in turn led him to become the personal physician to the First Earl of Shaftesbury, which led him, in turn again, to find himself embroiled in the major political turmoil of England's 1670s and 1680s. Suffice to say that these were not peaceful times, and Locke was forced to spend some years in exile in Holland. He returned to England in 1688, after the "Glorious Revolution" finally diminished the royal power and increased the parliament's. Along the way, Locke composed important works in philosophy and political theory, becoming a significant early proponent of the then-radical ideas of liberty and tolerance.

The Favorite Uncle of Modern Philosophy?

As we saw in the previous chapter, the great French thinker René Descartes is often called the father of modern philosophy—not so much for his accomplishments in philosophy but rather in what we would today call science. A generation behind Descartes and an English Channel away, his British near contemporary John Locke was almost as influential, not so much in developing that science himself, but in working out some of its philosophical implications. If Locke does not quite deserve paternity credit for modern philosophy, then we here bestow upon him the next best thing.

Let's begin by briefly reminding ourselves of the science in question.

The Mechanical Philosophy, Again

It was *the mechanical philosophy*, and its major components were *dualism* and *mechanism*.

Dualism was the doctrine that minds and bodies are different sorts of things: the former are nonphysical and characterized by their capacity for thought and consciousness, while the latter *are* physical and *lack* the capacity for thought and consciousness, and are characterized by having purely passive spatial properties, such as size and shape.

Mechanism was the doctrine that physical matter operates purely mechanically: being intrinsically passive, it cannot move itself but is caused to move only by minds, by God, and/or by the laws of nature.

The mechanical philosophy then becomes the theory that all natural phenomena may be explained in terms of dualism and mechanism. Got any questions about the soil, the water, the air? About fire or light? Or chemistry, biology, physiology, cosmology? The answers will be given in terms of how various pieces of matter, of various sizes and shapes, get moved around either by minds or by the newly discovered laws of motion. Armed with just those conceptual tools and being very good at mathematical computation, Descartes spent much of his life explaining nearly everything.

You wouldn't think that the mechanical philosophy should be particularly controversial. Well, all right, there were some problems with its implications about animal minds, as we saw. But at least the powerful seventeenth-century Catholic Church was probably all right with those implications.

There were other implications with which it was rather less comfortable.

Galileo, Anyone?

If you don't know much about the famous Italian mathematician and physicist Galileo (1564–1642), then that topic should be next on your reading list.

But chances are you know at least a little. To jog your memory, Galileo was the guy who got into deep trouble with the Catholic Church, in Descartes's own century, for supporting the theory of *heliocentrism*—that the earth moves around the sun—over that of *geocentrism*—that the sun (and the rest of the universe) moves around the earth.

But here is what is less well known.

Galileo was one of the early developers of the mechanical philosophy. Indeed, Descartes himself was quite aware of Galileo's work and may even have met the great man personally during a trip to Italy. And, in fact, Descartes also used the mechanical philosophy to defend heliocentrism over geocentrism, in a book he was just about to publish in 1633, when he heard about Galileo's troubles with the church down there in Italy. This book Descartes had called *The World*, a title meant to convey his humble opinion that he had explained pretty much everything that needed explaining. Imagine how frustrating that must have been when he realized, in light of Galileo's tribulations, that he needed to suppress the book! Descartes ended up choosing, probably wisely, not to publish it at all during his lifetime.

But that meant that he was aware that the mechanical philosophy could stir up trouble—big trouble, such as the business with the motion of the earth, but also, as we'll next see, some even bigger trouble too.

Aristotle and the Medieval Christians

Here's a slightly brief sketch of the history of Western philosophy.

First there was Plato, and then there was Aristotle. Plato said that we obtain all knowledge ultimately by reasoning, and Aristotle said that, no, perceptual experience plays an important role as well.

Then fifteen or sixteen centuries went by.

Then the very religious medieval thinkers—Jewish and Muslim, too, but we'll focus on the Christians—decided that Aristotle was right about everything, except for all those parts where he contradicts Christian theology. So they spent four or five centuries synthesizing Aristotle and Christianity. By the time they were done, Aristotle was more or less a Christian, and Christianity itself was more or less expressed in the language of Aristotle.

They were just wrapping up that impressive project when the French father of modern philosophy showed up, along with, a little later, modern philosophy's favorite British uncle.

But Here's the Thing

Aristotle was keen on perceptual experience. The medieval Christians then inherited this keenness.

That's where the trouble begins.

Because think about what perception teaches us of the physical world. It teaches us (among many other things) that the physical bodies around us don't merely exist but also have many interesting properties, properties that we detect by our various senses. Have a sniff of this banana: it smells *banana-y*. Have a taste: it also tastes *banana-y*. Step on it: it sounds *squishy*. Oh, and before you toss that mushy mess in the trash, be sure to have a look at it: it looks *yellow*. All of this is obvious, at least if we trust our senses.

But all of this is precisely what the mechanical philosophy denies.

For according to the mechanical philosophy, physical bodies consist only of bits of matter with certain sizes and shapes moving in various ways, and nothing else. But size, shape, and motion are not the same things as smells, flavors, sounds, and colors. Or to put it more technically, the mechanical philosophy argues that the physical world may be completely understood in mathematical terms. That means that all genuine physical properties must be mathematical in nature. Size, shape, and motion fit the bill because you can describe them with numbers and with geometry: you can say just how big the thing is, what geometric shape, and just what speed it is moving. But smells, flavors, sounds, and colors are not mathematical in the same way. We smell that banana-y smell, but we can't assign a number to it. And if these are not mathematical, they are not genuine properties of physical objects.

So the banana, the physical object itself, is not *really* yellow. It merely *looks* that way to a perceiver but isn't that way in itself. The same is true for smells, flavors, and sounds (though we shall focus on colors). Physical objects do not *really* possess these properties; they only *seem* to, to a perceiver.

But then if that is so, Aristotle must be wrong in the fundamental role that he assigns to perceptual experience in the acquisition of knowledge.

And if Aristotle is wrong, then so is medieval Christian philosophy, which was largely expressed in Aristotelian terms.

And if medieval Christian philosophy is wrong, *then so is Christianity itself.*

Or at least that's how it seemed to the leading religious thinkers of the seventeenth century, as they grappled with the mechanical philosophy: they saw this simple-sounding scientific theory of the world as directly challenging the foundations of the entire religion.

So the proponents of the mechanical philosophy had their work cut out for them. Not only were they now promulgating a strange doctrine—physical bodies are not really colored (try telling *that* to common sense!)—but they also had to worry, by and large, about being burned at the stake for heresy.

They were definitely going to need some arguments.

Enter John Locke

Of course, Galileo, Descartes, and others were already making arguments for the mechanical philosophy. But these tended to be scientific in nature, while Locke took a more straightforwardly philosophical approach. Moreover, Locke's treatment of the issue (in particular of the nature of properties such as colors) is especially thorough, his arguments especially clear, and his terminology has become the standard for the debate.

Thus, his work shall be our main source for this chapter.

Ideas v. Qualities

"Whatever the mind perceives in itself or is the immediate object of perception, thought, or understanding," Locke writes, "that I call *idea*, and the power to produce any *idea* in our mind I call a *quality* of the subject in which that power is" (II.VIII.8).[1]

Given the dualism described earlier, an "idea" here is some sort of mental object, existing within a mind, that serves as the "immediate object" of perceptions and thinking in general: when you perceive a yellow banana, the yellowness you perceive is a mental "idea," and so too, when you later think about bananas, the idea of a "banana" is before your mind's eye, so to speak.

So understood, we obviously find ourselves aware of an ongoing stream of ideas during our normal waking hours and our dreams. This naturally raises the question of where these ideas come from, of what causes them, which dualists answer equally naturally by invoking physical bodies. As Locke puts it, sensations are "produced in us only by different degrees and modes of motion in [us] variously agitated by external objects" (II.VIII.4). Thus, the motions of external physical bodies cause motions in our sensory organs (such as our eyes), which then cause motions inside our bodies and brains, which ultimately results in our having the mental experience of sensing something such as the yellowness of the banana.

So our sensory ideas are typically caused by external physical bodies. That means that physical bodies have the causal powers to produce these mental ideas in perceivers. These powers Locke refers to as "qualities" in the physical body.

So "idea" refers to the entity in the mind during a sensation, and "quality" refers to the power that some body has to *cause* that idea or sensation. So described, the distinction seems straightforward, and ideas seem quite different in nature from qualities.

There's just one small complication.

A Wrinkle in the Distinction

It's this: in ordinary English, we rarely observe the distinction carefully and thus often use the same word to name both an idea and a quality.

Locke continues,

> Thus a snowball having the power to produce in us the *ideas* of *white, cold, and round*, the power to produce those *ideas* in us as they are in the snowball I call *qualities*; and as they are sensations or perceptions in our [minds] I call them *ideas*. (II.VIII.8)

Consider the word "white" in this example. We say that the snowball *is* white, that is, that the snowball has the power to produce in us a certain idea or sensation. So used, "white" refers to a quality of the snowball. But then we might ask, yes, but which idea or sensation is produced in us? Why, the idea of *whiteness*, of course: a white sensation or sensory idea! But here "white" refers not to something in the snowball but to something in us, our mental idea. We use "white," in other words, to refer both to our mental sensation (an idea) and to the physical snowball (its power to cause that idea in our minds).

No wonder ordinary people (i.e., commonsense people) are so easily confused into thinking of colors as properties of physical bodies! And not just ordinary people: Locke admits that sometimes he himself speaks loosely, not carefully distinguishing qualities (in bodies) from ideas (in minds).

Nevertheless, we must strive to do our best here: for when we are careful about distinguishing "color as we experience it" from the physical body's "power to produce that color sensation in our minds"—the idea from the quality—then we shall be more amenable to the strange idea that perhaps colors as we experience them are not really in bodies after all.

Primary and Secondary Qualities

Locke next turns to his most famous distinction.

He offers three major criteria for classifying the various qualities of bodies into these two categories. A quality is a *primary quality* if (1) it is "utterly inseparable" from the body, (2) it "really does exist" in the body, and (3) our idea of it resembles what's in the body. To the contrary, a *secondary quality* is one to which none of these apply but rather *is* separable from the body, it does not *really* exist in the body, and our idea of it does *not* resemble what's in the body.

So what does all this mean?

Locke elaborates on the first criterion as follows. No matter what you do to any given physical body, no matter what changes it undergoes, there are certain qualities that it will always have; similarly, no matter how small a physical body is, it will always display these qualities; and you cannot even *conceive* of any bodies lacking such qualities. Take a grain of wheat, for example, and divide it into two parts, and "each part has still . . . *extension*, *figure*, and *mobility*; divide it again, and it retains still the same qualities; and so divide it on until the parts become [invisible], they must retain still each of them all those qualities" (II.VIII.9). *Extension* is size, *figure* is shape, and *mobility* is motion; so what Locke is saying here is that every physical body, no matter how small, will always possess size, shape, and motion. These "primary qualities" are thus "inseparable" from body, just as the mechanical philosophy says.

Of course, in addition to these qualities, we have corresponding ideas, namely our *sensations* of the sizes, shapes, and motions of bodies. But by the second and third criteria, Locke is saying that it doesn't merely look to us this way but in fact really is this way: bodies *really do* possess size, shape, and motion, independent of our sensations (or ideas), and so our sensations really do *resemble* what is in the body itself. This doesn't mean that our sensations are always perfectly accurate: how big something looks may be different from how big it actually is. But that it has *some* size is always true, and what size, shape, and motion are as qualities in the body resembles, in general, what size, shape, and motion look like to our senses.

In contrast, secondary qualities—such as color, sound, and flavor, though again we'll focus on color—are "nothing in the objects themselves but powers to produce various sensations in us by their *primary qualities*" (II.VIII.10).

As we saw earlier, sensation occurs when physical particles cause motions in our sensory organs and brains, which in turn cause sensory ideas to arise in our minds. Some of these are sensory ideas *of* the size, shape, and motion of the external physical bodies, ideas that do resemble those bodies, which really have those qualities. But other sensory ideas do not resemble the bodies at all, since bodies do *not* really have those qualities: these are ideas of secondary qualities. We may see "yellow," true, but that sensation is caused by bits of matter of various sizes, shapes, and motions but which *are not themselves yellow*. Secondary qualities are "separable" from bodies, then, in the sense that bodies can and do exist without them. So color as we perceive it is not really a property of a physical body but exists only as an idea in the mind of the perceiver.

Now we need some reasons to believe this is true.

Five Arguments for the Distinction between
Primary and Secondary Qualities

(1) Science

The main idea is simply this. The most successful science of the day was the mechanical philosophy, but it endorsed the distinction between primary and secondary qualities! Its many successful explanations of phenomena proceeded by ascribing to physical matter only the qualities of size, shape, and motion. The mechanical philosophy therefore recognized no room for color or the other secondary qualities in the physical world, and if that's what your most successful science believes, then so perhaps should you. If colors exist at all, then the only place for them would be as ideas in the mind of the perceiver.

(2) Separability Considerations

The very criterion that Locke uses to distinguish primary and secondary qualities offers support for the distinction. For if indeed he is right that size, shape, and motion are inseparable from bodies while color and such are not, then that is an important difference between the two, one perhaps best explained by concluding that secondary qualities are not really in the bodies at all.

There is, however, an important weakness in this particular argument. Just because there can be bodies devoid of colors (clear glass, perhaps, or subatomic particles, etc.) does not necessarily mean that colors are not really properties of those bodies that *do* seem to have colors. Maybe color is not a *necessary* property of bodies, but that doesn't mean it's not a physical property at all, any more than the fact that some stones aren't round would mean that "roundness" isn't a genuine property of those stones which are.

(3) The Almond Argument

"Pound an almond," Locke writes,

> and the clear white *color* will be altered into a dirty one. . . . What real alteration can the beating of the pestle make in any body but an alteration of the *texture* of it? (II.VIII.20)

Assuming that the almond is uniform and homogeneous throughout—that it's clear white all the way through—then Locke's argument here seems to be this. If that clear white color were really in the almond itself, all the way through, then "pounding" the almond wouldn't change its color. Why not? Because pounding only changes its *texture*—that is, the particular arrangements of its molecules—and if all its molecules are really white, why should merely rearranging them affect the almond's overall white color?

Yet pounding does affect its color.

The best explanation seems to be that color is not really in the almond itself after all. Rather, some molecular arrangements cause clear white color sensations in us, the perceiver, and other arrangements of the same molecules cause "dirty" white sensations; pounding affects the arrangements and in this way affects the perceived color.

But then color is in the perceiver, not the body.

(4) The Analogy Argument

The same fire, Locke observes, which at some distance causes in us a pleasing sensation (or "idea") of warmth causes close up a sensation or idea of burning pain. But everyone agrees that pain is a sensation "in us," not a quality in the object: when you step on a nail, you never say, "I'm perceiving the pain in this nail!" You say, rather, that the qualities of the nail, its solidity and sharpness, cause a sensation of pain in *you*.

But now the sensory processes in the two cases are precisely analogous: in perceiving both the warmth of the fire and the pain of the burn, the size, shape, and motion (the primary qualities) of the fire particles cause changes in the primary qualities of our sensory organ (our skin), resulting in sensations in us. Thus, since everyone agrees that the resulting pain is in the perceiver, we ought to admit that the warmth is too.

Similarly, a spoiled piece of food may look (say) white to us and even taste perfectly sweet, but then upon being consumed it may cause in us very unpleasant feelings of nausea. Everyone agrees that nausea is a sensation "in us," not a quality in the food, but the physical processes of sensing the bread's color and taste are precisely analogous to the process by which we sense the nausea: the primary qualities of the object affect the primary qualities of our sensory organs.

So if nausea is merely a sensation in us, then so too are color and taste.

Again, secondary qualities are not genuinely properties of bodies.

(5) Relativity of Perception Argument

This argument, or rather family of arguments, is perhaps the most influential of them all. A "relativity of perception" argument is one with the following general form:

A perceived quality varies.
The object itself does not vary.

———————————

Therefore, the perceived quality is not in the object itself.

Locke's classic example is the "two hands in a bucket" case.

Imagine putting one of your hands in the freezer for a few minutes while you put the other hand in a mildly heated oven. You then simultaneously place both hands into a homogeneous, stirred bucket of water. Presumably, the freezer hand will feel a warm sensation while the oven hand will feel a cool sensation.

This scenario now fulfills the two premises. A perceived quality varies, here between the two hands: one perceives warmth while the other perceives coldness. But the object itself doesn't vary: it's the same bucket of water, of uniform temperature throughout.

But then the conclusion seems to follow that warmth and coldness are not qualities in the water itself but only in the perceiver. As Locke himself puts it, since warmth and coldness are opposites, they can't both literally be in the water, for that would be a contradiction. But if warmth and coldness are produced as sensations in the perceiver by various arrangements of moving particles, then we can understand how the same water might produce these opposing sensations when perceived in different circumstances (here, by the different hands).

Once you are aware of relativity of perception phenomena, in fact, you'll find them all over the place. The perceived color of an otherwise unchanging object can vary dramatically from perceiver to perceiver or from context to context (as the color of a shirt looks different in the store than at home); the quality of a sound can vary without the thing making the sound varying; how something tastes depends very much on who is tasting it and in what circumstances; and so on.

And in each case, the conclusion seems the same: colors (flavors, sounds, etc.) are secondary qualities, meaning that they are, in the end, not genuine properties of physical objects but merely sensations in the mind of the perceiver.

Then and Now

Locke's specific arguments have not all stood the test of time equally well.

The mechanical philosophy no longer has the position it once had; separability considerations are too murky to be very persuasive; and the almond argument is a little too idiosyncratic for many people's tastes. But as for the analogy argument and the relativity of perception arguments, well, it turns out that they are not perfectly strong as stated here; but when updated in various technical ways, they still do exert a strong pull on the contemporary intellect. So much so that, these days, with respect to color anyway—even when, or perhaps because, the science of color and color perception is so vastly advanced from Locke's seventeenth century—probably the majority of philosophers are persuaded that colors are really just in the mind.

So much so that, to most philosophers, anyway, this strange idea has pretty much just *become* their common sense.

Note

1. All quotations are from Locke's *An Essay Concerning Human Understanding.*

Primary Source

Locke, John. 1690. *An Essay Concerning Human Understanding.* From *Works*, modified by and appearing in *Modern Philosophy: An Anthology of Primary Sources* (2nd ed.), edited by Roger Ariew and Eric Watkins (Indianapolis, IN: Hackett, 2009).

Recommended Secondary Sources

Chappell, Vere, ed. 1994. *The Cambridge Companion to Locke.* Cambridge: Cambridge University Press.
Uzgalis, William. 2010. "John Locke." In *Stanford Encyclopedia of Philosophy*, edited by Edward N. Zalta. http://plato.stanford.edu/archives/win2010/entries/locke/.

9

Nicolas Malebranche

ON HONORING LEEKS AND ONIONS

STRANGE IDEA

No ordinary things, such as minds and bodies, have any causal powers. Instead, God Himself directly causes everything that occurs.

MAJOR PROPONENT

Nicolas Malebranche (1638–1715)

BRIEF BIOGRAPHY

Suffering from early frail health, Nicolas Malebranche was educated at home, in Paris, until sixteen but eventually went on to study theology at the Sorbonne. In 1660, he entered the oratory, a religious congregation, where four years later he was ordained a priest. Right around this time, he happened upon a book in a local bookstall by a man named Descartes, a book he found so exciting that he suffered violent cardiac palpitations from reading it. He subsequently immersed himself in Descartes's philosophy and then commenced his own prodigious philosophical output, soon becoming perhaps the most famous philosopher in France in his time. Some of his greatest work came from his decades-long, very acrimonious, and very public debate with Antoine Arnauld, a debate that produced between them several books, many articles, and innumerable letters. Their discord began over a small philosophical point but soon grew in scope and intensity to the point where the pope had to intervene to stop them from constantly calling each other a heretic. Malebranche's death in 1715, some speculate, was hastened by another unpleasant metaphysical debate with the up-and-coming Irish idealist George Berkeley (see chapter 11).

Cause and Effect

You strike a match, and it lights. A billiard ball collides with another, setting the second ball in motion. Someone hits you, and you feel pain. You think for a while about philosophy and start to get a headache. You feel hungry and set off in pursuit of a late-night snack from the refrigerator.

All of these are perfectly ordinary events in which one thing seems to cause another: the striking causes the lighting, the motion of the first ball causes the motion of the second, and so on. In some cases, a physical thing causes another physical thing (the billiard balls); in others, a physical thing causes a mental thing (the punch and the pain); in others, a mental thing causes a physical thing (the hunger and the walk); and in others, both cause and effect are mental (the thinking and the headache).

Or so it might seem, if all you've got is common sense.

But common sense was, apparently, in pretty short supply back in the medieval and early modern periods of philosophy.

The Ultimate Cause and Its Effects

In fact, the nature of "causation" was the subject of much intense discussion from early medieval times onward. The discussion had to be intense because it concerned, primarily, figuring out precisely what role to assign to God in the affairs of the created world. All parties believed that God had created the world, but the next question was, and then what?

You'll recall the strange idea from chapter 6, that God's creating wasn't a one-shot deal but is continuous and ongoing. But now we're asking something a little different. These creatures that God created or continues to create—exactly what are they capable of doing, on their own, if anything?

On one hand, some thinkers felt that God, in creating a thing, gives it some measure of independence from Him, a measure reflected in granting the creature causal powers to bring about various things on its own (such as the power to heat objects and cause motion and so on).

On the other, some felt that God, as the ultimate sovereign, must in fact be causally involved in literally *every* event in the created world.

Among these latter thinkers, some felt that you could grant God such involvement while simultaneously permitting creatures an equal causal role in various events, yet others disagreed and felt that you couldn't have both. Among *these* latter thinkers, in turn, some felt that God must have all the causal power and creatures none, while others felt that creatures' causal powers could not be completely denied, and so God's must be at least partly restricted.

In the midst of all this, there were disagreements, too, over precisely which doctrines applied to which sorts of creatures: some were inclined to grant causal powers to minds, for example, while denying them to bodies.

It's no surprise that the debates could get pretty complicated here.

But if there's one virtue of Nicolas Malebranche's position, at least, it's that it is clear and simple: he denies causal powers to *all* created things, minds and bodies, period.

What Are You Saying?

Really, this: that it's not the case, according to Malebranche, that the striking of the match causes the lighting or that the motion of the first billiard ball causes the motion of the second or even that your mental desire for a snack causes you or your body to move toward the fridge. None of these things are true or genuine causes of the events that follow them.

Rather, the first member of each pair is merely the "occasion" on which *God* causes the second member. The striking is the occasion upon which God lights that match; the collision is the occasion upon which God moves the second ball; and so on. Malebranche sometimes calls the first member of the pair the *occasional cause* of the second, and his doctrine was known as the *system of occasional causes*, or later, just *occasionalism*. But don't be fooled: an "occasional cause" is not a cause that only happens occasionally, as the English expression may suggest, and it most definitely is not a true or genuine cause of its apparent effect.

For no created thing is or could be a true cause of anything else.

Period.

Now why, exactly, would Malebranche believe this very strange idea?

Here Come the Leeks

Personally, I like leeks, especially when they're lightly fried with some garlic. But I wouldn't exactly be inclined to *worship* them, even despite my apparent affinity toward really strange things.

That's basically Malebranche's point.

As an ordained priest, Malebranche shares a motivation common to all deeply religious thinkers: one's system should reflect God's complete sovereignty over the created world. God created and continuously creates His creatures, which are therefore (obviously) profoundly dependent on him; but when you add in the occasionalism, too, their dependence on God becomes exhaustively complete.

And so it's no surprise that Malebranche begins his discussion by specifically invoking religious considerations.

The idea of a cause, he suggests, is the idea of something divine. For a cause is something with a power to act, and anything with a power to act has power over the thing upon which it acts. Thus, just as God's supreme power establishes Him as the supreme divinity, so too anything with lesser power is like a lesser divinity. We therefore treat creatures as being divine, to various degrees, when we grant them causal power over things.

Indeed, he continues,

> it is difficult to be persuaded that we should neither fear nor love true powers—beings that can act upon us, punish us with pain, or reward us with pleasure. And as love and fear are true adoration, it is also difficult to be persuaded that we should not adore these beings. (*Search* 6.2.3, 446)

It is a common idea that inferior things serve and even worship superior things, and anything with causal powers over us would therefore count as something we should serve and worship.

Now certain foods may taste very delicious and sometimes seem responsible not merely for generating gustatory pleasure in us but also for promoting our general health and welfare. But if we grant to them the genuine causal power of doing these, then we are treating them as superior to us, as objects worthy of adoration and worship, and, in effect, as if they were deities. But that is to provide them with a status that they simply do not have and to fail to recognize to whom true credit is due. For God is the only being *genuinely* worthy of our adoration and worship, and while certain creatures, or in this case vegetables, may seem to bring us various goods, as Malebranche puts it, "one should not render sovereign honor to leeks and onions" (*Search* 6.2.3, 447).

But that's what you'd be doing were you to grant them causal power of any sort over us. It would amount, in effect, to a form of idolatry.

Think about *that* the next time you sit down to supper.

Four Arguments for Occasionalism

Now the preceding considerations are not an actual argument for occasionalism; they merely underscore the need to develop such arguments, to demonstrate the truth of occasionalism, and thus to help us avoid what Malebranche calls "the most dangerous error" both of common sense and of the philosopher, namely the granting of true causal powers to ordinary objects.

To these arguments he next turns.

(1) Occasionalism Dissolves "The Mind-Body Problem"

You'll recall the doctrine of dualism from the preceding chapters: that mind and body are very different sorts of things. But now no sooner does one adopt dualism than one confronts the classic form of *the mind-body problem*: if bodies are spatial in nature while minds are not, then how could any body ever have causal influence over a mind, or vice versa?

Consider the paradigm case of commonsense causation, where two billiard balls collide. Clearly, the literal contact between them plays an important role in their interaction. But if minds are not spatial in character, then contact between minds and bodies is literally impossible: no mind (or mental state) could ever "collide" with a physical body or brain. But then any causation between bodies and minds is simply unintelligible. Thus, we cannot understand how a punch causes pain or how a desire causes a physical action, and so on.

Malebranche's occasionalism now dissolves this problem.

That is "dissolves" and not "solves," for it does not explain *how* physical things cause mental things and vice versa. Rather, it denies that they do, and thus, it removes the problem of explaining it altogether. The brain state (say) does not cause the subsequent mental state; it's merely the occasion on which God causes it. No problem! (Or at least no problem beyond what every theist already has to deal with, occasionalist or not, namely that of understanding how God Himself causes anything.)

So there's one advantage of occasionalism: if you're a dualist, it frees you of the mind-body problem.

(2) The Know-How Argument

This argument applies specifically to the mind → body domain, aiming to show only that minds do not have causal powers over bodies. A paradigm example of such a causal power would be our ability to move our arms: we mentally desire or "will" to move our arms, which subsequently results in our physical arm moving.

But Malebranche now asks exactly how we do this.

To move our arms, he writes,

> it is necessary to have animal spirits, to send them through certain nerves toward certain muscles in order to inflate and contract them. . . . And we see that [people] who do not know that they have spirits, nerves, and muscles move their arms, and even move them with more skill and ease than those who know anatomy best. Therefore, [people] will to move their arms, and only God is able and knows how to move them. . . . There is no man who knows what must be done to move one of his fingers by means of animal spirits. (*Search* 6.2.3, 449–50)

If you (i.e., your mind) really caused your body to move, then you must know *how* to make your body move. But truly knowing *that* requires knowing the anatomical structures and processes involved in that motion. According to the science of Malebranche's time, we had fine fluids (or "animal spirits") running through our veins that were responsible for the contractions of our muscles, but nothing rides on those outdated details. His point, put more modernly, is that no human being knows exactly what neurons must be fired, what nerves must be triggered, which muscles must be contracted, and so on, to move her body. And if we don't know exactly how to move our bodies, then we ought not to be given causal credit for doing so. That credit must go to the one being who does know all that, namely God.

There's an important implicit assumption in Malebranche's argument here: that "knowing how" to move our bodies requires our having explicit, conscious awareness of those details, which we surely lack. But while this was a widely accepted assumption in Malebranche's time, today, a century after Freud's theory of the unconscious mind, few thinkers still accept it, and so this particular argument has little contemporary pull.

But Malebranche has others.

(3) The Continuous Creation Argument

Like most thinkers of his time and like most religious thinkers of *our* time, Malebranche accepted the strange idea that God continuously creates the world. But he next argues that once you've accepted that strange idea, then you must also accept his strange idea.

God continuously creates the world, Malebranche begins, which means that for all things (minds and bodies), God is causally responsible for their existing at every moment in which they do exist. So if you exist at a given time, *t*, what explains your so existing is that God *wills* that you exist at time *t*. Now with respect to physical bodies, Malebranche notes,

> God [cannot] will that a body exist nowhere, nor that it does not stand in certain relations of distance to other bodies. Thus, God cannot will that this armchair exist . . . without situating it here, there, or elsewhere. (*Dialogues* VII.X, 115)

When God creates the armchair, He has to specify its location: He has to put it *somewhere*. That means that God is responsible not only for the existence of every physical body at every time but also for the specific locations of every physical body.

But now think about what it means for a given body to be either in motion or at rest. For it to be in motion is for it to be in different locations at different times: here at time *t*, then a bit to the left at *t* + 1, and further to the left at *t* + 2, and so on. For it to be at rest is for it to be in the same location over time: here at *t*, still here at *t* + 1, and so on. If God is fully responsible for the location of every body at every time, then He must also be fully responsible for whether every body is at rest or in motion, and if it's in motion, He's responsible not only for its direction but also for its speed.

But now according to the mechanical philosophy (as you'll recall from chapters 7 and 8), everything in the physical world may be fully explained in terms of the size, shape, and motion of all the physical bodies. If God continuously creates all bodies, then He is Himself fully responsible for their sizes and shapes at all times, as well as their motions. But then there is literally nothing left over for bodies themselves to be causally responsible for. *So bodies cause nothing in the physical world, and God causes everything.*

Thus, occasionalism is true.

When two billiard balls collide, then, the motion of the first does not cause the motion of the second. Rather, God first creates them at a certain distance apart, and then a little closer, and then in contact; and then a little apart, and then further apart, and so on. God is fully causally responsible for everything here; the balls themselves, the collision itself, do nothing but merely provide the occasion on which God then creates the subsequent motions.

Interestingly, Malebranche makes this argument using only purely physical things as his examples. But the argument certainly seems to generalize. For example, consider the case where you (mentally) desire to move your physical arm and your arm subsequently moves. Well, your arm is a physical object just like a billiard ball is. If God continuously creates your arm at every moment and creates it in whatever location it is, then God is again fully causally responsible for your arm's motion. But then it's God who causes your arm to move, not you or your desire. Thus, we get mind → body occasionalism too.

Similarly for the body → mind case: God also continuously creates souls or minds, including yours. But now when He creates a mind, He must create it in *some* state or another: thinking something, perceiving something, etc. But then it follows that God is fully causally responsible for the particular states of every mind at every time. But then we shouldn't say that physically putting your hand on the stove at time *t* was the cause of your mentally feeling that subsequent pain at *t* + 1. Rather, that is only the occasion on which God creates your mind, at *t* + 1, feeling that pain. So again, God causes everything, and nothing else does anything.

You get occasionalism in every domain, in other words, once you accept continuous creation.

And if you don't accept continuous creation?

Malebranche has an even stronger argument for you.

(4) The Necessary Connection Argument

To appreciate this one, we need a little background on what exactly we mean when we call one thing the "cause" of another.

It is this. To say that one thing, x, is the cause of another, y, is to say that x made or compelled y to happen; that is, given that x occurred in those circumstances, it was impossible for y *not* to happen. Thus—when we still had our common sense—we would say that the striking of the match caused it to light because it was impossible for the match *not* to light, in those conditions, once it was struck, and similarly for our other ordinary examples. To see this, imagine for a moment that it was *not* impossible for the match *not* to light in those conditions; that is, you could just as well have struck the match just so without its lighting. If that were so, then the fact that it did light would seem to be a random event, a chance pairing: you might strike the match in the same conditions next time and it wouldn't light. But then we'd be inclined to think of the lighting as a random accident, not as something the striking made or caused to happen.

When events are connected in this way, when the occurrence of the first makes it impossible for the second not to occur, philosophers say that the events are *necessarily connected*. To say that "x causes y," then, is to say that "there is a necessary connection between x and y": whenever x occurs in those conditions, y is guaranteed to occur, or alternatively, once x occurs, it's impossible for y not to occur.

That is a very plausible conception of causation, even today, and indeed it was one widely accepted in Malebranche's time (only coming under attack later, as we'll see in chapter 12).

But if that is what you think causation is, then watch out: you might have to be an occasionalist, too. For there are in fact no necessary connections between any pair of ordinary events, physical or mental.

Or so Malebranche now argues.

Think of any two events, such as your mental desire to get a snack and your subsequent bodily motion toward the fridge. We can easily conceive of circumstances in which you might have that same desire and yet that motion fails to occur: you might be paralyzed or restrained, or you might only be dreaming about the fridge, or, in the extreme case, you might only *be* a mind and not even *have* a body, and so on. Most of all, if you are a theist, then you must recognize that it's always within *God's* power to override any desire you might have, so He could always prevent your body motion. But if it's even possible to have the desire without the motion, then there is not a *necessary* connection between them, and if not, then the desire cannot be said to cause the motion.

Similar reasoning applies to any other pair of events.

Any theist would grant God the power, even if miraculous, of overriding the normally expected sequence of events. So no physical event ever guarantees any subsequent physical event, nor does any physical event (such as the firing of one's neurons) ever guarantee any subsequent mental event (such as a perception), nor, as in our first example, does anything mental ever guarantee anything physical.

There are no necessary connections and, thus, no true causation between any pairs of ordinary events.

Indeed, necessary connections are to be found only in one place, as Malebranche observes:

> But when one thinks about the idea of God, i.e., of an . . . all-powerful being, one knows there is such a connection between His will and the motion of all bodies, that it is impossible to conceive that He wills a body to be moved and that this body not be moved. (*Search* 6.2.3, 448)

There is actually a contradiction in the idea that an infinitely powerful being (God) might will for something to happen and yet that thing doesn't happen. After all, "infinite" power is by definition power without limits, so nothing *could* override it. So if that being wills something, that thing must occur. But that is just to say that there *is* a necessary connection between the will of God and whatever it is that He wills, which means that only with respect to God do we ever find genuine causality.

So given what we mean by causation (necessary connection), no ordinary things ever cause anything, and God causes everything.

Occasionalism anybody?

No, Seriously, Occasionalism Anybody?

To be sure, occasionalism does have its philosophical problems.

Many philosophers worry whether it is consistent with humans having free will: after all, God seems here to be inflicting our own mental states on us. Others worry that in its eagerness to respect God, it is really quite *dis*respectful to the world that God has created and thus actually reflects poorly on God. Others, still, worry that it seems to involve perpetual miracles, since God is causally involved in every event in the world, or that it suggests that God is actually incapable of just creating a world that could operate on its own. Some of these problems are more difficult than others, and Malebranche in fact made impressive strides toward responding to many of them.

The important point, though, is that these problems are worth responding to in the first place.

For Malebranche's greatest achievement may be in simply making it clear that occasionalism is a serious contender. True, that doctrine may be as far removed from common sense as any of the other strange ideas we have been discussing. But Malebranche shows rather compellingly that you really should believe in occasionalism if you accept any one of a number of other ideas. Obviously, if you are not a theist, if you reject God's existence, then occasionalism will be a nonstarter for you. But if you are a theist, then you will need to work out God's causal relationship to His creatures; and as you do that, you will have to entertain very seriously the idea of continuous creation; and once you do *that* you will be practically all the way there toward occasionalism. Moreover, if you think there's any causation in the world at all, and causation really is a matter of necessary connection—ideas that are not so strange—then, again, you just may have to accept occasionalism.

Not that these arguments could *cause* you to accept occasionalism, of course, but they just might be the occasions upon which God causes you to.

Primary Sources

Dialogues = Dialogues on Metaphysics and on Religion
Search = The Search after Truth
Jolley, Nicholas, and David Scott, eds. 1997. *Nicolas Malebranche: Dialogues on Metaphysics and on Religion*. Cambridge: Cambridge University Press.
Lennon, Thomas, and Paul Olscamp, eds. 1997. *Nicolas Malebranche: The Search after Truth*. Cambridge: Cambridge University Press.

Recommended Secondary Sources

Nadler, Steven, ed. 2000. *The Cambridge Companion to Malebranche*. Cambridge: Cambridge University Press.
Schmaltz, Tad. 2009. "Nicolas Malebranche." In *Stanford Encyclopedia of Philosophy*, edited by Edward N. Zalta. http://plato.stanford.edu/archives/win2009/entries/malebranche/.

10

G. W. Leibniz

SYNCHRONICITY

STRANGE IDEA

Each thing in the universe runs entirely on its own internal program, in perfectly coordinated harmony with every other thing—with no causal interactions between them.

MAJOR PROPONENT

G. W. Leibniz (1646–1716)

BRIEF BIOGRAPHY

What can you say about a man whose work was so wide-ranging, deep, and most of all *original* that even the great French thinker Denis Diderot wrote, a century later, that comparing one's own talents to those of Leibniz makes one want to throw away all one's books and just go die quietly somewhere? Born and raised in Leipzig, Leibniz completed a doctorate of law in 1667. But rather than pursue a legal career, he secured a position with the elector of Mainz, in whose court he began the career that would produce Diderot's later depression. In 1672, the elector sent him on a diplomatic mission to Paris, where he met many of the major intellectuals of the era and where his access to unpublished manuscripts by Descartes and mathematician Blaise Pascal inspired his own work on what would become the calculus. He returned in 1676 to a new position as librarian for the Duke of Brunswick, in Hanover, where he stayed for the rest of his life. His final years, however, were marked by a protracted and ugly dispute with British mathematician and physicist Isaac Newton over who had invented the calculus first, and Leibniz slowly fell out of favor with his own court; and when his employer departed in 1714 to become King George I of England, Leibniz was left behind in Hanover, where he died in relative obscurity.

Like Clockwork

No philosophy is stranger, or more brilliant, than that of G. W. Leibniz. And no philosophical idea is quite as strange, or perhaps as brilliant, as Leibniz's famous doctrine of *preestablished harmony*.

To explain it fully would require technical details better avoided, but we can, with some simplifying assumptions, get the basic idea across. For our purposes, we shall thus treat Leibniz as accepting *dualism* (the doctrine that the mental and the physical are fundamentally different sorts of things) and present preestablished harmony as applying to all pairs of things or events, mental or physical.

So assumed, we may sketch the idea as follows.

Imagine two perfectly made grandfather clocks, exactly identical in every way, wound the same way, and set to the same time. What we'd expect to see, over time, is a perfect correlation between the two clocks: when the first reads 12:13, so too would the second, and so on. But, of course, this perfect correlation does not result from any direct causal relationship between the clocks. Neither clock causally influences the other; the readings on one clock in no way cause the readings on the other. Rather, their respective readings are caused purely internally, by the internal mechanisms of each clock, by their structures, their springs, and so on. The correlations obtain between them because their internal mechanisms have been (in this case) externally coordinated. They run in perfect parallel, in a kind of harmony of correlation, yet causally separated from each other.

That is Leibniz's picture of the world as a whole.

There *appears* (as we saw in the previous chapter) to be plenty of causal interaction between minds and bodies (for example). You mentally desire to get something to eat, and your physical body starts moving toward the fridge. Someone physically punches your arm, and you have a mental perception of pain.

But this appearance, Leibniz says, is an illusion: the first event may be regularly correlated with the second event but does not in fact cause it.

Instead, each individual thing causes its own sequence of internal states. Your mind causes itself (i.e., you!) to go through a sequence of mental states, including desires, thoughts, perceptions, and so on. It runs on a purely internal program, as each grandfather clock did above. Meanwhile, the physical world is running on *its* own internal program, going through a sequence of states (where different bodies are in different states of motion and so on). And those two sequences of events are all perfectly correlated with each other: at the moment your mind's program produces your desire for food, your body's program produces its motion toward the fridge, and just when the physical world's program brings that fist into contact with your arm, your mind's program produces the perception of pain. Not only this but all individual minds, too, are in perfect correlation (or "harmony") with one another: at the moment your mind produces in you the perception of calling my name, my mind produces in me the perception of your voice calling my name.

Each individual runs its own internal program, yet everything is so perfectly correlated or harmonized that we appear to have causal interaction.

These are, clearly, some pretty fine clocks.

The Clockmaker

That would be God, obviously.

For who else could set up such a system involving the incalculable coordination of the internal programs of innumerably many distinct substances, mental and physical? A system in which it was established in advance, at the moment of its creation, that everything forever afterward would be perfectly correlated, a *preestablished harmony*, as it were?

Leibniz offers various dramatic statements of the doctrine:

> God originally created the soul . . . in such a way that everything must arise for it from its own depths, through a perfect *spontaneity* relative to itself, and yet with a perfect *conformity* relative to external things. . . . The perceptions or expressions of external things occur in the soul at a given time, in virtue of its own [internal] laws, as if in a world apart. ("New System," 143)

> Anything which occurs in . . . a substance . . . occurs in the substance spontaneously, arising out of its own depths; for no created substance can have an influence upon any other, so that everything comes to a substance from itself (though ultimately from God). (*New Essays* II.xxi, 210)

> According to this system, bodies act as if there were no [minds] . . . and [minds] act as if there were no bodies; and both act as if each influenced the other. (*Monadology* #81, 223)

A dramatic doctrine, indeed. But the question is, as usual, why anyone might believe it.

Could the Alternatives Actually Be Worse?

One indirect way to argue for a theory is to argue that all the competing theories are worse, because they are stranger, or beset by more difficult problems, or generally less plausible. It's hard to imagine any theory that's harder to believe than that of preestablished harmony, but then maybe that's only because our imaginations are not as powerful as Leibniz's.

So let's follow Leibniz in a little imagination stretching by exploring the main competing theories.

Two essential aspects of preestablished harmony are the claims that (1) individual substances do not truly causally interact and (2) yet they genuinely do have *internal* causal powers, as their internal programs cause their sequence of internal states. Competing theories, then, reject either of these claims. As we saw in the previous chapter, *occasionalism* is the doctrine that no ordinary creatures have any causal powers at all, so it therefore rejects claim 2, and we may dub as *interactionism* the doctrine that *endorses* true causal interaction between things and that therefore rejects claim 1. The former is associated with Nicolas Malebranche, of course, and the latter, with some caveats, with René Descartes.

Let's join Leibniz, then, in his critiques of both.

Leibniz's Critique of Interactionism

Leibniz focuses here on the case of mind ↔ body interactions and raises two problems.

(1) First, he argues, mind → body causal interaction is inconsistent with the laws of motion, which govern the entire physical universe.

To say that laws of motion govern the universe is to say that, given a particular physical state of affairs—a set of particular bodies moving in particular ways—strict rules determine what happens next. These laws dictate how the planets and stars move, how objects fall to the ground, how two billiard balls move upon collision, and so on. They also dictate (it was believed, for various reasons) that the total amount of motion in the universe always remains the same, a belief reflected even today in the law of the conservation of momentum.

But now suppose that a mental event were to cause a physical event: your desire to eat causes your body to move toward the fridge.

Presumably, this interaction is mediated by the brain: your desire influences motions in your brain, which in turn, by purely physical means, cause your muscles to contract. But the brain is itself a physical object, governed by the same laws of motion as every other physical thing. These laws already dictate precisely which sequence of motions should occur in your brain. If your desire in any way affects those motions, then it must be by overriding what the laws of motion already dictate! Moreover, this would amount to your desire adding new motion to the brain that wasn't already present and thus increasing the overall amount of motion in the world—which every scientist of the day agreed was impossible!

Mind → body interaction therefore violates the laws of motion and should be rejected.

(2) The second problem derives from the deepest core of Leibniz's worldview.

For Leibniz is a leading example of a school of thought known as *rationalism*, which here may be understood as the doctrine that human reason is capable of obtaining genuine knowledge of reality. But for Leibniz, this could only be so if in fact reality itself displays some kind of rational order: if it is *intelligible*, or *makes sense*.

His worry, then, is that mind ↔ body interaction would violate this constraint:

> When I began to meditate about the union of [mind] and body, I felt as if I were thrown . . . into the open sea. For I could not find any way of explaining how the body makes anything happen in the soul, or *vice versa*. ("New System," 142–43)

Why is mind ↔ body interaction so problematic?

Recall that we are working within the framework of dualism, according to which the mental and the physical are fundamentally different. In particular, the physical is spatial in nature, while the mental is not. Now as we saw in our discussion of *the mind-body problem* from the previous chapter, the paradigm cases of causal interaction involve contact or collision between cause and effect, as in the billiard balls example. But it is precisely this that is impossible, in the dualist framework, between the mental and the physical: if the former is nonspatial, then it can neither smash into, nor be smashed into by, the latter. Your (mental) desire to eat cannot literally collide with the molecules of your brain and set your body moving toward the fridge.

So how could it have *any* causal power over the molecules in your body?

No causal mechanism at all seems even imaginable. But that is just to say that we can make no sense of the idea of mind ↔ body causal interactions. If you insist on intelligibility, then you'll have to reject that interaction.

Of course, Malebranche used this same point as a reason to endorse occasionalism, which also denies that interaction. That would be very nice for Leibniz, as well, except that he now has some issues with occasionalism too.

Leibniz's Critique of Occasionalism

Leibniz had great respect for Malebranche personally but not very much respect for his occasionalism.

(1) First, we saw Malebranche's worry that to assign ordinary creatures causal powers was wrongly to elevate them, as if they were as gods having powers over others, including ourselves.

Leibniz thinks that Malebranche has this pretty much backward. To deprive creatures of all causal powers is to make them utterly impotent and worthless and thus *unworthy* of God their creator, who in creating them would certainly share some of His perfections with them (if, of course, in a limited measure). Thus, we must expect creatures to have *some* sort of true causal powers, though precisely what sort is yet to be seen.

(2) Second, next, recall Malebranche's "continuous creation" argument for occasionalism. When God continuously creates the universe (that argument went), He must create all creatures in their various specific locations and states and thus is fully causally responsible for every creature and every state. But then there is nothing left over for creatures to cause, and occasionalism is true!

But while Leibniz accepts God's continuous creation, he rejects Malebranche's occasionalist conclusion:

> No created substance . . . would remain numerically the same, and thus, nothing would be conserved by God, and consequently all things would be only certain vanishing or unstable modifications . . . of [the] one permanent divine substance. ("On Nature Itself" (8), 160)

If what God creates has absolutely no causal powers, then it wouldn't even have the intrinsic ability to persist in existence, even for a moment, on its own. But then it wouldn't *be* anything, for to exist as a distinct individual being is to exist for at least a moment. And if no creatures are distinct individual beings in this way, then we'd have to say that they really are just manifestations (or "modifications") of God Himself, the one permanent (i.e., persisting) substance or being.

If you deny creatures all causal powers, in short, then you deny them any independent reality, and you turn everything into a mere aspect of God. The resulting *pantheism*—the doctrine that everything ultimately is God—contradicts the traditional distinction between God and His creatures and in fact was scornfully repudiated by every major religious thinker in the long history of Western religious philosophy.

So if occasionalism entails pantheism, Leibniz concludes, then continuous creation cannot entail occasionalism, Malebranche's argument notwithstanding.

(3) Third, finally, there's that whole intelligibility thing again. Occasionalism ultimately fares no better here than interactionism.

"It is quite true," Leibniz writes,

> that . . . there is no real [causal] influence of one created substance on another. . . . But . . . it is not sufficient [simply] to . . . invoke [God]. For when one does that without giving any other explanation derived from the order of [natural] causes, it is . . . having recourse to miracle. ("New System," 143)

Leibniz agrees with the occasionalist that "there is no real [causal] influence" of one thing over another. His worry is rather with the occasionalist's next claim, that God does the causing, for to say that is not to explain how some thing happens but to admit that we *cannot* explain it. Suppose you hire a scientific expert to determine what caused a certain explosion, and after her lengthy investigation, she reports that "God did it." Would you pay the balance of her fee for that answer or instead sue her to return your advance? Well, it's not much different when we explain how the collision brought about the motion of the second billiard ball by saying "God did it": if we cannot explain these things on their own terms, with an "explanation derived from the order of [natural] causes," then we are simply saying that everything is a miracle.

But to say *that* is to say that the universe is unintelligible: understanding it on its own terms is not enough to understand it.

Indeed, on the occasionalist picture, whatever occurs is fundamentally arbitrary: God could freely choose to make any event follow any other event, to make your desire to move your body results in your sitting down, to make your striking of a match result in its turning into an elephant, and so on. That's what follows where there is no *intrinsic* reason why one event is followed by another, why striking matches typically results in their lighting. And that's precisely what it means for the universe to not be intelligible, which the rationalist Leibniz cannot accept.

What Leibniz needs, then, is a system that dispenses with causal influences between different substances but still ensures that everything that happens is orderly and intelligible.

What he needs is a little preestablished harmony.

Leibniz's Arguments for Preestablished Harmony

But of course a good rationalist also needs reasons to believe the things he believes, so let's consider a couple of reasons to believe in preestablished harmony.

(1) First, conveniently, the problems confronting interactionism and occasionalism also reveal the advantages of preestablished harmony. As Leibniz writes,

> therefore, since I was forced to agree that it is not possible for the [mind] or any other true substance to receive [causal influence] from without.... I was led ... to a view that surprised me, but which seems inevitable, and which, in fact, has very great advantages and rather considerable beauty. ("New System," 143)

Preestablished harmony provides everything the other theories lacked.

For it rejects the causality between substances: every individual thing operates on its own internal program, in parallel with everything else. It thus avoids the "laws of motion" and "intelligibility" problems for interactionism by denying that the mind does have causal effects on the body. But then it also offers what occasionalism specifically lacked: it grants substances some causal powers, if only "internal" ones, *within* the substance, for it holds that each substance causes its own internal states. In granting this, it avoids the first two problems for occasionalism: God's creatures "share" His perfections (insofar as they do have genuine causal power) and thus are "worthy" of Him, and since they cause their own sequence of states, they are responsible (at least in some sense) for their own persistence over time—or at least enough to count as being distinct from God and therefore to avoid the dreaded pantheism.

But now preestablished harmony also avoids the other intelligibility problem.

For each substance genuinely causes its own sequence of states: that means that the intrinsic nature of the substance makes or compels its states to occur in their appropriate order. And what that means is that anyone who sufficiently understood the substance would see or understand precisely why its states occur in just that order and not some other. But that is just to say that the sequence of states "makes sense," or is intelligible. We may not ourselves ever succeed in reaching this level of understanding, of course; we may never be able explicitly to confirm the intelligibility of the sequence of events in the universe. But in adopting preestablished harmony, we are holding that, in principle, there *is* an underlying order and that a being properly equipped could grasp that order, as, no doubt, according to Leibniz, God Himself does.

(2) Finally, preestablished harmony follows from the nature of truth itself.

What, you may ask, is "truth"? (It's about time we asked that question: we are philosophers, after all!)

Well, truth is something that at least some sentences enjoy, while others do not. The question is what accounts for the difference between those that do and those that don't. The answer begins by observing that the relevant sentences standardly come in the form of a *subject* combined with a *predicate*: the subject is the thing the sentence is about, and the predicate is what is being said about the subject. In the sentence "Snow is white," for example, "snow" is the subject and "is white" is the predicate.

But now, Leibniz writes, " All true predication has some basis in the nature of things. . . . Thus the subject term must always contain the predicate term" (*Discourse* 8, 41).

A true sentence has a "basis in the nature of things," that is, in reality itself. Thus, to say that, in such a sentence, the predicate term is "contained in" the subject term is to say that what you say about the subject really is *in* the subject. For "snow is white" to be true, then, whiteness, the thing referred to by the predicate "is white," must really be a feature of the snow itself.

Plausible enough, surely.

But now let's consider some other true sentences.

Imagine, for a moment, that we are contemporaries of the ancient leader Alexander the Great. He lived from 356 BCE until 323 BCE, a mere thirty-three years (if you can count backward there); let us imagine that we are with him during his teenage years, say, in 340 BCE. It turns out that, here in 340 BCE, there are many true sentences that could be uttered about this gangly pimply boy: "He was born in Macedon," "He was tutored by the famous philosopher Aristotle," "He is currently sixteen years old," "He will become king in four years," "He will shortly conquer most of the known world," "He will eventually become a legendary figure in the myths of Greek culture," and so on. Notice the tenses: some of these sentences are in the past tense, some in the present, and some in the future. Of course in 340 BCE, we wouldn't be in a position to *know* those truths that are about his future, but those were true sentences at that time anyway, as our actual twenty-first-century perspective teaches us.

But now truth, Leibniz tells us, "has some basis in the nature of things."

If those sentences are all true, then their respective predicates must be "contained" in their shared subject.

But that means that, in 340 BCE, it is already "contained" in Alexander himself that he *will* become king and conquer the world and be featured in Greek myth. Indeed, everything that will ever happen to him after 340 BCE is already "contained" in him, just as whiteness is contained in snow that is currently white.

But then *that* is to say that nothing could ever come into him from outside, or causally affect him, later on, for if some effect (or property) were only to come in from outside later, then it wouldn't already be contained in him now. But then it follows that everything about his future, if it is already contained in him now, must be generated from within him, just as preestablished harmony says.

To make this even clearer, let's shift our perspective: to you.

Right now you are having certain visual perceptions, such as that of reading this page. A little later you will be having different visual perceptions, such as that of putting down this book. Weeks or months or years from now, you'll have who-knows-what sorts of perceptions; we're not in a position to know our futures. Nevertheless, whatever specific perceptions will happen to you in the future, at those different times, it is true right now that you *will* have those perceptions exactly when you have them, even if we don't know it.

But now a true sentence is one where the predicate is contained in the subject.

If so, it follows that all those future perceptions of yours must already be contained in you in some sense or another. What makes the sentence "Snow is white" true right now is that whiteness is contained in snow; what makes "You will have perception *p* at later time *t*" true right now is that *the fact that you will have that perception at that time is itself already contained in you.*

But if the fact that you will have all those future perceptions is already built into you now, then we cannot say that those perceptions will, later, only be caused in you by something external to you.

And to say that is just to say that nothing at all has causal influence over you and your perceptions. And, of course, similar considerations apply to every single individual thing and to everything that will happen *to* every single thing.

And that is precisely what preestablished harmony asserts.

The very idea of truth, then, supports the preestablished harmony—which is about the most powerful endorsement any strange idea could ever wish for.

Primary Sources

Discourse = *Discourse on Metaphysics,* in Ariew and Garber (1989).

Monadology = *The Principles of Philosophy, or, the Monadology,* in Ariew and Garber (1989).

New Essays = *New Essays on Human Understanding*

"New System" = "New System of Nature," in Ariew and Garber (1989).

"On Nature Itself," in Ariew and Garber (1989).

Ariew, Roger, and Daniel Garber, eds. 1989. *G. W. Leibniz: Philosophical Essays.* Indianapolis, IN: Hackett.

Remnant, Peter, and Jonathan Bennett, eds. 1982. *Leibniz: New Essays on Human Understanding* (abridged edition). Cambridge: Cambridge University Press.

Recommended Secondary Sources

Jolley, Nicolas, ed. 1994. *The Cambridge Companion to Leibniz.* Cambridge: Cambridge University Press.

Look, Brandon C. 2008. "Gottfried Wilhelm Leibniz." In *The Stanford Encyclopedia of Philosophy, edited by* Edward N. Zalta. http://plato.stanford.edu/archives/fall2008/entries/leibniz/.

11

George Berkeley

To Be Is to Perceive or Be Perceived

STRANGE IDEA

There is no physical world: all that exists are minds and their perceptions.

MAJOR PROPONENT

George Berkeley (1685–1753)

BRIEF BIOGRAPHY

Born near Kilkenny, Ireland, the future philosophical idealist was exposed to the works of Descartes, Locke, and Malebranche as a student at Trinity College, Dublin, then got himself ordained in the Anglican church. Through his twenties, he produced some of his most enduring philosophical writings, which brought him not only some notice at the time but also a pleasant gig as a private tutor for a wealthy family during their four-year-long grand tour of Europe. After a few more years at Trinity as a fellow, he became enthused about a scheme for founding a Christian college in Bermuda. Realizing that the place would need some food, Berkeley sailed in 1728 for Newport, Rhode Island, to establish some farms, but the whole project soon foundered, and he returned to Britain in 1731. In 1734 he was made bishop of Cloyne, Ireland, where he composed the best selling of his works (in his day), a book defending the medical virtues of a concoction called tar water. He died in 1753, shortly after moving to Oxford to supervise the education of one of the only three of his children (out of seven) to survive their childhoods.

Red Pill or Blue Pill?

The job of the philosophy professor got a lot easier after 1999, the year of the groundbreaking film *The Matrix*. If you somehow haven't seen it yet, then stop reading right now and go watch it: it will also make your job as a reader of this chapter a lot easier.

For the strange idea of this chapter, George Berkeley's strange idea, is (with a caveat or two) beautifully illustrated by that film: the universe according to Berkeley is pretty much the universe as it is experienced by those poor souls plugged into the matrix. What exists for those people exists entirely inside their minds, exists *only* inside their minds, as a set of perceptions. The buildings and streets and even other people of the city in which they live—in which they think they live—don't really (i.e., physically) exist at all; all that exists are their *perceptions* of these buildings and streets and other people. The only difference between the Berkeleyan world and that of *The Matrix* is that the creator of the former does not take his conception of reality, as being entirely within the mind, as a fiction.

Rather, for Berkeley, the universe of the mind is all the universe there is. There are minds, and there are perceptions within minds, and nothing else.

Or, as he puts it in his famous slogan *esse est percipi*, "to be is to be perceived." Everything that exists does so only insofar as it is perceived by some mind. True, we might quibble and note that in addition to the perceptions, the things perceived, there also exist the minds doing the perceiving; so, strictly speaking, "to be is to be perceived *or* to be a percei*ver*." But then again that is a mere quibble: since minds are always aware of themselves, they are always perceiving themselves. Thus, to be, to be real, to exist, for Berkeley, is always simply to be perceived.

This doctrine, that all that exists are minds and their perceptions, the latter more commonly called *ideas*, is known as *idealism*. What made *The Matrix* such fantastic entertainment was how literally incredible such a purely mental universe was. But for Berkeley, this strange idea is not only *not* incredible but is, rather, something that careful and powerful argument shows us we *must* believe. And not only that: it is also, in the end, just plain old *common sense*.

That latter is no doubt the strangest claim of all.

But we'll get there in due course.

Materialism

To appreciate his idealism, we need first to get clearer on just what it is up against. Its main competitor, which Berkeley calls *materialism*, is this doctrine:

Materialism: In addition to nonphysical minds, the universe contains mind-independent, spatially extended physical objects that are perceived indirectly by means of ideas, some of which resemble those objects and some of which do not.

So stated, materialism is no stranger to strangeness itself, and indeed we've already encountered some of its own components in previous chapters. You may recognize first what we've called *dualism*, the doctrine that the mental and the physical are very different sorts of things. You may also recognize part of *the mechanical philosophy* from chapter 7, here the claim that physical matter is characterized by being "spatially extended," literally just "taking up space." And, finally, you may also recognize the distinction between *primary* and *secondary qualities* from chapter 8: some of our sensory perceptions (or "ideas") truly resemble what's in the physical body (such as our perceptions of size, shape, and motion, the primary qualities), while others do not (such as our perceptions of color, flavor, and the other secondary qualities).

There's really only one new doctrine here, namely the claim that we perceive physical objects "indirectly, by means of ideas." To say this is to say that what we actually perceive, for example when we are looking at a tree, isn't the physical tree itself but some mental representation or image (or "idea") of the tree. This strange claim could get its own chapter, of course, but here let's just observe that when we dream, we are clearly perceiving not real objects but only mental images thereof; so perhaps it's not too outlandish to grant that the same is true during waking perception, which is often quite indistinguishable in nature from dream perception.

At any rate, all the major thinkers of Berkeley's period endorsed this claim, including Berkeley himself: as an idealist, he agrees that what we perceive "directly" are only our own mental representations or ideas. The difference between the idealist and the materialist is that the former stops there (there are only minds and ideas), while the latter then adds the claim that there are also mind-independent physical objects out there causing those ideas.

And in adding this claim, Berkeley thinks, these materialists—including René Descartes and John Locke, his primary targets—have simply gone too far.

Three Arguments against Materialism

Berkeley thinks that materialism is wrong in almost every way, and he offers three arguments to show why.

The first involves concerns about *skepticism*. A *skeptic* is one who questions whether it's possible to know certain things. Berkeley will claim that materialism leaves several crucial aspects of the world "unknowable" and thus engenders skepticism. In the early eighteenth century, when it was widely held that the whole reason that God gave us minds in the first place was for us to know the world, any theory that leaves the world unknowable in fundamental ways would be very unpopular.

The second involves various attacks on the distinction between primary and secondary qualities, a distinction central to materialism.

The third argues that materialism is not merely false but in fact contradictory: it couldn't even *possibly* be true.

Let's examine each in turn.

Argument 1: Materialism Engenders Skepticism

Berkeley argues that materialism leaves at least two important things unknowable: the *sensible qualities* of physical bodies and whether those bodies even exist outside the mind at all. By "sensible qualities," he means all the properties of bodies that we are able to sense or perceive (such as their sizes, shapes, colors, etc.), and we'll see why materialism leaves them unknowable a bit later. Here we'll see why he thinks the *existence* of physical bodies is unknowable, and to do that, we must first look at the arguments that materialists such as Descartes and Locke make to prove that physical bodies *do* exist.

(1) First, they observe, when we call up mental images from our memories or imagination, they are always faint and occur voluntarily. But when we open our eyes, we *involuntarily* experience *vivid* sensory perceptions. The best explanation of this difference is that the former are purely in our minds and that external physical bodies, independent of our minds, cause the latter—in which case they must exist.

(2) Second, they note, it surely *seems* to us that our perceptions come from external bodies, and God would be deceiving us if in fact they didn't. But of course God, a perfectly good being, could be no deceiver. So our perceptions must come from external bodies, just as they seem to, and bodies must therefore exist.

Berkeley thinks both of these arguments stink.

The first merely suggests that *something* exists externally to our minds, causing our perceptions, but it doesn't show that these must be physical bodies. In fact, the cause of our perceptions could just as well be other nonphysical minds and/or God Himself! So the argument doesn't prove that there is an external *physical* world, as materialism claims.

The second argument, meanwhile, assumes that it "seems to us" that our perceptions come from external bodies. But all we ever experience, Berkeley replies, are the perceptions, the ideas; we don't experience the bodies themselves. So how could the former "seem to" come from the latter, when we don't even experience the latter? Rather, perceptions simply arise in our minds and don't "seem to" come from anywhere. So God wouldn't be deceiving us if there aren't any physical bodies after all.

In fact, Berkeley concludes, there are no good arguments to believe in the existence of an external physical universe. So materialists posit the existence of something whose existence cannot be demonstrated or known.

Thus, the skepticism—and strike 1 against materialism.

Argument 2: Contra the Distinction between Primary and Secondary Qualities

Again, this is the distinction between those qualities that physical bodies really do have (the "primary qualities" of size, shape, and motion) and those that really only exist in the mind of the perceiver (the "secondary qualities," such as color, flavor, and so on). This distinction is essential to materialism because the primary qualities are allegedly mind independent, which would mean that they are grounded in something outside the mind and thus physical.

Berkeley challenges the distinction in two steps.

(1) First he emphasizes what he shares with his materialist adversaries: the view that the secondary qualities are really only in the mind of the perceiver and not in the bodies. He even borrows some arguments to this effect directly from Locke, including the "relativity of perception" arguments we examined in chapter 8.

But then he adds some new arguments. For example, everybody agrees that pain and pleasure exist only as sensations in the perceiver's mind and that they are not properties in bodies themselves. But now extreme heat and cold are just kinds of painful sensations; if pain is only in the mind, then extreme heat and cold sensations must also be only in the mind. Furthermore, moderate degrees of these are kinds of pleasurable sensations; so, if pleasure is only in the mind, then moderate heat and cold sensations are also only in the mind. But extreme and moderate sensations are all there are, so heat and cold are really just properties of perceivers' minds, and not of bodies.

(2) Next, Berkeley argues that similar arguments apply to materialism's primary qualities—in which case, even *they* must exist only in the mind as well!

Recall, in particular now, the earlier relativity of perception arguments. These were arguments with the following general form:

A perceived quality varies.
The object itself does not vary.
_____

Therefore, the perceived quality is not in the object itself.

Locke's classic example was the "two hands in a bucket" case. Put one hand in a freezer and the other in a warm oven, then place both in the same bucket of water: the perceptions of temperature will vary between the hands, but it's the same water, so the conclusion was (as it was earlier) that warmth and coolness are not in the water but in the mind of the perceiver.

Well, Berkeley observes, if "relativity of perception" shows that certain qualities are really in the mind, so much the worse for primary qualities: they are subject to the same relativity!

Consider size. A dust mite appears small to our eye and its foot even smaller. But the mite's foot would appear to the mite itself as being some moderate size and would appear as even larger to any creatures smaller than the mite. But then the perceived quality (size) is varying between perceivers, while the alleged body itself, the mite's foot, is not varying; therefore, the perceived size must not belong to the body itself. So the "primary quality" of size is, after all, in the mind of the perceiver!

Similar arguments may be made about shape and motion. Whether a motion is fast or slow, for example, is a function of how much distance is covered over a certain time. But the perception of time is notoriously subjective: a given interval may seem very short to one perceiver and very long to another. Thus, a motion that the former perceives as swift would be perceived by the latter as slow. (One reason it's so hard to swat a fly, apparently, is that what looks like the murderously quick motion of the swatter to you looks like a long, slow, leisurely descent *to the fly*.) But, of course, it's allegedly the same single, unvarying motion. Therefore, again, the "primary quality" of motion is in the mind and not in the body!

There's no real distinction between primary and secondary qualities after all, Berkeley concludes: all qualities are in the mind. But then there's nothing left over to exist "out there," in the mind-independent physical world posited by the materialist.

Strike 2 for materialism.

Argument 3: The Inconceivability Argument

But it gets worse.

Materialism isn't merely false, it's actually logically contradictory: there are no conceivable circumstances under which it could possibly *ever* be, have been, or become true.

For is it even logically possible for a mind-independent physical object to exist or come into existence?

To say that something is "logically possible" is to say that it may be conceived without contradiction. But now try to conceive of something existing outside of all minds, Berkeley urges. Try to conceive of some tree (for example) existing independently or outside of all minds. You can't do it, for the very act of conceiving of it ensures that it is in some mind, namely yours! To say that you are conceiving of some object existing outside all minds is to say that you have *in* your mind an object *outside* all minds: a clear contradiction. Thus there is a contradiction in the very idea of a mind-independent object, in which case, mind-independent objects are logically impossible. But then, obviously, so is materialism, which believes in such objects.

Strike 3 for materialism.

But Wait—the Catcher Dropped the Ball!

For the strikeout to count in baseball, the catcher must hold on to the ball.

We actually left out one piece of Berkeley's attack on materialism.

The first argument was that materialism engenders skepticism on two fronts, but we haven't yet explained the first, namely why Berkeley thinks that the "sensible qualities" of bodies remain unknowable on materialism.

Until we close that gap, a glimmer of life may remain for the materialist.

Argument 1 and Relativity of Perception, Revisited

It turns out that argument 1 and the relativity of perception arguments from argument 2 are closely related.

The latter Berkeley used to show that not only "secondary" but also "primary" qualities were in the mind. But let us now ask ourselves an important question: are relativity of perception arguments actually valid arguments? Does their conclusion, that the perceived quality is "not in the object itself," actually follow from their premises?

The answer, perhaps unexpectedly, is no: in fact, it's possible for the premises to be true yet the conclusion false.

This could happen if, say, one of the relative perceptions is simply mistaken. In the "two hands in a bucket" case, if the hand feeling "warmth" were *mis*perceiving, then we could explain why the perception varies between the hands without placing the perceived quality in the mind. The water "really is" cold in itself, we could say, and any other perception is just an error. In this way, both premises of the argument could be true and yet the conclusion false. So relativity of perception arguments are actually invalid and fail to prove their conclusions!

But here's the interesting point: Berkeley actually knows they are invalid.

In his 1710 work *The Principles of Human Knowledge*, he quite explicitly observes that relativity of perception arguments do not prove their conclusion, as just described. Yet, oddly, in his 1713 work *Three Dialogues*, which is the source of the material presented here, Berkeley uses relativity of perception arguments all over the place to prove that primary and secondary qualities are all in the mind. Yet how could he do that, just three years after *explicitly noting their invalidity?*

Answer: he uses them *ad hominem* against Locke.

Ad hominem means "to the person," and that is a fancy way of saying that when Berkeley uses relativity of perception arguments in 1713, he does so not because he thinks they are valid (he does not) but because he is addressing his arguments specifically "to the person" of Locke, and because *Locke* (wrongly) thinks that they are valid. What he is trying to show Locke, in fact, is that *if* you accept these arguments as valid (as Locke does), then you have to reject the distinction between primary and secondary qualities (because relativity of perception arguments apply equally to both).

Of course, Berkeley himself thinks they are invalid.

But, then, if these arguments are invalid, they leave Locke (and materialism) with a different problem. One hand tells us the water is cold, the other tells us the water is hot, and perhaps one hand is misperceiving; but the new problem is that *sensation leaves us no means of determining which hand is perceiving correctly and which is misperceiving.* The relativity of perception may not prove that all qualities are "in the mind," after all, but it does mean that we can never know by sensation which of the differing perceived qualities is the true one.

So, relativity of perception leaves us with the skepticism we left out from argument 1: the true sensible qualities of bodies are unknowable.

We may represent Berkeley as confronting Locke with a *dilemma* here. Relativity of perception arguments are either valid or invalid. If they are valid (as Locke thinks), then all qualities are in the mind, and materialism is false. If they are invalid, then the sensible qualities of bodies are unknowable, which is a skeptical strike against materialism. Thus, either way materialism is in trouble.

Strike 3, this time, for real: materialism is out.

It Isn't All Negative

Berkeley's strategy, that is.

For while he does thoroughly dismantle materialism as we've just seen, he recognizes that to win some converts to his strange idealism, he must do more than just destroy its competitor. In the next stage, then, he provides a more positive argument to support idealism.

We may present that argument in four steps.

(1) Sensible Qualities Are by Their Nature Perceived

To say that sensible qualities are "by their nature perceived" is to say that they are the kinds of things whose essence consists *in* being perceived: they exist when and only when they are being perceived. The paradigm example might be something such as pain, for "pain" clearly only exists insofar as someone is actively feeling pain. More controversial examples might be properties such as flavors and sounds and colors: perhaps (say) sodium chloride has its molecular structure even when no minds are around but that salty flavor or sensation exists only when someone is tasting it. Of course, materialism already grants that "secondary qualities" exist only in the mind, so Berkeley needs little argument here. And given his earlier arguments against the distinction between secondary and primary qualities, he now takes *all* sensible qualities to exist only when perceived.

(2) Thus, Sensible Qualities Are Perceived Directly

Perceiving "directly" contrasts with "inferring": we hear a sound directly but only infer that there is a car out there causing the sound. But now, if sensible qualities were perceived *in*directly—that is, only inferred to exist and not directly perceived—then they would in fact exist while being themselves unperceived. But then by claim 1, it has been argued that sensible qualities only exist when being perceived. It therefore follows that we *cannot* perceive them indirectly, in which case we must conclude that they are perceived directly.

(3) Bodies Are Just Bundles of Sensible Qualities

There are, in philosophy, two major competing views about the relationship between a given object (say, an apple) and its properties. On the first, an apple just is its bundle of properties: roundness, redness, sweetness, moistness, and so on. There is nothing more to the apple than that completed list. On the second view, held at least by the materialist Locke, an apple is something distinct from its bundle of properties: it is the "thing" that *has* those properties. This "thing" is often called a *substratum*, or "something lying beneath": it is what "lies beneath" the roundness, redness, and so on.

Berkeley, here, is endorsing the first view.

He offers various arguments, but the most important is perhaps the skeptical concern from argument 1. Properties such as "roundness, redness," and so on, we can observe with our senses, he notes, but once you insist that the substratum is distinct from all those sensible qualities, then it instantly becomes something we are *incapable* of sensing. But then we can never confirm its reality: it becomes unknowable, and that, of course, is very bad.

It's better, therefore, to reject the substratum view and instead hold that a given body is nothing more than a bundle of sensible qualities.

(4) Thus, Bodies Are by Their Nature Perceived, and Perceived Directly

This conclusion follows directly from the previous steps. If sensible qualities are by their nature perceived and perceived directly, and if bodies just are bundles of these qualities, then bodies themselves are by their nature perceived and perceived directly.

And to say that, of course, is to say that everything that exists does so only insofar as it is being perceived, that is, insofar as it exists within a mind. So there is no mind-independent physical world after all. What we previously took to be "bodies" just are bundles of perceptions, existing within minds— and minds and their perceptions are all that really exists.

We've got our idealism.

Uncommon Sense?

Okay, so Berkeley has now dismantled materialism and bolstered idealism, but really, for many people, idealism simply crosses the line of believability. You may be willing to grant that reality is stranger than you thought, but to actually deny the existence of the physical universe and claim that everything exists only in our minds? Surely, common sense must put *some* constraints on what we believe, and idealism simply violates common sense too violently to be accepted.

Or does it?

Surprisingly, Berkeley doubles down here. Instead of simply insisting that sometimes good arguments must override common sense, he opts to suggest that in comparison to materialism, *idealism itself better fits common sense.*

This may sound even more preposterous, but it just may work if you ask precisely what common sense actually believes about the relevant things. Perhaps do a quick survey, and ask a few normal people (i.e., not philosophers) the following questions:

Do you perceive bodies directly?
Do you believe the world is fundamentally unknowable?
Is fire hot?

Most will likely answer yes, no, and yes.

Then think about how materialism answers these questions.

Materialism's physical bodies are perceived only indirectly; what we perceive directly are our ideas. The substratum "lying beneath" a body's properties can never be perceived and is thus unknowable; nor (if Berkeley's arguments are right) can we know the true sensible qualities of bodies or whether bodies even exist at all. And, finally, according to materialism, fire is some physical object "out there" while "heat" is a secondary quality existing only in the mind; so, strictly speaking, the fire is not itself hot but merely causes heat sensations in us.

Or, in other words, no, yes, and no.

Not much of a fit with common sense.

How does idealism do here?

Well, a body (according to idealism) is just a bundle of sensory perceptions and is therefore perceived directly. Since all that exists is what is perceivable, there is nothing left over to the world that could be unknowable in any way. And since the object "fire" is itself just a bundle of sensory perceptions, including heat, then the fire itself is indeed plenty hot.

Yes, no, and yes.

'Nuff said.

Primary Sources

The Principles of Human Knowledge = *A Treatise Concerning the Principles of Human Knowledge*, in *The Works of George Berkeley*, edited by G. N. Wright (London, 1843), reprinted with modification in *Modern Philosophy: An Anthology of Primary Sources* (2nd ed.), edited by Roger Ariew and Eric Watkins (Indianapolis, IN: Hackett, 2009).

Three Dialogues = *Three Dialogues between Hylas and Philonous, in Opposition to Skeptics and Atheists (1713)*, in *The Works of George Berkeley*, edited by G. N. Wright (London, 1843), reprinted with modification in *Modern Philosophy: An Anthology of Primary Sources* (2nd ed.), edited by Roger Ariew and Eric Watkins (Indianapolis, IN: Hackett, 2009).

Recommended Secondary Sources

Downing, Lisa. 2011. "George Berkeley." In *Stanford Encyclopedia of Philosophy, edited by* Edward N. Zalta. http://plato.stanford.edu/archives/spr2011/entries/berkeley/.

Winkler, Kenneth, ed. 2005. *The Cambridge Companion to Berkeley.* Cambridge: Cambridge University Press.

12

David Hume

Stercus Accidit

STRANGE IDEA

Nothing can be explained, and you can't even make reasonable predictions about anything that will happen—even in the next few seconds.

MAJOR PROPONENT

David Hume (1711–1776)

BRIEF BIOGRAPHY

Scottish philosopher David Hume entered Edinburgh University at the tender age of eleven. Upon finishing there, he spent several years composing his first great work, *A Treatise of Human Nature*, which was published in 1739 but which fell, in his own words, "dead-born from the press," not even exciting a "murmur among the zealots." He didn't give up, however, and over the next decade rewrote the material and published it anew to much greater murmuring. The zealots were primarily concerned about Hume's apparent atheism and general skepticism, and it was enough to prevent him from ever obtaining any academic posts. Instead, he became librarian to the Edinburgh Faculty of Advocates, where he began work on what was to become a six-volume, best-selling history of England. This success gave him financial independence, which he enjoyed to great advantage by traveling, socializing, and playing a lot of billiards. On learning that he had intestinal cancer, he wrote a brief and beautiful autobiography and then made sure to arrange for posthumous publication of his most zealot-exciting book, one deeply criticizing religious belief, before departing from this world in 1776.

The Lollipop

Nothing can coax out the philosopher in you more quickly than an inquisitive toddler.

If you really think about any one of her endless "why" questions, in fact, you'll probably realize you don't actually have a satisfactory answer. "Why is the sky blue?" Hmm—the sky isn't a thing at all—there are only some gases up there, which aren't themselves blue. "Why do dogs bark?" Um, well, they feel like barking? "Why does the phosphorus on a wooden match combust upon striking in the presence of oxygen?"

Actually, weirdly, David Hume does provide us with an answer to this last one, but it's not what you'd expect.

The world seems to be filled with causation, as we saw in chapter 9. You strike that match, and it lights. Billiard balls collide and move. Someone hits you, and you feel pain. And, indeed, we typically invoke causation to explain *why* things happen: you opened the fridge *because* you were hungry and were seeking a snack.

But then we encounter Hume.

For Hume argues, in a way influenced by his predecessor Nicolas Malebranche, that no two events in the world are in fact related as cause and effect, which therefore means that we cannot adequately explain the occurrence of any event by citing its "cause." And since predictions about what's going to happen next also rely on causation, we can never justifiably make any predictions either. You're probably familiar with the financial proviso that "past results are no guarantee of future performance." Well, Hume applies this point to *everything*. No causation, no explanations, no predictions: we've got *nothing*.

Or, as he himself famously put it, causation is like "the cement of the universe" keeping the whole thing together (*Treatise*, 662): remove it and the universe effectively falls apart, at least from a philosophical point of view.

So when you are asked by your toddler why something happened, why it *really* happened, your only answer will have to be: have a lollipop.

So What Is This Thing, Which Hume Says Isn't?

To appreciate Hume's critique of causation, naturally, we'll have to get clearer on just what causation is supposed to be.

And to see this, let's begin with what it is *not*.

What it is not, is merely one event happening to follow after another. The lighting of the match may have followed immediately upon its being struck, but that alone is not enough to make the striking count as the cause of the lighting.

To see why, consider how defendants in some legal cases may attempt to deny that their actions have caused various harms to the plaintiffs. Fast-food restaurants may deny that their products cause obesity; tobacco companies long denied that their products cause cancer; and the U.S. government, a few years back, denied that veterans' service in the first Gulf War was the cause of their various subsequent illnesses. The government, in the latter, pointed to the numerous veterans of that war who did *not* subsequently become ill. Why? Because, the thinking goes, if one thing is truly the cause of another, then it should be impossible to have the first without the second. And since many people served in the war without getting those illnesses, then, they concluded, their service did not cause the illness.

Now we're not here concerned with the overall validity of the government's claim, merely with the way it illustrates what we mean by the notion of *causing*. And as we saw in chapter 9, it means more than merely that one event followed another but also this: the first event must have *made* the second happen. The striking *compelled* the lighting to occur; once the striking occurred, the lighting *had* to occur; it was *impossible* for the striking to occur in just those conditions without the lighting occurring.

Or, there was a *necessary connection* between the striking and the lighting.

That's what causation is, then, a necessary connection; and, as we'll next see, what Hume argues is not. For he claims there are no two events in the world that are necessarily connected in this way.

First Argument against Causation: Conceivability

For there to be a necessary connection between event *x* and event *y* is for it to be impossible for *x* to occur without *y*. But to say something is impossible is to say that it involves a contradiction, since anything not involving a contradiction is possible at least in principle. But now, Hume insists, there is never any contradiction in conceiving of any one distinct event occurring without another.

He writes,

> When we . . . consider merely any [event] or cause as it appears to the mind . . . it never could suggest to us the notion of any distinct [event], such as its effect, much less show us the inseparable and inviolable connection between them. (*Enquiry* IV.I, 544–55)

Every event is a distinct entity from every other event, so contemplating any one event cannot lead the mind necessarily to contemplating any other event. But that is just to say that any event can be conceived to occur without any other event, which is to say that it is always possible for any given event to occur without any other given event. But then no two events are necessarily connected, and nothing causes anything else.

So, for example, it's easy to conceive of our match striking in just those same conditions but without lighting: you just did, with no contradiction to be found! But then we must say that it is possible for the match to strike without the lighting, in which case we cannot say the striking caused the lighting.

You may be tempted to object: "But given the laws of physics and chemistry, if you strike that match in those conditions it *is* impossible for it not to light!"

But now what exactly are these "laws of nature"?

These laws, Hume argues, are discoverable only through sensory experience and observation and not by pure logical reasoning; so to say that there is a law linking the striking and the lighting here, is really only to say that we have seen many similar strikings followed by similar lightings in the past. But such laws are merely patterns of past behavior and therefore carry no necessity with them: they won't allow us to say that the strikings *compel* the lightings. And in any case, it is just as easy to conceive of the laws of nature themselves as not existing or as being different from what they are. No contradiction there! If you can conceive of that, then you can conceive of the match striking without lighting, in which case, again, it's not impossible to have the first without the second. So, again, the first does not cause the second.

Similar considerations apply to all our commonsense examples of causation. Hume writes,

> When I see, for instance, a billiard ball moving in a straight line towards another . . . may I not conceive that a hundred different events might as well follow from that cause? May not both these balls remain at absolute rest? May not the first ball return in a straight line or leap off from the second in any line or direction? (*Enquiry* IV.I, 544)

Of course, most of these unusual outcomes are never observed to occur, but Hume's point is just that as far as we can conceive, they *could* occur. But that is to say that no event ever guarantees any other, that no two events are ever necessarily connected—that no event is ever the cause of any other event.

Second Argument against Causation: Deducibility

The second argument is a variation on the first. Let's begin with some of Hume's examples (all from *Enquiry* IV.I, 543):

Adam [i.e. the first human being], though his rational faculties are supposed entirely perfect . . . could not have inferred from the fluidity and transparency of water that it would suffocate him, or from the light and warmth of fire that it would consume him.

Present two smooth pieces of marble to a man who has no [scientific knowledge]; he will never discover that they will adhere together in such a manner as to require great force to separate them in a direct line, while they make so small a resistance to a lateral pressure . . . nor does any man imagine that the explosion of gunpowder or the attraction of a [magnet] could ever be discovered by [pure reasoning].

We fancy that were we brought, all of the sudden, into this world, we could at first have inferred that one billiard ball would communicate motion to another upon [contact] and that we did not need to have waited for the event in order to pronounce with certainty concerning it.

We are never able to infer or deduce, by pure reasoning alone, any one event from any other; that's what these examples illustrate. The first time you saw water, you simply could not infer or know that it would suffocate you; the first time you observed billiard balls about to collide, you could not infer what would happen next. But now why is this? Because the contemplation of any one event never compels us, necessarily, to contemplate any other event; given that each event is distinct from every other, we can always conceive of any one event occurring without any other; thus, from any one event, nothing at all follows, logically, about what must happen next, and that's why we cannot perform these inferences.

But to say all this is once again to say that no two events are necessarily connected and, thus, that no event ever is the cause of any other.

Third Argument against Causation:
The Very Idea of Necessary Connection

Or rather the lack of that idea:

All events seem entirely loose and separate. One event follows another, but we never can observe any tie between them. They seem *conjoined*, but never *connected*. And as we can have no idea of anything, which never appears to our outward sense or inward sentiment, the . . . conclusion *seems* to be that we have no idea of connection or power at all and that these words are absolutely without any meaning. (*Enquiry* VII.II, 562)

To appreciate this point, let's note, first, that Hume is a traditional representative of the philosophical school known as *empiricism*, which here amounts to the doctrine that all our concepts or ideas ultimately derive from our perceptual experience. The question he now asks is this: if the idea of causation (necessary connection) does not come from pure reasoning about events, then where exactly does it come from? How did people even generate the idea in the first place? Well, if not from reasoning, there is only one other source, the empiricist's favorite: perceptual experience.

The problem is, experience provides no such thing.

Do we derive the idea of necessary connection from our observations of the external, physical world?

> When we look about us towards external objects . . . we are never able . . . to discover any power or necessary connection, any quality which binds the effect to the cause and renders the one an infallible consequence of the other. We only find that the one does actually in fact follow the other. The impulse of one billiard ball is attended with motion in the second. (*Enquiry* VII.I, 557–58)

We never literally observe any one physical event compelling any other; we merely observe the second event following the first. We see the match struck, and it lights; we don't see the match making it impossible for the lighting not to occur. So our perceptual experience of the external world does not give us the idea of necessary connection.

Nor do we get it from our awareness of our own inner mental states and processes. We desire to move our body, and our body moves; we are aware of the former and of the latter but not of the former compelling the latter. We may similarly observe our thoughts or feelings or desires occurring in various sequences, but we are never aware of ourselves actually controlling or compelling those sequences of mental states: they just happen.

So the idea of necessary connection does not come from pure reasoning nor from perceptual experience, either outer or inner. But since these are the only possible sources of ideas, then the conclusion is inevitable: we don't really have the idea of necessary connection after all!

The whole suggestion that one event could be necessarily connected to another, that there is causation in the universe, turns out to be *unintelligible nonsense.*

The "I Do So!" Objection

You may have found yourself resisting the preceding by insisting that you understand perfectly well what necessary connections would be and, thus, that you do *so* have such an idea. And anyway, how could so many people have believed for so long that there are necessary connections between events and then turn out to have been so fundamentally misinformed about their own ideas?

Hume has an answer to this too.

The "You Sort of Do, but Not Really" Reply

It's that people, including you, have been mistaken about what "necessary connection" means. In fact, there *is* something in perceptual experience to which we refer when we think of necessary connections: it's just not necessary connections.

To see this, let's now note the reason why all of Hume's examples, in the second argument, stressed the "first" time you observe something. For the first time you observe something, you wouldn't have any inkling of a necessary connection: you'd see the striking and the lighting, the first ball colliding with the second, and merely observe that the events followed each other with no thought of necessary connection. But then experience accumulates: you observe many strikings followed by lightings. And over time you come to feel that the first does compel the second, that there *is* a necessary connection between them. But of course this feeling is, in the end, illusory: if necessary connection was not literally observable in the first instance, it wouldn't be observable in any subsequent instances either.

So something else must be going on:

This idea of a necessary connection among events arises from a number of similar instances which occur, of the constant conjunction of these events. . . . But there is nothing in a number of instances, different from every single instance [alone] . . . except only that after a repetition of similar instances the mind is carried by habit, upon the appearance of one event, to expect its usual attendant and to believe that it will exist. This connection, therefore, which we *feel* in the mind . . . is the sentiment or impression from which we form the idea of . . . necessary connection. (*Enquiry* VII.II, 563)

We think there is a necessary connection between the striking and lighting, because after having observed many strikings followed by lightings, we *psychologically come to anticipate* the lighting on the occasion of a striking—and we then mistake that purely *subjective* feeling of anticipation, within our minds, for the allegedly *objective* necessary connection between the events themselves. That is why you think you have a genuine idea of necessary connection, because there *is* something to which you refer with that notion; except, what that is, is not genuine necessary connection "out there" in the world but merely some subjective feelings *entirely within you*.

There are no necessary connections out there. There's just a sense of anticipation, in here.

Again, there is no causation in the universe.

Time to Reach for That Lollipop?

Maybe not.

Or so you may be thinking.

Okay, fine: there is no causation. Nothing that occurs ever guarantees what occurs next; your financial advisor has already justified losing most of your money by reminding you that past results can't guarantee future ones.

But does that mean we have *nothing*?

For even if there is no causation, strictly speaking, even Hume admits that we still have all those past results, those past patterns of paired events that triggered us to think there were necessary connections. We've observed plenty of strikings followed by lightings, so even if we should not say that the strikings cause the lightings, isn't it at least reasonable to predict, and to believe, that the next time we strike a match in similar conditions, it will be followed by a lighting? Perhaps not a guarantee but something, at least, to go on?

The answer is no.

Justifiably Predicting the Future

It's about to get *really* strange.

Consider, for our working example now, your trip to the kitchen this morning to make breakfast. You surely were confident that the ground would support your weight in every step that you took. (If you thought you might disappear into a sinkhole with your next step, would you have dared to move?) And what justified you in believing, of the future, that your "next" step wouldn't be into a brand new sinkhole? Well, past results are no guarantee: it is always at least possible that the next step will be your last. But doesn't the ground's fine record of supporting your previous billion steps (say) at least make it *reasonable to believe* that it will support your next step?

To say it is "reasonable to believe" is to say that you have some good reason for believing it, that you have some *justification* for believing it. And common sense surely tells us that the results of our past billion steps provide at least some justification for feeling optimistic about our next step.

But then again, common sense does not itself have such a great track record, at least based on the previous eleven chapters of this book.

Sadly, the past performance of common sense here may well indicate the future result.

Take a Walk on the Wild Side

Or just to the kitchen.

And along the way, ask yourself again: does the fact that the ground has supported your previous billion steps give you good reason, or even *some* reason, to believe that it will support your next step?

It would, Hume observes, only on one condition: if you may justifiably assume that the future will in fact be like the past. For if it won't be, after all, then you would probably want to rethink your little excursion.

But then the question becomes this one: how would you justify that very assumption itself, that the future will be like the past?

Let's spell this out in some detail. Imagine the following argument:

The ground supported step 1.
The ground supported step 2.
The ground supported step 3.

_____

Therefore, the ground will support my next step.

It surely looks, to the untrained eye, that the truth of those premises at least increases the likelihood of the truth of the conclusion. But as we train our eye, we realize that this argument actually requires a hidden premise, namely that assumption that the future will be like the past. We'll call that assumption *the uniformity of nature* and abbreviate it with a *U*:

The ground supported step 1.
The ground supported step 2.
The ground supported step 3.
U: The future will be like the past.

_____

Therefore, the ground will support my next step.

To see that this additional assumption is necessary, imagine for a moment that it's false: the future will not be like the past. Well, if the ground has supported all your previous steps and the future will *not* be like the past, then that surely wouldn't increase the likelihood that the ground will support your next step! So if the original premises are to support the conclusion at all, it must be that we are assuming that *U* is true, as we indicated.

But now: how can we defend *U* itself?

Well, so far, the world has been pretty consistent: in the past, the future has always been like the past with respect to things like the ground supporting our steps. So don't we have good reason to believe that, in the future, the future will continue to be like the past?

To represent this as an argument, we might say,

Relative to three days ago, the future was like the past.
Relative to two days ago, the future was like the past.
Relative to yesterday, the future was like the past.

Therefore relative to today, the future will be like the past.

That is,

Three days ago, U was true.
Two days ago, U was true.
Yesterday, U was true.

Therefore, today U will be true.

To say that three days ago, the future was like the past is to say, roughly, that from the perspective of three days ago, what came afterward followed the same patterns as what came before. Insofar as the world has remained pretty consistent, then, these premises all seem to be true.

The problem, however, is that even so, these premises cannot support the crucial conclusion, U, that the future will *continue* to be like the past. Why not? Because just as we saw with the earlier argument that we needed to include U as a hidden premise, so too *here* we must include U as a hidden premise:

Three days ago, U was true.
Two days ago, U was true.
Yesterday, U was true.
U: The future will be like the past.

Therefore, today U will be true.

Why? Because, in effect, if U is false and the future won't be like the past, then the fact that it was like the past, in the past, won't mean that it will be like the past, in the future! (Got that?) Or to put it another way: the argument in question merely assumes that past patterns—now, about the future being like the past—will continue to hold into the future. *But that is the very assumption we're trying to justify in the first place!* And you can't justify something merely by assuming it's true. You can only justify something by giving some other, independent reason to believe it is true.

Hume's profound insight, then, is that there is no way to justify your belief that the future will be like the past without merely *assuming* that the future will be like the past—which means that you actually have no good reason at all to believe that the future will be like the past. The future could just as easily be different from the past as like it—which means that past results don't merely not guarantee future performance: *they don't give you any guide to it all.*

Now if only your financial advisor had told you *that* before absconding with your money.

We Got *Nothing*

If Hume is right, then, we can't explain why anything happens. And we have no good reason to believe that things will continue to happen the way they have been nor, for that matter, that they won't continue to happen that way. We have no idea, basically, why things have happened the way they have and why they will happen the way that they will, however that is.

They just do.

Or in short: *stercus accidit*, to use an elegant Latin phrase for what, in English, is far less elegant.

S*** happens.

Time for that sucker.

Primary Sources

Enquiry = *An Enquiry Concerning Human Nature*, in *The Philosophical Works of David Hume*, edited by T. H. Green and T. H. Grose (London: Longmans, Green, 1898), reprinted with modification in *Modern Philosophy: An Anthology of Primary Sources* (2nd ed.), edited by Roger Ariew and Eric Watkins (Indianapolis, IN: Hackett, 2009).

Treatise = *A Treatise of Human Nature* (2nd ed.), edited by L. A. Selby-Bigge and P.H. Nidditch (Oxford: Clarendon Press, 1978).

Recommended Secondary Sources

Morris, William Edward. 2011. "David Hume." In *Stanford Encyclopedia of Philosophy*, edited by Edward N. Zalta. http://plato.stanford.edu/archives/fall2011/entries/hume/.

Norton, David Fate, and Jacqueline Taylor, eds. 2008. *The Cambridge Companion to Hume* (2nd ed.). Cambridge: Cambridge University Press.

13

Friedrich Nietzsche

Philosopher, Psychologist— Antichrist?

Strange Idea

Pretty much everything we believe about morality is false.

Major Proponent

Friedrich Nietzsche (1844–1900)

Brief Biography

Perhaps the greatest writer in any discipline ever—really!—Nietzsche was born near Leipzig, to a long line of Lutheran ministers who would have turned over in their graves if they knew what he was up to. At the University of Leipzig, he discovered the work of the philosopher Schopenhauer, which, despite its "cadaverous perfume," captured him powerfully. In 1868, he was captured even more powerfully when he met the famous composer Richard Wagner and began the stormy, decade-long quasi-father-son relationship with the older man, which would provide much fodder for later psychoanalysts. In 1869, the University of Basel appointed him a professor of philology at the unheard age of twenty-four, beginning his stormy, decade-long relationship with academia itself. This concluded with his resignation in 1879, at age thirty-four, due to extremely bad health. The remaining decade of Nietzsche's sanity was spent meandering through various European cities, composing, along the way, some of the most stunning philosophical and literary works ever produced (really!). On January 3, 1889, in Turin, he suddenly threw his arms around the neck of a horse being beaten by a coachman and collapsed, providing further fodder for later psychoanalysts. He then spent the decade of his insanity under the care of his mother and sister, before finally dying in 1900.

"God is dead. . . . And we have killed him."

Now that I have your attention.[1]

There was no shortage of strange ideas bubbling about even in the pre-insane brain of Friedrich Nietzsche. Indeed, in choosing his idea about morality to be the subject of this chapter, I actually got quite depressed about all the fantastic strange ideas that had to be left behind.

But there was at least one good reason for this choice.

Every philosopher struggles not merely to figure out her views but then to communicate them effectively, to be understood. Philosophy can be difficult, and neither of these tasks is easy. But some philosophers have *particular* difficulty in being understood, and perhaps no philosopher has been more misunderstood than Friedrich Nietzsche. And, certainly, no particular idea has been more *tragically* misunderstood than his strange idea about morality.

To be sure, Nietzsche invites this misunderstanding.

He may be one of the greatest writers ever. His prose is rich, deep, inspiring, gorgeous. No one creates sharper, more incisive, more elegant sentences and aphorisms. Certainly, no one competes with him for the sheer number of italics and exclamation points! He is also the most quotable writer you can imagine. Here's another of his many famous lines: "In reality there has been only one Christian, and he died on the Cross."[2] Talk about expressing a profound and debate-provoking thesis in just a few words!

But these same virtues are also the source of the problem.

The pursuit of rhetorical excellence may lead one to express things in ways not always clearly indicative of what you believe. It can lead you both to oversimplify and to make more complex what you really believe. And very quotable people are especially easy to quote out of context. And without the appropriate context, someone like Nietzsche is incredibly easy to misunderstand.

Tragically misunderstand, as I said.

For, quite infamously, Nietzsche's philosophy became something like the official philosophy of the Nazis, and we all know what followed from that. It is also easy to see why, out of context, this might be so. Nietzsche has many profound things to say about power, and race, and morality, and Aryans, and Jews, and he is quite easily read as supporting the idea of a master race of human beings not subject to the same moral restrictions as inferior races. Nazi propagandists could easily remove passages from their contexts and trumpet them in support of their own ideology. As a consequence, Nietzsche's name was quite soiled for many years after World War II and the Holocaust. Almost no reputable philosopher would go near him.

There was only one problem. Nietzsche in fact would have despised the Nazis.

He would have despised their nationalist fervor and their anti-Semitism. He has critical things to say about ancient Judaism (as we'll see), but he had even worse things to say about Christianity. He speaks about a "master race" but would have denied that twentieth-century Aryans were an example of it. He occasionally refers to the master race as the "blond beast," but in fact he is making a literary reference not to Aryans but to *lions* and applies the term not only to studly Vikings and Goths but also to Arab and Japanese nobility. And so on.

I said that "almost" no reputable philosopher went near him for a while. In fact, one or two did. Most important of these was Princeton philosopher Walter Kaufmann, who in 1950 published the important book that inspired the title of this chapter—*Nietzsche: Philosopher, Psychologist, Antichrist*—and then went on to translate many of Nietzsche's writings into English. Thanks to Kaufmann (and others), Nietzsche's works were soon being carefully studied and his reputation rehabilitated. Nietzsche is now widely considered to be one of philosophy's deepest and most original thinkers.

Let's see why.

The Greatest Weight

What, if some day or night a demon were to steal after you into your loneliest loneliness and say to you: "This life as you now live it and have lived it, you will have to live once more and innumerable times more; and there will be nothing new in it, but every pain and every joy and every thought and sigh and everything unutterably small or great in your life will have to return to you, all in the same succession and sequence—even this spider and this moonlight between the trees, and even this moment and I myself. The eternal hourglass of existence is turned upside down again and again, and you with it, speck of dust!"

Would you not throw yourself down and gnash your teeth and curse the demon who spoke thus? Or have you once experienced a tremendous moment when you would have answered him: "You are a god and never have I heard anything more divine." (*The Gay Science* #341, 273)

This passage contains another of Nietzsche's strange ideas, that of the *eternal recurrence*: the idea that everything that has happened will happen again and again, in precisely the same sequence and manner. Whether he actually endorsed this idea literally is a question for scholars, but for our purposes, as we'll see, it offers a glimpse of his vision of the proper, or best, attitude that a human being should take toward life.

He continues:

If this thought gained possession of you, it would change you as you are or perhaps crush you. The question in each and every thing, "Do you desire this once more and innumerable times more?" would lie upon your actions as the greatest weight. Or how well disposed would you have to become to yourself and to life *to crave nothing more fervently* than this ultimate eternal confirmation and seal? (*The Gay Science* #341, 274)

What Nietzsche seeks, then, is an attitude of life affirmation, of the profoundest sort: where you are so well disposed toward yourself and your life, no matter who or what you or your fortune might be, that you would gladly embrace the prospect of reliving your life exactly as it is, over and over again.

Keep this idea in mind as we now work our way through Nietzsche's very strange ideas about morality.

Not Your Ordinary Family Tree

For ease of exposition, we'll focus on Nietzsche's famous book *On the Genealogy of Morals*.[3]

And what, you may ask, is a "genealogy" of morals?

A genealogy is an account of the origins of a thing, and many people enjoy constructing their own genealogies, to see how far back they can trace their family trees. Nietzsche now wants to do something analogous with our basic moral concepts. These concepts—of good, of bad, of right and wrong, evil, guilt, punishment, and so on—do not arrive from nowhere, he thinks: they have a history, and he aims to illuminate that history.

But even that statement reflects how radical his ideas are.

For morality is often treated as rather sacred, as if right and wrong are beyond investigation, as if they are handed to us by God or derived by us from pure reason and thus enjoy a kind of eternal status that can never be challenged. Consequently, we merely assume that our moral distinctions (between right and wrong or good and evil) are themselves intrinsically good or valuable and beyond reproach. To even suggest that they *have* a genealogy, an origin in and evolution through human history and experience, is already to reject that transcendent nature and thus to question their *actual* value.

> Under what conditions did man devise these value judgments good and evil? *and what value do they themselves possess?* Have they hitherto hindered or furthered human prosperity? Are they a sign of distress, of impoverishment, of the degeneration of life? Or is there revealed in them, on the contrary, the plenitude, force, and will of life, its courage, certainty, future? (Preface #3, 453)

What is at stake, Nietzsche continues, is the value of morality itself, "the value of the 'unegoistic,' the instincts of pity, self-abnegation, self-sacrifice": values that people treat as absolute values, and on the basis of which they in fact come to say "*No* to life" (Preface #5, 455):

Let us articulate this *new demand*: we need a *critique* of moral values, *the value of these values themselves must first be called in question*—and for that there is needed a knowledge of the conditions and circumstances in which they grew, under which they evolved and changed. (Preface #6, 456)

We've merely assumed that our values are valuable, that "the good person" is more valuable than "the evil person." But what if the reverse were true?

What if a symptom of regression were inherent in the "good," likewise a danger, a seduction, a poison, a narcotic, through which the present was possibly living *at the expense of the future?* . . . So that precisely morality was the danger of dangers? (Preface #6, 456)

The only way to find out? Provide a history—a genealogy—of morality.

The Good, the Bad, and the Ugly

What is the origin of the moral concepts of "good" and "bad," according to Nietzsche?

It was "the good" themselves, that is to say, the noble, powerful, high-stationed and high-minded, who felt and established themselves and their actions as good, that is, of the first rank, in contradistinction to all the low, low-minded, common and plebeian. (I.2, 461–62)

Long ago—Nietzsche is not very specific—the noble class, the "best" people, the most powerful ones, the wealthy ones, saw themselves as "good," as "first-rate," and in contrasting themselves to the less fortunate, the less impressive, referred to the latter as "bad." "Good" and "bad" were thus originally and roughly akin to "us" and "them," with the implication that what *we* are is preferable to what *they* are.

This kind of morality, reflecting "knightly-aristocratic" values, Nietzsche suggests,

presupposed a powerful physicality, a flourishing, abundant, even overflowing health, together with that which serves to preserve it: war, adventure, hunting, dancing, war games, and in general all that involves vigorous, free, joyful activity. (I.7, 469)

Though I personally also enjoy some dancing and war games now and again, the idea here is that early morality was generated by the aristocratic class and amounted to praising the attributes of that class as good while dispraising the lack of those attributes as bad.

Nietzsche's characteristically provocative name for this original morality is *master morality*: morality as understood and promoted by the "master" class, or the superior class, of people. This is where the family tree begins, with master morality. But that was, of course, just the beginning—because morality, like everything else, evolved.

The Good, the Evil, and the Enslaved

If only society consisted of just the aristocrats, the noble, the rich!

Unfortunately, there are also the rest of us.

There were also the powerless, the weak, the poor, the brooding masses. And they too developed, in time, their own conception of morality, which Nietzsche correspondingly refers to as *slave morality*: morality as understood and promoted by the "slave" class, the lower class, of people.

This morality was deeply different from master morality. In its details, slave morality naturally promoted being humble and meek and weak as being better, as more virtuous, than being strong and powerful and rich. If this sounds familiar, it should: as we'll see in a moment, ordinary Christian morality (according to Nietzsche) *is* slave morality.

But slave morality also differs with respect to its motivations. Master morality was all about physicality and vigor and health and flourishing. It was motivated primarily by intense self-affirmation, a saying Yes to life: easy to do, of course, when "life" for you is so wonderful.

Slave morality comes from a contrary attitude. As Nietzsche puts it, the main promulgators of slave morality, the *priests* of slave morality, are to master morality its

> *most evil enemies*—but why? Because they are the most impotent. It is because of their impotence that in them hatred grows to monstrous and uncanny proportions, to the most spiritual and poisonous kind of hatred. . . . In opposing their enemies and conquerers [they] were ultimately satisfied with nothing less than a radical revaluation of their enemies' values, that is to say, an act of the *most spiritual revenge.* (I.7, 469–70)

In opposition to master morality's self-affirmation, the priests of slave morality were driven by the need to *negate the other*. Suffering from impotence, they developed a profound, gripping hatred of the master class. Since they could not physically overthrow their masters—the whole weak and meek thing—they did the only thing they could do, a *spiritual* thing, to satisfy their hatred. They simply inverted the masters' moral code:

[They] dared to invert the aristocratic value-equation (good = noble = powerful = beautiful = happy = beloved of God) and to hang on to this inversion with their teeth, the teeth of the most abysmal hatred (the hatred of impotence), saying "the wretched alone are the good; the poor, impotent, lowly alone are the good; the suffering, deprived, sick, ugly alone are pious, alone are blessed by God, blessedness is for them alone—and you, the powerful and noble, are on the contrary the evil, the cruel, the lustful, the insatiable, the godless to all eternity; and you shall be in all eternity the unblessed, accursed, and damned!" (I.7, 470)

Here the earlier "good v. bad" distinction of master morality becomes something more profound: the "good v. *evil*" distinction. While the "masters" were pleased with themselves and glad not to be "slaves" (who wouldn't be?), their "good v. bad" distinction did not carry any heavy moral judgment. It was merely an expression of their self-affirming preference. But the priests didn't merely invert this by preferring the weak to the strong: they also added to this inversion that heavy, even transcendental, moral judgment. It wasn't merely bad (i.e., undesirable) to be noble, powerful, and so on.

It was *evil.*

In which case, it followed, as an afterthought, that they, the weak, must be *good.*

Who Is Nietzsche Talking About?

Only those people responsible for the whole moral code of Western civilization, to put it mildly. Not that Nietzsche ever puts anything mildly. So what he says is something more exciting:

With the Jews there begins *the slave revolt in morality*: that revolt which has a history of two thousand years behind it and which we no longer see because it—has been victorious. (I.7, 470)

You can easily see the Nazi propagandists eagerly cutting and pasting here. But all Nietzsche is saying here is that the rise of Western monotheism reflected the profound moral inversion that his genealogy has discovered. Where previously *this-worldly* strength and power were praised, by the master class, with monotheism the new virtues became *next-worldly*: the meek and the humble were to be rewarded in the *afterlife.* And while he traces this "inversion of values" to the ancient Jews (who developed monotheism), he notes that the Old Testament itself reflects far more of the "master morality" than does the New Testament. Indeed, it's the latter that represents the *fullest* expression of the slave morality, which "has been victorious." Nietzsche's real target, in other words, is not "the Jews" but—as the "history of two thousand years" remark makes clear—Christianity. For it is that religion, with its complete rejection of *this*-life virtues in favor of a *next*-life salvation, that has entirely dominated Western civilization and that represents the utter victory of slave morality.

"Antichrist," anyone?

Masters, Slaves, and the Shrink

Nietzsche next goes on to earn the second component of Kaufmann's subtitle, namely that of the psychologist:

> The slave revolt in morality begins when *ressentiment* itself becomes creative and gives birth to values: the *ressentiment* of natures that are denied the true reaction, that of deeds, and compensate themselves with an imaginary revenge. (I.10, 472)

Slave morality is motivated by *ressentiment* (French, for resentment), as the weak and powerless resent those who stand over them in power and status. Since they cannot overcome their disadvantage through direct action, they take that far more subtle spiritual revenge, an "imaginary" one: they invert the master values.

> While every noble morality develops from a triumphant affirmation of itself, slave morality from the outset says No to what is "outside," what is "different," what is "not itself"; and *this* No is its creative deed. This inversion of the value-positing eye—this *need* to direct one's view outward instead of back to oneself—is of the essence of *ressentiment*: in order to exist, slave morality always first needs a hostile external world; it needs . . . external stimuli in order to act at all—its action is fundamentally reaction. (I.10, 472–73)

Master morality is about self-affirmation, love of self, Yes to self, with a disregard to what is exterior: if you're fulfilled by yourself, then who cares about others? But slave morality is about negation of the other, hatred of the other, No to the other, contrasting oneself with the other. Master morality is therefore about acting, about developing self, while slave morality, in pitting itself against the other, is about *re*acting:

> The "well-born" *felt* themselves to be the "happy"; they did not have to establish their happiness artificially by examining their enemies, or to persuade themselves, *deceive* themselves, that they were happy (as all men of *ressentiment* are in the habit of doing). (I.10, 474)

Master mentality reflects the mind-set of individuals comfortable with themselves, happy and satisfied, and thus with no need to "deceive" themselves about who or what they are. Slave mentality, to the contrary, reflects the mind-set of those who must deceive themselves to carry on: I *appear* weak and poor and miserable, so therefore I must really, on some deeper level, be happy and good!

> To be incapable of taking one's enemies, one's accidents, even one's misdeeds seriously for very long—that is the sign of strong, full natures. . . . Such a man shakes off with a *single* shrug many vermin that eat deep into others; here alone genuine "love of one's enemies" is possible. . . . How much reverence has a noble man for his enemies! . . . For he desires his enemy for himself, as his mark of distinction; he can endure no other enemy than one in whom there is nothing to despise and *very much* to honor! In contrast to this, picture "the enemy" as the man of *ressentiment* conceives him—"the evil enemy," "*the Evil One*," and this in fact is his basic concept, from which he then evolves, as an afterthought . . . a "good one"—himself! (I.10, 475)

The master's mentality is so self-satisfied that he cannot take his enemies or misdeeds seriously; he even embraces and praises his enemy! The slave's mentality of *ressentiment*, to the contrary, despises his enemy, is consumed by hatred of his enemy, thinks of him as "evil"—and then only subsequently classifies himself as "good." Again, the master is fundamentally motivated by self-affirmation, the slave by other-negation.

No wonder Sigmund Freud, the inventor of psychoanalysis, cited Nietzsche as one of his influences.

The Blond Beast and the Herd

One last observation.

The master mentality, Nietzsche thinks, is deeply individual in nature, marking a person who is comfortable with himself *as* an individual. It is characteristic of real leaders, people who are active, constructive, on the move, not unlike (in one of those memorable phrases) "the splendid *blond beast* prowling about avidly in search of spoil and victory" (I.11, 476–77). By this phrase, again, Nietzsche was not referring to the Nazi Aryans but to the psychological state of a wild, uncaged lion. In contrast, the slave mentality is that of a follower, a member of the "herd," a domestic animal that finds security only in numbers.

It is this slave mentality, Nietzsche thinks, that has conquered European thought and culture, leaving in its wake a herd of human beings who are "tame," "hopelessly mediocre and insipid," "ill-constituted, sickly, weary and exhausted," who are no longer capable even of living life, much less affirming it (I.11, 479).

So much for his opinion of nineteenth-century Europe!

Is Nietzsche Just a Big Downer?

It's easy to think so.

Slave mentality and morality has won. It dominates the culture of his time, which is therefore characterized by deep hatred and resentment, by self-rejection, by impotence, by a profoundly life-negating attitude. This man is not someone, you'd think, whom you'd want to invite to your parties.

But maybe think again.

For Nietzsche isn't merely interested in diagnosing the malaise of the world but in *treating* it; he thinks that slave mentality is a psychological illness, but (in another famous phrase) "an illness as pregnancy is an illness" (II.19, 524). It is a stage, a phase, a long one but nevertheless a finite one, through which humanity is going. And in keeping with his great discovery that morality has a genealogy, that it has evolved, he suggests that even this stage will eventually end: like a pregnancy, it will result in the birth of something new.

As for the details, well, that's not Nietzsche's department. But as usual, he provides us with some gripping imagery:

> But some day, in a stronger age than this decaying, self-doubting present, he must yet come to us, the redeeming man. . . . This man of the future, who will redeem us not only from the hitherto reigning ideal but also from that which was bound to grow out of it, the great nausea, the will to nothingness, nihilism; this bell-stroke of noon and of the great decision that liberates the will again and restores its goal to the earth and his hope to man; this Antichrist and antinihilist; this victor over God and nothingness—*he must come one day.* (II.24, 532)

Whoa.

Nietzsche uses religious language here, but of course he comes not to praise the reigning religious ideals but to bury them. "This man" may, but need not, refer to some individual person; what Nietzsche really has in mind here is the rise of a new mind-set in humankind as a whole.

Not the Western monotheistic mind-set, the Christian one, obviously. For that one *negates* this life, devalues it, minimizes it in favor of what he thinks is a purely delusional next life. What Nietzsche seeks instead is the mind-set that "liberates the will again," that "restores its goal to the earth" and its "hope to man." Since Christian life negation is the problem, the mind-set he seeks is that of—the "Antichrist."

Did we already say "whoa"?

So Nietzsche is not actually a downer, it turns out: he is an *antidowner*. For he is against all those who downgrade our existence right here in this life. He calls for the overthrow of the mentality and morality that, in the end, *are* antilife. He demands the *affirmation* of life.

You should *definitely* invite him to your next party.

A Return to the Masters?

So is Nietzsche merely calling for a return to master morality, to a culture promoting the upper over the lower, the stronger over the weaker, the haves over the have-nots?

I don't think so.

Nietzsche obviously does not condemn those features manifested by the noble class, the power, the strength, and so on. But less obviously, I think, he is not actually quite so critical of those features of the lower classes, the weakness, the meekness, and so on.

What really matters to him is not how you are or what you have but rather how you think or feel about how or what you are or have. It's about being able to affirm yourself—your life and life in general—*no matter how or what* you are or may have.

Sure, it was easy for the noble class to be self-affirming, because they had many easily affirmable features. But people misread Nietzsche when they read him as affirming those very things *rather than the affirmative mind-set itself.* And when you realize that it's the mind-set that matters, not the things, you realize that, though it may be more challenging, that very mind-set could be had *even by the very worst off.*

Let us return to that wonderful passage with which we began, "The Greatest Weight." "How well disposed would you have to become," Nietzsche asks, "to yourself and to life *to crave nothing more fervently* than [the] ultimate eternal confirmation and seal?" namely the prospect of the eternal recurrence—of everything in your life repeating over and over again, for all eternity? Would you curse this prospect—or would you welcome it—even going so far as to answer the demon proposing it by saying, "You are a god and never have I heard anything more divine!"

So here is Nietzsche's message.

It doesn't matter who or what you are or what you have.

If you can throw yourself into your life with this attitude, embrace your life, and life in general, with this profound and eternal YES, then *you* are the "redeeming person" that he so desperately longs for.

Can you?

Notes

1. *The Gay Science* #125, 181.
2. *The Anti-Christ* #39, 151.
3. All quotations are from *On the Genealogy of Morals* unless otherwise indicated.

Primary Sources

The Anti-Christ, translated by R. J. Hollingdale (Harmondsworth, England: Penguin, 1968).

The Gay Science, translated by Walter Kaufmann (New York: Vintage Books, 1974).

Genealogy = *On the Genealogy of Morals*, in *Basic Writings of Nietzsche*, edited and translated by Walter Kaufmann (New York: Modern Library, 1966).

Recommended Secondary Sources

Kaufmann, Walter. 1950. *Nietzsche: Philosopher, Psychologist, Antichrist* (4th ed.). Princeton, NJ: Princeton University Press.

Magnus, Bernd, and Kathleen Higgins, eds. 1996. *The Cambridge Companion to Nietzsche*. Cambridge: Cambridge University Press.

Wicks, Robert. 2011. "Friedrich Nietzsche." In *Stanford Encyclopedia of Philosophy*, edited by Edward N. Zalta. http://plato.stanford.edu/archives/sum2011/entries/nietzsche/.

14

John McTaggart

TIME DOES NOT FLY EVEN *WHEN* YOU'RE HAVING FUN

STRANGE IDEA

The passage of time is merely an illusion: in fact, time is not real.

MAJOR PROPONENT

John M. E. McTaggart (1866–1925)

BRIEF BIOGRAPHY

John McTaggart Ellis McTaggart—no, that isn't a typo—achieved notoriety early, when he refused to play soccer at his British preparatory school and simply lay down in the middle of the field instead. Managing to excel at school despite occasional bullying (imagine!), he studied philosophy at Trinity College in Cambridge, where he joined the Cambridge Apostles, a secret discussion group whose members would eventually include some of the greatest philosophers of the twentieth century. McTaggart never left Trinity, becoming after his graduation first a Prize Fellow and then a lecturer, a position he held until almost his death. McTaggart was once described as what you'd get if you could combine an eighteenth-century English Whig, a mystic, a medieval philosopher, a lawyer, and a French mathematician. He also had a tendency to shuffle down hallways, his back to the wall, as if he were anticipating a sudden kick from behind. Apparently, he saluted cats whenever he met them. His preferred mode of transportation was an oversized tricycle. And strangest of all: he denied the reality of time.

Don't Ask, Don't Tell

"What is time?" the great Christian thinker Augustine (354–430) famously wrote. "If no one asks me, I know; if I want to explain it to a questioner, I do not know."[1]

When we're not asked, nothing is more familiar to us than our experience of time.

"Time flies when you're having fun," they say—though, of course, it also moves, if apparently more slowly, when you're not. And you should "seize the day!" they also say, because, after all, "What's here today is gone tomorrow." These expressions convey the flow of time or perhaps the flow of events *through* time: events that move from far off in the future into the present and then forever recede from us into the past.

But while the experience of time may be familiar, a little philosophical reflection quickly shows just how mysterious it is. Imagine, for a moment, that the universe is entirely empty, devoid of all things, and ask yourself whether time would still flow in such a universe. It's surely tempting to say yes. After all, we can imagine the universe remaining empty for (say) a minute, or an hour, or a million years, but it couldn't do that unless time were actually passing while it remained empty. But then wait a moment: it's an *empty* universe; there is nothing in it. If there is nothing in it, then nothing can be happening, nothing can be occurring, and, most of all, nothing can really be moving. So how exactly can time be passing in an empty universe?

And not just passing: if the universe is empty, if there's nothing in it, then how could there be *time* in it in the first place? Just what *is* time, anyway?

Augustine wondered the same thing. Time, he observed, seems to be composed of the past, present, and future. But the past does not exist; if it did, it would be present! Nor does the future yet exist, for the same reason. So if time exists at all, it is only as the present. But what is the present? Only an instant of absolutely zero duration, composed of no time at all. Time is only the present, in short, but the present consists of no time.

But something composed of nothing must itself be nothing.

So there is no time.

Or as Augustine memorably puts it,

> where is [time] from?—obviously from the future. By what way does it pass?—by the present. Where does it go?—into the past. In other words it passes from that which does not yet exist, by way of that which lacks [duration], into that which is no longer.[2]

Perhaps it would have been better not to ask.

Fifteen Unreal Centuries Later . . .

"It doubtless seems highly paradoxical to assert that Time is unreal," McTaggart concedes in his famous 1908 article. Indeed, "so decisive a breach with [the] natural [commonsense] position is not to be lightly accepted" (94).[3]

Fortunately, we need not accept it lightly, for McTaggart next provides an argument against the reality of time that has dominated all philosophical discussion of the subject ever since.

Two Types of Temporal Facts

We begin with his distinction between two different ways of thinking about temporal matters. We may think of any given event as being either

A: past, present, or future; or as
B: earlier than, later than, or simultaneous with some other events or times.

These "A-facts" (that a given event is past, present, or future) and "B-facts" (that the given event is earlier than, later than, or simultaneous with some other event or time) may not seem so different, but they are.

Most important, A-facts reflect a *dynamic* or *moving* aspect of time, the phenomenon of time *passing*: events are always "in motion" from future to present to past, continuously changing their respective positions. The event of your finishing this chapter is in the near future, for example, but will soon be present (as you finish it) and then will become past, first a little bit past, then more, and eventually a lot.

To bring out this dynamic element more clearly, imagine that you were tasked with maintaining a continuously up-to-date list of all the A-facts. You'd immediately notice that such a list is constantly changing: what is "seven days future" today is only "six days future" tomorrow, then becomes "present" in a week, and then becomes "one day past" and "two days past," and so on. You would also notice that an accurate list of A-facts depends precisely on when you compile it. The list of A-facts you make today will differ from the list you make tomorrow and next year: yesterday's list had some events as "one day future," which are "present" on today's list, and so on.

In contrast, B-facts reflect a *static*, or unchanging, aspect of time.

Consider, for example, the B-fact that the event of Plato's death (in 347 BCE) is twenty-five years "earlier than" the event of Aristotle's death (in 322 BCE). That fact can and will never change: Plato's death will *always* be twenty-five years earlier than Aristotle's death. Were you creating a list of the B-facts, too, you would need to list all the events that have occurred in history, ordered according to which events were earlier than, later than, and simultaneous with other events, that is, in chronological order. And then you would notice two things that immediately contrast with your A-fact list. First, your list of B-facts never changes, for once events have occurred in that order, they always remain in that order. Consequently, second, an accurate list of B-facts does *not* depend on when you compile it: the list you make today of history's events will be the same as the one you make tomorrow or next year. Plato's death remains eternally, unchangingly, twenty-five years earlier than Aristotle's and so on for every event on the list!

A-list making is an ongoing occupation, in short, while B-list making is a one-time job.

An Obvious but Wrong Objection

Now you might be tempted to object here that your B-lists *will* change depending on when they are compiled: for tomorrow's B-list will include the events of the next twenty-four hours, while today's will not. More dramatically, your B-list today will differ greatly from one drafted by Aristotle, long ago, not least in including Aristotle's own death a quarter century after Plato's. So aren't B-lists and the corresponding B-facts just as dynamic as A's?

No.

As a practical matter, perhaps: as finite beings, we are always limited in knowledge, so of course, Aristotle could have no idea what events were to occur after his death and so could not have included them on his list. Nor are we ourselves able to include on the B-list that we make today even the events that will occur in the next twenty-four hours: we just do not know.

But since when are philosophers concerned about practical matters? It is *in principle* that B-lists do not change, even if we are in practice incapable of composing them.

To see this, you might recall from chapter 2 our discussion of truths about the future. We may not be able to know right now what is true about the future, we saw there, but nevertheless there are indeed such truths about the future, right now, even *if* we can't know them. Suppose that Sasha Obama is elected U.S. president in 2048. Even though our lack of a good crystal ball precludes us from including this fact in the B-list we compose today, if in fact she *is* elected in 2048, then it has been true all along that she *would be*—and thus true *right now* that the event of her election is forty years "later than" the event of her father's election. But then that event would indeed be on the complete list of B-facts right now, if only we had the means to generate that list.

So the true complete B-list, in principle, never does change, even if, in practice, the ones we draw up ourselves do.

So much for the objection.

We've now got something bigger to grapple with.

A World without A-Facts

A world in which time does not actually move.

Before we get to the argument, let's get clearer on just what kind of world McTaggart is arguing for.

McTaggart acknowledges that our *experience* of time seems to include both A-facts and B-facts or (as he sometimes puts it) that events seem to constitute both an "A series" and a "B series." However, he continues,

> It is possible . . . that this is merely subjective. It may be the case that the distinction introduced among positions in time by the A series—the distinction of past, present and future—is simply a constant illusion of our minds, and that the real nature of time only contains the distinction of the B series—the distinction of earlier and later. (95)

It's possible that the dynamic aspect of time, the passing of time, is merely a subjective illusion—that all that's objectively real is that events occur in a certain order, not that time is actually *flowing*.

But what could this mean?

If time is not really passing, then there is no significant distinction between what's "past," "present," and "future." Take some "past" event, such as the year 1964. If time is not really passing, then we cannot say that 1964 came into being, lasted a while, and then went out of being, for that would require the passing the time. Similarly, with some "future" event, such as Sasha Obama's election in 2048, we cannot say that it *will* come into being, last a while, and then go out of being, for *that* would require the passing of time. If time is not really passing, then we cannot say that 1964 has truly gone and that 2048 is truly yet to come. Instead, we must say that all events—all years and the events occurring therein—exist in some sense timelessly or eternally.

An analogy might be useful here.

Imagine a film strip, the kind that used to be run through a projector. Each frame of the film contains, we might say, a snapshot of the events occurring at that instant in time, and successive frames contain the events of successive moments. If you were to lay the entire strip out before you, the order of frames from left to right would contain the order of events from earlier to later. The frames on the far left (say) show you arriving at the coffee shop to meet your friend Fred; the next frames show you ordering your coffees; the next show you deeply engrossed in your debate about time; the next show the beginning of the fisticuffs; and so on, all the way to Fred's hasty departure in the ambulance.

The film strip represents, in short, a visual B-list.

Except now note one more thing: the entire film strip exists "all at once," the "earlier" frames along with the "later" frames. There is no significant difference between earlier and later events other than their different locations in the series: they are all equally *real*. We might say that all the events in the film exist timelessly or eternally, with your meeting of Fred being just as real as the later moment you were arrested for assaulting him.

Now make each frame of the film be a moment in time and the contents of each frame be the events which occur at that time, and you've pretty much got a world without A-facts. The "first" frame of the film is as real as the "last," and the actual events themselves in the first frame are as real as all those in all the subsequent frames.

Your arrival at the coffee shop exists as timelessly and eternally as your landing of that impressive knockout punch.

Wait a Minute—Literally

You'd probably like to stop time (if it *were* flowing) to process this point a little. Perhaps, it will help to develop the analogy a bit further.

Suppose the film strip is now run through a projector, which illuminates the frames in sequence as they pass before its lamp. We may think of the act of illuminating as corresponding to the motion of time, the moving "now" so to speak: that frame that is momentarily being illuminated contains the events that are "present," while the frames preceding it are the "past," and those yet to come are the "future." This, of course, corresponds to our "ordinary experience" of the passing of time in the first place. When the frame with your coffee shop arrival is being illuminated, then that is the event occurring "now," while earlier frames are past, and later frames are future; when the frame with your fingerprints being taken is illuminated, then the frame with your coffee shop arrival is past, and others are future, and so on.

This expanded analogy puts two ideas in play: that all times and events exist timelessly (the entire film strip exists all at once) and that the passage of time is genuinely real (since the frames are really being illuminated in sequence). The former corresponds to the B series (all events exist eternally in sequence), while the latter corresponds to the A series (events "take turns" existing);

thus, our expanded analogy nicely correlates with the way that our ordinary experience seems to include both.

But now *seems* is the operative word here. For perhaps we don't need actual or *real* sequential illumination to explain our apparent *experience* of the passing of time.

You, Now and Then

Consider more closely, now, the contents of each frame of the film.

In each of those frames, you are perceiving whatever is in that same frame with you, and you are aware of whatever is on your mind at that moment. Similarly, in each frame, you have memories of what occurred in *earlier* frames and perhaps anticipations of what may come in *later* frames. In frame 1, for example, you are arriving at the coffee shop. In frame 39 (say), you are perceiving the empty chair across from you and wondering why Fred is incapable of being punctual; in frame 137, you are hearing Fred make that same tired argument about the unreality of time, and you are thinking that you probably shouldn't have had so many cups of coffee while waiting for him; in frame 211, you are feeling the handcuffs snap shut behind your back and thinking the same thought about the coffee; and so on.

In each frame, you are fully aware of what you take to be "now" or "present" (the contents of that frame), what you take to be "past" (the contents of your memory), and what you take to be "future" (whatever you think is to come). In each frame, you are aware of what feels like a real difference between past, present, and future and thus of what feels like the passing of time.

Except for one thing.

There is no projector, no lamp, no sequential illumination.

All the frames exist together, eternally, with their distinct contents. *There is in fact no really passing time.* You will sincerely believe that time really does pass, because in each frame you distinguish between what you *take* to be past, present, and future. But you in frame 39, thinking that Fred is late, and you in frame 211, being booked, in fact both exist timelessly and eternally, even while you both individually, and *wrongly*, believe that time is really passing!

As McTaggart noted earlier, the passing of time just might be "simply a constant illusion of our minds" (95). That's what a world without A-facts would be like and why even if time doesn't actually move, it may seem to us as if it did.

Now we need some reason to believe that our world is such a world.

McTaggart's Argument against A-Facts

Here's the reason:

> Past, present, and future are incompatible determinations. Every event must be
> one or the other, but no event can be more than one. . . . But every event has
> them all. If [event] M is past, it has been present and future. If it is future, it will
> be present and past. If it is present, it has been future and will be past. Thus all
> the three incompatible terms are predictable of each event, which is obviously
> inconsistent with their being incompatible. (105)

We may reconstruct this argument as follows:

1. The A-properties of being past, present, and future are mutually incompatible: no more than one can apply to any event.
2. If any one of them were to apply to some event, then they all would (which is impossible, by premise 1).

_____

3. Therefore, none of them applies to any event.

The conclusion, 3, is the rejection of A-facts and, thus, the rejection of the
flow of time.

Let's consider each proposition in turn.

Premise 1: The Incompatibility of Past, Present, and Future

This premise is straightforward: the very idea of some specific event M's
being past excludes its being present or future, as its being present would exclude its being past or future and its being future would exclude its being present or past. To say that M is past is precisely to say it already *was,* in which case
it couldn't be occurring *now* or *yet* to occur and so on. Whichever A-property
we want to say that a given M has, therefore, it can only have one of them.

Premise 2: If One, Then All

But now premise 2 is where all the action is.

McTaggart elucidates it as quoted: "If M is past, it has been present and
future . . ." and so on. And this much does seem true: no event could truly
count as "past" if it weren't previously "present" and even earlier "future."
And it also seems right to say that no event could truly count as "future" if it
weren't at some point going to be "present" and then later be "past" and so
on. It thus does seem that if any one of these properties applies to some event,
then they all do.

1-2-3: The Conclusion That There Are No A-Facts

Well, it seems to follow.

By premise 1, no more than one of those properties may pertain to event M, but by premise 2, if any one does pertain, then they all do, which premise 1 rules out as impossible. The only way to avoid that impossibility is therefore to deny that *any* of them truly pertain to any event, which, of course, is the conclusion, 3.

So nothing is truly past, present, or future; there are no A-facts; time does not really move.

But no doubt you're already itching to object.

Another Obvious Objection

McTaggart himself promptly observes that there's an obvious objection to his argument as so far stated.

You only get a problem, the objection begins, when incompatible properties apply to some thing *at the very same time*. For example, the property of being exactly six feet tall and the property of being less than six feet tall are incompatible: nothing could have both properties at the same time. But there is no problem in having them at different times. After all, someone who is exactly six feet tall now was once less than six feet tall.

Similarly, now, for the properties of being past, present, and future. They *are* incompatible in one sense, but those who accept the reality of A-facts will observe that no event ever has more than one of them *at a time*. Indeed, McTaggart's statement of the argument reflects this. He writes, again, but this time with italics added:

> If M *is* past, it *has been* present and future. If it *is* future, it *will be* present and past. If it *is* present, it *has been* future and *will be* past. (105)

So at the times when "past" applies to M, "present" and "future" do not; when "future" applies to M, "present" and "past" do not; and so on.

But, then, no event *does* have more than one of them at any given time.

Thus, there is no problem with A-facts after all.

Obvious, but—McTaggart Replies—Wrong Again

Leave it to a philosopher to reject the obvious.

McTaggart offers several replies to the "obvious objection," but we'll only look at one here: that the objection just described commits the logical fallacy known as *begging the question*.

In ordinary speech, to "beg the question" often means something like "invite the question." But to beg the question, in philosophy, means something different: it is to make some argument that implicitly assumes the very thing you are trying to prove. For example, suppose you're having another debate with Fred, this time about whether the physical world really exists. Fred says to you, "Of course it exists. Just open your eyes and you see physical objects!" But Fred here is assuming that your ordinary perceptions are *of* external physical objects—whereas you who deny the external world no doubt also hold that our ordinary perceptions are more like dream images and thus no more prove the existence of anything than your dream of a unicorn proves the existence of unicorns. The very point in contention between you, in other words, is whether perceptions are "of" external objects or not. For Fred to invoke perception in his defense of the external world is thus to assume the very thing he's trying to prove, and thus to beg the question.

And why is this a fallacy? Because if your argument that there is an external world begins with the *assumption* that there is, then you haven't proven anything at all.

And that, McTaggart asserts, is what the second "obvious objection" is doing. He puts it this way:

> To meet the difficulty that my writing of this article has the characteristics of past, present and future, [objectors] say that it is [now] present, has been future, and will be past. But "has been" is only distinguished from "is" by being existence in the past and not in the present, and "will be" is only distinguished from both by being existence in the future. Thus [their] statement comes to this—that the event in question is present in the present, future in the past, past in the future. And it is clear that there is a vicious circle if we endeavor to assign the characteristics of present, future and past by the criterion of the characteristics of present, past and future. (105–6)

But we can put all that more simply.

The objector said that there is no problem with A-facts because no event has the properties of past, present, and future at the same time. But to say that, McTaggart replies, is to say that when event M has the first property, it doesn't have the second and third and so on: if M *is* now present, then it *was* future, and it *will be* past. But now the difference between *is*, *was*, and *will be* just *is* the difference between present, past, and future. The objector is therefore helping herself to the difference between past, present, and future to defend the past, present, and future from McTaggart's attack!

Or in a sentence: the objector *assumes* the motion of time to object to McTaggart's argument that time does not move.

And that's to beg the question.

The objection fails.

The Upshot (and the Downside)

On the plus side, those wonderful events (and those wonderful but perhaps now departed people) from your childhood: well, they're still there, eternally, frozen in time. There's no place like home, and, in one sense, you've never left yours.

On the downside, that awkward miserable teenager you used to be, with that awful skin and hair and very questionable choices of behavior and clothes, is still around too.

For everything that is, was, or will be—just is, always, eternally.

For time does not really pass; events and people do not really come into being, linger a while, and then depart.

It only seems that way.

Notes

1. *Confessions*, book 11, chapter 14, translated by Frank Sheed (Indianapolis, IN: Hackett, 1993), reprinted in *Time*, edited by Jonathan Westphal and Carl Levenson (Indianapolis, IN: Hackett, 1993), 15.

2. *Confessions*, book 11, chapter 21, 20.

3. All McTaggart quotations are from "The Unreality of Time," *Mind* 17 (1908), as reprinted in *Time*, edited by Jonathan Westphal and Carl Levenson (Indianapolis, IN: Hackett, 1993), 94–111.

Primary Source

McTaggart, J. M. E. 1908. "The Unreality of Time." In *Mind* 17 (1908), as reprinted in *Time*, edited by Jonathan Westphal and Carl Levenson (Indianapolis, IN: Hackett, 1993), 94–111.

Recommended Secondary Sources

Le Poidevin, Robin. 2005. *Travels in Four Dimensions: The Enigmas of Space and Time.* Oxford: Oxford University Press.

McDaniel, Kris. 2010. "John M. E. McTaggart." In *Stanford Encyclopedia of Philosophy, edited by* Edward N. Zalta. http://plato.stanford.edu/archives/fall2010/entries/mctaggart/.

15

Ludwig Wittgenstein

THE VOICE IN MY HEAD IS
SPEAKING NONSENSE

STRANGE IDEA

There could be no such thing as a meaningful private language.

MAJOR PROPONENT

Ludwig Wittgenstein (1889–1951)

BRIEF BIOGRAPHY

Most philosophers would give anything to produce an important book; Wittgenstein produced *two*, and, better yet, the later one refuted the earlier! Born in Vienna, Wittgenstein studied engineering and mathematics before going to Cambridge University to study philosophy. After quickly both irritating and impressing everyone there—thanks to his utterly idiosyncratic way of doing philosophy—he assembled his first important book, *Tractatus Logico-Philosophicus*, "assemble" being the appropriate word because the book consisted entirely of a series of numbered propositions. Having solved all philosophical problems (he thought), he retired from philosophy in 1919 and became a school teacher. This did not work out very well, especially for the schoolchildren whose ears he apparently boxed when they failed to master their lessons. Fortunately (for him and them), the repute of the *Tractatus* got him invited back to Cambridge in 1929. He spent the next decade doing some utterly idiosyncratic but remarkably profound philosophy while also rethinking his earlier opinions. With the outbreak of World War II, he volunteered to work at a London hospital. Two years after the war, he resigned from Cambridge to work on his writing but soon fell ill and died of cancer in 1951. Two years later, some of his former students assembled (partly from notes he'd left behind) what became his second important book, *Philosophical Investigations*.

"One Gets to the Point Where One Would Like Just to Emit an Inarticulate Sound"

And no one gets us to that point more quickly than Wittgenstein, who made that comment about philosophizing itself in *Philosophical Investigations* (§ 261).

Indeed, it's hard to imagine a philosopher of the last century who is deeper, more inspiring, but also more maddening than Ludwig Wittgenstein, and it is hard to imagine any of his particular *ideas* that is deeper, more inspiring, or more maddening than his famous argument against the possibility of a private language. The "deep" and "inspiring" are due to his original and controversial probing of some of the weightiest issues in contemporary philosophy (linguistic meaning, thinking, normativity, knowledge, and so on).

The "maddening" is due to his manner of doing so.

For Wittgenstein proceeds in a literary manner, by presenting a series of brief, almost aphoristic remarks in which he seems to argue with himself: one remark may assert an idea, while the next ones raise questions or challenges or demand clarifications, while the next ones, still, move on to other issues entirely before suddenly returning to the original assertion. Some remarks simply raise questions without ever offering any answers. It can often be quite difficult, in fact, to determine "who" is speaking: is it Wittgenstein himself asserting a point or some imagined objector *critiquing* something that Wittgenstein asserts? Nor does it help that the remarks are often extremely concise, consisting of just a few sentences. They thus often raise their tantalizing points without going far toward explaining or defending them.

As a result, there is, unsurprisingly, much disagreement among philosophers on almost every point of Wittgenstein's argument against private language. Philosophers are not entirely sure where the argument exactly begins and ends in his writings, nor is there much consensus on just what points Wittgenstein is actually making, what his specific conclusions are, and certainly not on how persuasive the argument ultimately is. Much of the scholarly literature consists of philosophers merely trying to figure out precisely what the argument actually *is*.

Thankfully, we will be able to ignore those complications.

Instead, we'll simply have a look, here, at perhaps the most traditional way of understanding Wittgenstein's argument. And since nothing could substitute for Wittgenstein's own inimitable style, we'll have our look here by means of as many of Wittgenstein's own famous (and maddening) remarks as possible.

So What Is a "Private Language" Anyway?

But could we also imagine a language in which a person could write down or give vocal expression to his inner experiences—his feelings, moods, and the rest—for his private use? . . . The individual words of this language are to refer to what can only be known to the person speaking; to his immediate private sensations. So another person cannot understand the language. (§ 243)[1]

A private language, then, is one that contains words referring to "immediate private sensations" (or more generally, private mental states), and insofar as these sensations and states are "private" to the individual experiencing them, no one else could be said, strictly speaking, to understand those words.

To appreciate Wittgenstein's rejection of the possibility of such a language, then, we'll need some background on the nature of mental states and sensations and of the ordinary language terms that concern them.

Two Extreme Views about Mental States and Mental Language

The first view may be called *Cartesianism*, after the famous René Descartes (1596–1650).

According to Descartes, an individual's mind is like a private inner space to which only that individual has access. Only I can immediately and directly *know* that I am sensing pain (say); others can at best infer or guess it. Moreover, while others can be mistaken about just which mental state I am in, I myself cannot be: if I believe that I am in pain, then I am in pain. As for mental language, a word such as "pain" naturally gets its meaning by *referring* to that private inner sensation. So described, Cartesianism is perhaps not far removed from common sense.

In contrast is the strange-in-its-own-right view known as *behaviorism.*

According to behaviorism, the words that we use for our mental states refer *not* to our private inner states but instead refer, indirectly, to our publicly observable behaviors. To say of Darleen that she (mentally) "desires" a vacation, for example, is just an indirect way of saying that she is likely to request time off from work, buy an airplane ticket, get a dog-sitter, and so on: "desire" here refers to a large complex of possible observable behaviors. Similarly, to say that Fred is in "pain" is to refer not to what is occurring privately inside him but instead indirectly to the observable fact (say) that he has just stepped on a nail and is screaming.

Note how behaviorism gives up the special private access that Cartesianism suggests we have to our own mental states: we all have equal access to one another's observable behavior, at least in principle, in a way we don't to one another's "inner" states.

Wittgenstein Rejects Both Extremes

First, Cartesianism.

Cartesianism, in treating mental states as private items, implies that no one else can genuinely know whether (say) you are in pain. But, Wittgenstein writes,

> If we are using the word "to know" as it is normally used (and how else are we to use it?), then other people very often know when I am in pain. (§ 246)

> Just try—in a real case—to doubt someone else's fear or pain. (§ 303)

In ordinary circumstances, there's no problem knowing when others are in pain; if Cartesianism suggests otherwise, so much the worse for Cartesianism.

More important, if Cartesianism were right, then we could never learn to understand and speak mental language.

For consider how you teach a child the meaning of a word such as "tree": you say the word while perhaps pointing at a tree. But if "pain" got its meaning by referring to something inner, then you couldn't teach it to a child, since you have no way of literally pointing at painful sensations either in you or in the child. Nor could anyone else ever know what you mean when you use the word, since no one has access to your inner mind: for all anyone knew, what goes on inside you when you speak of pain has no resemblance to what goes on in them when they speak of pain. Since we obviously do learn and understand mental language, then, again, so much the worse for Cartesianism.

Now while behaviorism may avoid these problems—if mental language really refers to observable behaviors—it suffers from others.

First, it seems that we know pretty clearly what we mean when we say that Fred is in pain even when we cannot state explicitly all the possible behaviors that would be deemed "painful behaving." This suggests that "Fred is in pain" *means* more than merely that Fred is exhibiting some such behaviors.

Moreover, while Cartesianism wrongly suggested that knowledge of other people's mental states should be impossible, behaviorism seems wrongly to go to the opposite extreme: since your behaviors are as accessible to anyone else as to you, in principle, there should be no difference between your own access to your mental states and that enjoyed by others.

And yet surely there is:

Other people very often know when I am in pain.—Yes, but all the same not with the certainty with which I know it myself! (§ 246)

So neither Cartesianism nor behaviorism gives an adequate account of mental states and mental language. It's in the quest for some alternative view, next, that Wittgenstein enters into the private language argument.

The First Premise: Words, Meanings, and Rules

As noted earlier, it's not possible to "point out" one's inner mental states to someone else nor to "point" at someone else's. But that raises the question of whether we can "point out" our own inner states *to ourselves*, so to speak, and so develop a purely *private* language:

> Let us imagine the following case. I want to keep a diary about the recurrence of a certain sensation. To this end I associate it with the sign "S" and write this sign in a calendar for every day on which I have the sensation. (§ 258)

Seems straightforward enough, yes?

Maybe to common sense, but this is philosophy.

To examine this idea of "naming" our private sensations, let us turn to the first premise of Wittgenstein's argument:

(1) For a word to be used meaningfully, there must be a rule or standard for its correct application.

For a word to be used meaningfully, it seems, two related conditions must be met: the word must be used *consistently*, and so, therefore, there must be a difference between using it *correctly* and using it *incorrectly*. If the word applies to an entity of a certain kind at one time, then it must apply to entities of the same kind at all other times: that is the consistency. Similarly, it can't just be applied to any old thing you like: once it has its meaning, there will be things that it correctly applies to and things that it may only incorrectly be applied to.

Consider the word "chair," to illustrate. For you to use that word meaningfully is for you to apply it consistently, to everything that is a chair and to only things that are chairs. When you apply it to chairs, we say that you have used it correctly, and should you apply it to something else, we say that you have used it incorrectly. Putting these together, then, your grasping the meaning of the word amounts to your grasping the rule that governs what the word correctly applies to.

Or, in reverse: if you don't know which things the word correctly applies to and which not, then you don't know the meaning of the word.

So far, so good.

The Second Premise: No Private Rules

(2) No purely internal or private rule exists for the application of mental words such as "pain."

Consider, first, how we learn the rules governing words for ordinary external objects, such as chairs. The question confronting a child learning the language might be put like this, said while pointing to some object: Does "chair" apply to *that*? To learn the meaning of the word is to learn to apply it to the correct things, and to this end, the child is greatly aided by two facts.

First, other people can correct her usage. When she calls a chair a "chair," they can applaud her; when she calls the sofa a "chair," they can correct her. Other people can do this here, of course, since chairs are publically accessible external objects: we can all look at, observe, and interact with the same chairs.

Second, objects such as chairs endure over time. If the child isn't sure whether the object in question is a chair, she can look it over, inspect it, come back a little later, and verify whether it's a chair. Indeed, she can verify whether it's the same item that it was yesterday, perhaps; she can often even verify whether it's the same kind of thing as something else she saw in the past, by going back and explicitly comparing it to the earlier item.

Well, now, neither of these facts obtains with respect to private sensations such as pains. As we've seen, no one else can access your own pains, so no one can teach you how to use the word "pain" or correct your usage of it. Nor do such sensations endure appropriately. You may have some sensation to which you apply the word "pain," but you're not able to "look it over," "come back later," and "verify" it. Your inner states come and go and cannot be double-checked later.

It therefore seems that we're *not* in a position to learn how to use sensation words consistently and correctly after all—in which case, given the first premise, we're not in a position to use such words meaningfully.

So far, *not* so good.

The Memory Objection to the Second Premise

But wait a moment: with respect to the second premise, anyway, can't we just use our memory to verify whether the (now departed) sensation was in fact a "pain"? Or more generally, can't we just use our memory to determine whether our current sensation is the same kind of sensation as ones we've had previously, and thus merits the same name of "pain"?

It turns out that the answer is no.

Forget the Memory Objection

Wittgenstein continues the passage:

> I want to keep a diary about the recurrence of a certain sensation. To this end I associate it with the sign "S" and write this sign in a calendar for every day on which I have the sensation. . . . Can I point to the sensation? Not in the ordinary sense. But I speak, or write the sign down, and at the same time I concentrate my attention on the sensation—and so, as it were, point to it inwardly. . . . In this way I impress on myself the connexion between the sign and the sensation.—But "I impress it on myself" can only mean: this process brings it about that I remember the connexion *right* in the future. But in the present case I have no criterion of correctness. One would like to say: whatever is going to seem right to me is right. And that only means that here we can't talk about "right." (§ 258)

There's a lot here, but let's tease out what we need.

Can we just use our memory to determine whether today's sensation is the same kind as yesterday's? Well, if you wish to associate a sign (such as the word "pain") with a particular sensation, then you must do it in such a way that the two remain associated consistently and correctly in the future. And there's something about the use of memory here, to "remember the connexion" between the word and the sensation, that fails to provide us with the required consistency and correctness.

To see what this is, consider this passage:

> Let us imagine a table (something like a dictionary) that exists only in our imagination. A dictionary can be used to justify the translation of a word X by a word Y. But are we also to call it a justification if such a table is to be looked up only in the imagination?—"Well, yes; then it is a subjective justification."—But justification consists in appealing to something independent.—"But surely I can appeal from one memory to another. For example, I don't know if I have remembered the time of departure of a train right and to check it I call to mind how a page of the time-table looked. Isn't it the same here?"—No; for this process has got to produce a memory which is actually *correct*. If the mental image of the time-table could not itself be *tested* for correctness, how could it confirm the correctness of the first memory? (As if someone were to buy several copies of the morning paper to assure himself that what it said was true.) (§ 265)

To use the word "pain" meaningfully, again, is to use it today to refer to exactly the same kind of thing that it was used to refer to yesterday. But sensations of previous days are accessible only by memory, and nothing guarantees that our memories of past sensations are actually *correct.* In fact, we have *no* independent means to verify whether our memories of past sensations are truly trustworthy. But then we have no means of knowing whether we are applying the word "pain" consistently and correctly over time. And if we're unable to know that, then we cannot say that we truly grasp the rule for correctly applying the word.

The second premise of the argument stands.

The Immediate Conclusion of the Private Language Argument

Well, if we cannot say that we truly grasp the rule for correctly applying mental words, as the second premise suggests, then, by the first premise of the argument, it follows that we cannot say that we know the *meanings* of any such words either.

This yields the immediate conclusion:

(3) Therefore, mental words such as "pain" do not derive their meanings by virtue of applying to purely internal or private objects.

If "pain" did get its meaning by applying to some inner sensation, then we run into the problems just mentioned: we cannot say that we grasp the rule governing its application and thus can't say that we grasp its meaning. If a "private language" is one in which an individual has meaningful words for his private mental states, then such a language is impossible—for there is no way to guarantee that he is using such words consistently and correctly.

But, of course, Wittgenstein thinks, we do know the meanings of our "sensation words": we use them all the time without any problem, and we communicate with others perfectly well.

There must therefore be some *other* means by which mental words get their meanings, other than by referring to our private inner states.

The argument continues.

Wittgenstein's Own Account of Mental Language

In one of his most famous passages, Wittgenstein writes,

Suppose everyone had a box with something in it: we call it a "beetle." No one can look into anyone else's box, and everyone says he knows what a beetle is only by looking at *his* beetle.—Here it would be quite possible for everyone to have something different in his box. One might even imagine such a thing constantly changing. But suppose the word "beetle" had a use in these people's language?—If so it would not be used as the name of a thing. The thing in the box has no place in the language-game at all; not even as a *something*: for the box might even be empty.—No, one can "divide through" by the thing in the box; it cancels out, whatever it is. (§ 293)

Whatever gives the word "beetle" its meaning here, it is not the actual contents of the box but something else. This passage thus suggests that mental words such as "pain" might be perfectly useful and meaningful *without* referring to what's "inside the box," that is, some private, internal entity.

Indeed, in ordinary circumstances, we're not even tempted to think of sensation words as referring to things "within" us:

> Look at the blue of the sky and say to yourself "How blue the sky is!"—When you do it spontaneously—without philosophical intentions—the idea never crosses your mind that this impression of colour belongs only to *you*. . . . And if you point at anything as you say the words you point at the sky. I am saying: you have not the feeling of pointing-into-yourself. (§ 275)

As we saw in chapter 8, colors are generally thought (by philosophers) to be paradigm sensations: colors exist "in our minds" much as pains do. Yet when we are being nonphilosophical (i.e., normal) with respect to color words, at least, we never feel we are "pointing inward" in using them. Applied to our current case, this suggests that we ordinarily "point outward," too, with respect to other sensation words such as "pain."

And what "outer thing" might we be pointing to?

> What would it be like if human beings shewed no outward signs of pain (did not groan, grimace, etc.)? Then it would be impossible to teach a child the use of the word "tooth-ache." (§ 257)

There's the clue: behavior.

We return to the "extreme view" of behaviorism and may now imagine the behaviorist adding two more lines to our argument:

> (4) There are *external* standards or rules for the application of mental words such as "pain."

After all, it's by means of the "outward (behavioral) signs of pain," as Wittgenstein just suggested, that we learn how to use such sensation words in the first place. This additional point would then lead to the final conclusion:

> (5) Therefore, mental words such as "pain" are meaningful by virtue of their outer (behavioral) manifestations.

To say, "Fred is in pain," then, again, is not to say anything about what's going on privately inside him; instead, it's to refer in some indirect way to his various behaviors (such as screaming or crying upon stepping on a nail).

The position does have a number of advantages. It explains how we can learn mental language. It explains how we can understand one another when we use mental language. It fits nicely with the fact that we apply mental terms only to beings that behave much as we do. (We never ascribe feelings, say, to things such as rocks.) And it would dissolve the famous "mind-body problem," as we saw in chapter 9, the problem of understanding how nonphysical "private" minds could be causally related to physical bodies and brains. Since behaviorism dispenses with referring to such minds, it simply doesn't have this problem.

But wait a minute.

Didn't Wittgenstein already reject the aforementioned behaviorism?

Wittgenstein's *Really* Own Account of Mental Language

Behaviorism pure and simple is not quite Wittgenstein's actual position. For in addition to his earlier criticisms, he writes this:

> "But you will surely admit that there is a difference between pain-behaviour accompanied by pain and pain-behaviour without any pain?"—Admit it? What greater difference could there be?—"And yet you again and again reach the conclusion that the sensation itself is a *nothing*."—Not at all. It is not a *something*, but not a *nothing* either! The conclusion was only that a nothing would serve just as well as a something about which nothing could be said. (§ 304)

If behaviorism denies the reality of mental sensations, then it's mistaken: there is more to being in pain than just displaying "pain behavior." But then, Wittgenstein has argued that the meaningfulness of "pain" does not come by referring to the inner sensation: thus, the pain itself becomes a "something about which nothing could be said," since our relevant words simply don't refer to it.

What he seeks, then, is some way of retaining the behaviorist insight that mental language is closely connected to outer behavior without simply holding that mental words indirectly refer *to* that behavior.

Wittgenstein merely hints at the solution:

> Here is one possibility: words are connected with the primitive, the natural, expressions of the sensation and used in their place. A child has hurt himself and he cries; and then adults talk to him and teach him exclamations and, later, sentences. They teach the child new pain-behaviour. (§ 244)

Mental words such as "pain" are not referring expressions: they do not get their meanings by referring to anything at all, internal or external. Rather, a word like "pain" is an *expression* of pain: it's a learned response, a behavioral response, to being in pain, just as a cry or the exclamation "ouch!" might be. No one thinks that the word "ouch" *refers to* pain, after all: its exclamation is just how we behave when in pain. Saying "I am in pain," then, is a fancy, grown-up way of crying or grunting: it isn't referring; it's just *doing*.

And if the word "pain" isn't referring, then it's out of place to talk about "rules for applying it" and so on. As such, mental words function quite differently from many other words in our language.

If this works, then Wittgenstein has steered a middle path between Cartesianism and behaviorism. For he preserves both what Cartesianism got right (that we do have a genuine mental life to which we have some privileged access) and what behaviorism got right (that there's some close link between our mental language and our behaviors); and yet by insisting that mental words do not *refer* and thus refer neither to inner states nor to external behaviors, he avoids the problems confronting both those positions.

So if this works, then we may have an adequate account of mental language. At least, that is, if all this *is* what Wittgenstein is saying.

Note

1. All quotations are from *Philosophical Investigations.*

Primary Source

Wittgenstein, Ludwig. 1953. *Philosophical Investigations* (3rd ed.), translated by G. E. M. Anscombe. New York: Macmillan.

Recommended Secondary Sources

Biletzki, Anat, and Anat Matar, 2011. "Ludwig Wittgenstein." In *Stanford Encyclopedia of Philosophy*, edited by Edward N. Zalta. http://plato.stanford.edu/archives/sum2011/entries/wittgenstein/.

Sluga, Hans, and David Stern, eds. 1996. *The Cambridge Companion to Wittgenstein.* Cambridge: Cambridge University Press.

16

Hilary Putnam

THINKING OUTSIDE THE (CRANIAL) BOX

STRANGE IDEA

Thoughts are not, strictly speaking, inside the head.

MAJOR PROPONENT

Hilary Putnam (b. 1926)

BRIEF BIOGRAPHY

American philosopher Hilary Putnam grew up in Philadelphia and studied mathematics and philosophy at the University of Pennsylvania, graduating in 1946. He promptly began his stunning academic career, receiving a PhD in 1951 from the University of California at Los Angeles and then teaching at Northwestern University, Princeton University, and the Massachusetts Institute of Technology before settling, in 1965, into his long and productive tenure at Harvard University. In 1965, he was elected a fellow of the American Academy of Arts and Sciences; in the 1960s and 1970s, he was very politically active; in 1976, he served as president of the American Philosophical Association; along the way, he occupied several senior positions, culminating in his being appointed, in 1977, as the Walter Beverly Pearson Professor of Modern Mathematics and Mathematical Logic; and he wrote and published prolifically, on topics ranging from philosophy to politics to mathematics, logic, and science. He retired from Harvard in 2000 but continued for the next decade to teach an annual seminar at Tel Aviv University.

Who'd Have Thought?

You would think that your thoughts are "inside your head."

After all, the mental activity of thinking surely seems closely related to brain activity: if not identical to it, as some believe, then at least directly caused by it (as almost everyone believes). And brain activity is obviously inside your head, where your brain is! So, therefore, should thinking be—such that were two individuals to have exactly identical brains, operating in exactly identical fashions, they would have to be in exactly identical mental states as well. If one individual is thinking something like "Water sure would quench my thirst!" then the other, with identical brain activity, must also be thinking, "Water sure would quench my thirst!"

How strange, then, is Hilary Putnam's claim that thoughts are *not* entirely inside the head?

We begin with some background.

Inside and Out

In chapter 7, we saw René Descartes's strange idea that animals do not have minds. But, of course, one of the motivating factors behind that idea was another idea, which has arisen in other chapters as well, namely that of *dualism*: the view that the physical and the mental are two fundamentally distinct kinds of things. The physical comprises everything surrounding us in space, all the bodies and objects with which we interact, including our own physical bodies; the mental comprises minds, or mental states, including such states as our thinking and perceiving and imagining and so on. Though dualism is not popular in the academy these days, when many want to deny that our minds are anything other than our brains, it still has some passionate contemporary adherents, and it is still, perhaps, the commonsense view among the nonprofessionals as well.

But our concern here is not with whether dualism is true.

For even if you reject dualism, it remains difficult to give up an idea closely associated with it, one we touched on in chapter 15: that we somehow approach the physical world from "inside out." Whatever the ultimate metaphysical story, our minds seem packaged "inside" our bodies, in their own private mental spaces, and all we really have *direct* access to are our own mental thoughts and perceptions. We do, of course, attempt to build up a picture of the physical world outside us, to understand what exists outside us and what its nature may be, but we always do so *indirectly*, on the basis of judgments or inferences that we make from the mental perceptions and experiences of which we're directly aware in that physical world.

To say all that is to say that our mental life, our thoughts and experiences, is insulated in a way from their physical surroundings. Not causally insulated: no one really doubts that the external physical world (including the brain) frequently causes and is causally affected by our mental states. Rather, *logically* insulated: it is the *representational contents* of our mental states, what our mental states are of or about, that seem to be purely internal, inside the mind, even if we are caused to go into states with those contents by external physical states.

We, our minds, our thoughts, are inside; everything else, the physical, even the brain, is outside.

Or so it seems.

Inside but Not Out?

Or more than just seems. Descartes, for one, bolstered this picture with some additional considerations. These he framed in the form of a skeptical worry, that is, a worry about our ability to know the world.

We may feel confident in our knowledge of the physical world, Descartes observes, but perhaps we shouldn't be. For how do we know that there isn't (say) some all-powerful evil being who aims to deceive us about everything, and whose power is so great that perhaps everything we believe about the physical world is simply false, including that it even exists at all? Or if the evil deceiver idea is too much for you, might it not be the case, Descartes wonders, that our existence is really just a long, detailed dream, a purely mental affair, in which all our purely mental thoughts and perceptions simply fail to correspond to anything "out there" in the physical world? Think, as we did in chapter 11, about the experiences of the poor unenlightened people in the original film *The Matrix*, and then simply remove the part about their bodies being hooked up as batteries in a pod. Our mental states might be exactly as they are, with the same representational contents they have, even if there's no external world at all out there—including our own bodies and brains.

No one is arguing that this *is* the case, that there is such a deceiving being, or that we are in fact only dreaming about the world. Rather, it's that the very possibility of these possibilities, the fact that we can even conceive of them *as* possibilities (however unlikely), shows that we conceive of the mental as being distinct or insulated from the physical.

Brains in Vats

The same is true even if, more reasonably, you're not particularly skeptical about the existence of the physical world. We may even just grant that the physical brain is necessary for the existence of any mental activity at all, so there couldn't be a mind whose whole existence was a dream without there also existing at least some physical brain. But even so, we can illustrate the insulation of the mental with a little more science fiction.

Imagine, now, that a molecule-for-molecule duplicate of your brain is created and kept alive in a vat, being periodically stimulated electrically by a clever neuroscientist. In so doing, she causes this brain to go into various physical states exactly like the physical states your brain goes into when you're enjoying particular thoughts and experiences. Suppose, on some occasion, you think to yourself, "This falafel tastes delicious!" The neuroscientist stimulates the duplicate brain to go into exactly the same state that your brain is in when you have that thought. The question then is this: does the duplicate brain also then have the very same thought, "This falafel tastes delicious!"? Does it, indeed, have the entire perceptual experience you are having with that thought, namely the sight, the smell, that delectably falafelish taste?

As a skeptical problem, that is, a problem for our ability to know, we might phrase this question differently. We might ask whether you can be certain that you yourself *are*, after all, a normal person with a normal body walking around the physical world having experiences, such as buying and consuming some delicious falafel. Can you really be sure that you're not in fact just a brain in a vat being stimulated to have these experiences?

But our question here is not the skeptical one. It's rather about the precise relationship between our mental states and our brain states in particular. Most people, with their common sense, are inclined to believe that a brain and its molecular duplicate would indeed share mental states: your brain and its duplicate would both be thinking, "This falafel tastes delicious!" The different external environments of the two brains—yours in your skull, itself atop your body as the latter moves around the world, while the other is merely floating in a vat of nutrients with a lot of wires sticking out of it—seem to be irrelevant to the precise contents of the brains' thoughts. But to say this is just to say that our mental states are, in that way, insulated from the external world: *what* we are thinking, the contents of our thoughts, depends only on what our brains are doing, inside our heads, and thus our thoughts would count as being entirely "inside our heads."

This is the commonsense view that Putnam is about to challenge.

Internalism and Externalism

The commonsense view that our mental states are "in the head"—and, thus, that two exactly identical brains should be in the same mental state—goes by the name of *internalism*. To the contrary, *externalism* holds that external context, including how things are in the world outside the head, is indeed relevant to determining just which mental states a being (or a brain) is in. According to externalism, it is therefore possible that two exactly identical brains might *differ* in their mental states, as long as their external contexts are relevantly different.

So why should we accept, with Putnam, the strange doctrine of externalism?

Back to the Vat

Let's probe that brain-in-the-vat scenario a bit more deeply.

We imagined that brain as being a molecule-for-molecule duplicate of you, but of course, that restriction isn't entirely necessary. Let's loosen it a bit here and imagine instead that our clever neuroscientist has grown some other perfectly functioning, otherwise "normal" human brain, entirely in the vat. Maybe she grew it from someone's DNA; maybe she combined various individuals' DNA; it doesn't matter. What matters is only that we now have a fully sized, fully functional human brain hooked up to a bunch of electrodes stimulating the neurons of that brain to fire in the same ways or patterns that our own brains fire as they navigate around the world, perceiving it and thinking about it.

Our question is, what exactly is this new brain thinking about and perceiving?

The internalist's answer would be, well, it depends on what states the brain is in. When this brain is firing in the way that your brain fires when you are thinking about delicious falafel, then it too is thinking about delicious falafel; when this brain is firing in the way that your brain fires when it is moving your arm and fingers toward the telephone to have some delicious falafel delivered to your apartment, then this brain too is moving (or attempting to move) corresponding arms and fingers toward a telephone to order that falafel. Of course, there's a catch: this brain is not hooked up to any body, to any arms or fingers, nor (we may suppose) is it near any telephone. In fact, if it isn't located in a reasonably sized city, it probably also isn't near any falafel restaurants!

But so what, the internalist says: the vat brain still has *those* mental states, the intentions to "move arm and fingers to the telephone," "dial this number and order falafel," and so on, even if there aren't any relevant arms or fingers or telephones nearby. What matters is how it feels "from the inside," from "within the brain," and just as *your* mental states, including these intentions, result from your brain firing in that way, so too the vat brain's mental states result from *its*. Mental states are "in the head," so the state of the brain fully determines the corresponding mental states, independent of the external context.

Except for one thing, Putnam suggests.

It's rather hard to believe that the vat brain has any genuine mental states at all, such as those thoughts and intentions just described.

For the mental states in question are all allegedly "about" things and, as we'll now see, nothing can be about *anything* unless it's hooked up in the right causal way to the things it is about.

Thoughts and Aboutness

What is a "thought," exactly?

I shall use the word "thought" as an umbrella term for a large category of mental states, namely those that are characterized by their "aboutness." Here are some: thinkings, believings, hopings, fearings, desirings, intendings, and so on. Whenever we engage in any of these activities, our mental states are always about something, directed *toward* something, something that is often best expressed as a sentence or proposition. Thus, you may think that this falafel is delicious; you may believe that the United States' current foreign policy is disastrous; you may hope that tomorrow is a better day, fear that it won't be, desire that your escape plan will succeed when it turns out not to be, and so on. Thinking, believing, desiring, and such are not the same kinds of states or activities, of course, but what they all share is that when we engage in them, it always makes sense to ask what it is we are engaged *about*.

An important point now follows from this one.

For if a thought is a mental activity about something, then the thing that the thought is about determines just *which* thought it is. If you and I are thinking about the very same thing, then we have the very same thought: we are in the same mental state. If you and I are thinking about different things, then we are thinking different thoughts and are in different mental states. (The fancy philosophical way of expressing this point is to say that thoughts are *individuated by their contents*: different contents, then different thoughts.)

If thoughts are entirely "in the head," as the internalist suggests, then exactly identical brains should be thinking the same thought. Or to put that in our new way: exactly identical brains should be having thoughts about exactly the same things. And the vat brain should be thinking about just what you think about when your brain is firing in just that way.

Except when it's not.

Causal Relations and Aboutness

Aboutness, Putnam now suggests, requires causal relations.

Nothing can genuinely be "about" a thing, in other words, unless it's causally connected to that thing in the right way. And since thoughts are characterized by what they are about, as we just saw, then being able to think about a given thing would require, in turn, that the mind (or the brain) be causally connected to that thing in the right way. But, of course, the vat brain is not causally hooked up to the world at all, in any way: it just floats there with its wires sticking out. Lacking those causal connections, the vat brain could not have thoughts about *anything* after all, much less thoughts about the same things as you.

An example from philosopher Daniel Dennett, much in keeping with Putnam's points here, helps make this clear.

Dennett imagines for a moment that, entirely randomly, a molecular duplicate has arisen not merely of his own brain but of his whole body. Would duplicate Dennett enjoy the same mental states that original Dennett has? Well, *he* (original Dennett) has lots of thoughts (beliefs, desires, etc.) about his wife, Susan, not least of which is the belief that he is married to her. But duplicate Dennett, just formed moments ago, could not have *those* thoughts, Dennett suggests. Sure, the duplicate might have thoughts qualitatively just like original Dennett's thoughts: from "inside," as it were, duplicate Dennett might be thinking and perceiving in ways indistinguishable from original Dennett. But duplicate Dennett has never even met Susan, much less interacted with her in any way. How could he therefore have any thoughts that are genuinely about *her*, that very person, when he's had no genuine interaction with her?

But now consider the vat brain.

Such a brain has had no causal relations whatsoever with the external world, besides perhaps the wires and electrodes and the neuroscientist herself. You may be thinking about falafel, which you are able to do because falafel has genuinely (and so deliciously) causally affected your senses and your brain, but a vat brain even identical to yours has never enjoyed those causal relations and thus is incapable of having thoughts genuinely about falafel. Again, it may have qualitatively indistinguishable thoughts, thoughts "just like" falafel thoughts. It may even be able to enjoy those delicious falafel-y sensations. But in being causally isolated from the world, a vat brain cannot have thoughts genuinely *about* anything in the world.

This means that it cannot be having the same thoughts that you are having, after all, when you are thinking about the world. Thus, just which thoughts a being or a brain is having will depend on more than just the state of the brain in question.

Internalism, holding that thoughts are "in the head," is therefore false.

Time for Twin Earth

The science fiction keeps coming.

In 1975, Putnam introduced another little thought experiment that changed the direction of contemporary philosophy quite dramatically—not to mention that it turned common sense, with its internalist inclinations, on its proverbial head.

Imagine, Putnam asks us, another entire whole *planet* exactly like Earth, somewhere else in the cosmos. Same size, same shape; indeed, you can even imagine a molecule-for-molecule duplicate of our own happy home, including its inhabitants, and even imagine that it goes (or has gone) through an exactly identical sequence of events, in its history, as we have in ours. Thus, as you read these words, there is a molecular duplicate of yourself reading corresponding words in a duplicate copy of this book; and just as you were born of your parents, your duplicate was born of parents molecularly duplicate to yours, all the way back to the bubbling puddles of chemicals constituting Earth's earliest prelife days. Let's call that planet "Twin Earth," and note that Twin Earth is exactly like Earth in every way, including in the languages that the respective inhabitants all speak.

Except, that is, for one thing.

"One of the peculiarities of Twin Earth," Putnam (1975, 223) writes,

> is that the liquid called "water" [there] is not H_2O but a different liquid whose chemical formula is very long and complicated. I shall abbreviate this chemical formula simply as XYZ. I shall suppose that XYZ is indistinguishable from water at normal temperatures and pressures. In particular, it tastes like water and it quenches thirst like water. Also, I shall suppose that the oceans and lakes and seas of Twin Earth contain XYZ and not water, that it rains XYZ on Twin Earth and not water, etc.

So Twin Earth is just like Earth, to the point even that were you transported there in your sleep, you would never notice the difference; and we may even imagine that the difference between XYZ and H_2O is so slight that even our best chemists (and theirs!) couldn't tell the difference with any tests available to them. Nor could anyone (you or some scientist) discover the physical difference between you and your own personal twin, no matter what tests were performed.

What seems to follow from this little science fiction?

Only everything.

Inside the Twins' Heads

You have finished your falafel and are now feeling quite thirsty.

You come upon an appealing fountain. Your throat parched, you promptly think, "Mmm, water," and then indulge yourself liberally in its thirst-quenching glory. But while you are doing this, your twin on Twin Earth has just finished *his* falafel and is suffering from the same thirst, qualitatively speaking. He, too, is looking at an appealing fountain (a molecular duplicate of your fountain) and thinks to himself, "Mmm, water," before indulging himself liberally in *its* thirst-quenching glory, just as you are doing with your fountain.

Except that his thirst is being quenched by XYZ, while yours is being quenched by H_2O.

But that is all the difference in the worlds, so to speak.

What we shall grant is that you and your twin have molecularly duplicate brains (we may safely ignore the H_2O v. XYZ compositions of your respective brains). We shall grant that both you and your twin use the word "water" to express your thought. But what is different is this: on Earth, the word "water" refers to H_2O. On Twin Earth, "water" refers not to H_2O but to XYZ. But what that means is that your thought, expressed with the word "water," is about H_2O, while your twin's thought, though expressed with the same word, is about XYZ.

Yours and your twin's thoughts are about different things.

But, then, by our earlier discussion in "Thoughts and Aboutness," they count as different thoughts.

So two beings with identical brains (not to mention identical bodies, and on nearly identical planets!) are capable of thinking different thoughts and thus of being in distinct mental states.

Everything inside their heads is the same, in short, but their mental states are different. So thoughts, to adapt Putnam's memorable phrase, "just ain't in the head!" (227).

So much for internalism!

One More Time

The reasoning here admittedly moves a little swiftly. There is plenty more that could be said, much of which *ought* to be said, and quite a lot that actually has been said, by philosophers, in the almost four decades since Putnam introduced his strange idea. We'll just glance at a little of it as we go through it briefly once again.

Let's go back to that moment where you and your twin are both expressing thoughts with the words "Mmm, water." Let us ask again whether you and your twin are "thinking the same thought" in that moment. There is no question that many people will want to say yes. Given that everyone agrees on the qualitative similarity between your mental state and your twin's—they would feel the same "from the inside"—there are strong intuitions identifying the respective mental states. Given, too, that everyone agrees about the role that the brain plays in producing our mental processes, combined with the fact that you and your twin would surely count as being in the same brain state in this moment (again ignoring the H_2O v. XYZ difference), there is even further intuition supporting the internalist view that you share mental states. It is not for nothing, after all, that the internalist analysis (on which mental states are "in the head") was the dominant one in philosophy before Putnam and most surely is the commonsense one.

And yet we must also return to the idea that *thoughts are individuated by their contents*: that just which mental state you are in depends on just what the state is about. Thoughts about different objects are then, by definition, different thoughts. Given the difference in nature between H_2O and XYZ, it seems undeniable that these are different things, different molecules. It seems equally undeniable that your thought is ultimately about H_2O, while your twin's is about XYZ. You live on Earth, you have interacted with H_2O your entire life, and you have never been near XYZ; your twin lives in an XYZ world without ever having encountered H_2O. Nor does it seem to matter that H_2O and XYZ are indistinguishable to you and your chemist friends: while interesting wrinkles are established by this fact, it still seems to be true that H_2O is different from XYZ and that your thought is about the former while your twin's is about the latter, even though neither of you is in a position to know it.

And so we are back to the conclusion of *externalism*.

There is more to determining just which mental states you are in than what is merely "in the head," or in the brain. What's external—and, in particular, what your overall causal context is—also matters. And since you and your twin are in different external, causal contexts (you being around H_2O and he being around XYZ), then even with identical brains you count as differing in mental states.

So mental states, in short, just ain't in the head.

Primary Sources

Dennett, Daniel. 1987. *The Intentional Stance*. Cambridge, MA: MIT Press.

Putnam, Hilary. 1975. "The Meaning of 'Meaning.'" In *Language, Mind and Knowledge*, edited by Keith Gunderson (Minneapolis: University of Minnesota Press), reprinted in Hilary Putnam, *Mind, Language, and Reality: Philosophical Papers*, vol. 2 (Cambridge: Cambridge University Press, 1975). Page numbers refer to the reprinted version.

———. 1981. "Brains in a Vat." In *Reason, Truth, and History*. Cambridge: Cambridge University Press.

Recommended Secondary Sources

Lau, Joe, and Max Deutsch. 2010. "Externalism about Mental Content." In *Stanford Encyclopedia of Philosophy*, edited by Edward N. Zalta. http://plato.stanford.edu/archives/fall2010/entries/content-externalism/.

Pessin, Andrew, and Sanford Goldberg, eds. 1996. *The Twin Earth Chronicles: Twenty Years of Reflection on Hilary Putnam's "The Meaning of 'Meaning.'"* Armonk, NY: Sharpe.

17

David Lewis

THE INCREDULOUS STARE

STRANGE IDEA

There are other possible worlds—literally.

MAJOR PROPONENT

David Lewis (1941–2001)

BRIEF BIOGRAPHY

There is no possible world in which the work of American philosopher David Lewis would not be judged to be remarkable. Lewis did his undergraduate work at Swarthmore College and was particularly inspired to study philosophy during a year abroad at Oxford University. He received his PhD from Harvard, writing a dissertation that would become his first published book. After teaching at the University of California at Los Angeles, he moved to Princeton University in 1970, where he remained until his death. Along the way, he made major contributions to the philosophy of language, of mathematics, of science, of mind; to logic and decision theory; and to metaphysics and epistemology. His work has become essential reading in perhaps all of these fields and more. In addition to receiving a number of honorary doctorates, he was a fellow of the American Academy of Arts and Sciences, a corresponding fellow of the British Academy, and an honorary fellow of the Australian Academy of the Humanities.

Don't Blink

"I once complained," David Lewis writes in his famous book *On the Plurality of Worlds*, "that my [doctrine] met with many incredulous stares, but few argued objections" (133). If your doctrine makes even professional philosophers react with an incredulous stare, then you know it has to be pretty strange.

The thing about incredulous stares, though: they may be rhetorically quite devastating to your doctrine, but they do not amount to a rational objection. And so Lewis responded to them as a true proponent of uncommon sense, by making a long detailed *argument* for his strange idea, which we'll look at shortly.

But first, what is this stare-provoking doctrine? As usual, we'll need some background.

Modes of Truth

Propositions, it turns out, can be more than merely just "true" or "false." For truth itself comes in more than one kind or mode. To see this, consider two different true propositions:

(A) The New York Mets won the 1986 World Series against the Boston Red Sox.
(B) $2 + 2 = 4$

Both A and B are equally true, but there is an important difference between them. For while A is true, it didn't *have* to be; it *could have* been false; there are circumstances that could have obtained (although they didn't) in which A *would have* been false. (In this case, perhaps, had that crucial ground ball not gone through Red Sox first baseman Bill Buckner's legs, then Boston would have won that game and the series.) Philosophers mark this by referring to A as being not merely true but *contingently* true.

But B is not like this. B is not merely true but *has* to be true; it *could not have been* and *never could be* false; there are *no* circumstances that could obtain in which it *would* be false. B is not contingently but *necessarily* true.

So both A and B are true but in different ways or modes. The study of these modes is called *the philosophy of modality*.

What Modes of Truth Are There?

To elaborate now, the main modes of truth (the main *modal concepts*) are these: possibility, contingency, impossibility, and necessity. We apply these concepts primarily to propositions, although also sometimes (as we'll see) to objects.

We might say of a given proposition P, therefore, that it is *possibly true* (or *possibly false*), *impossibly true* (or *impossibly false*), or *necessarily true* (or *necessarily false*). We'll focus on the "true" versions to simplify our discussion.

To say that P is *possibly true* is to say that there are conditions under which it could or would be true. Every actually true proposition is also possibly true, since if P is actually true, then the conditions under which it *would* be true have obviously been met! Much to Bostonians' eternal regret, A is both actually true and possibly true.

But some propositions that are actually false may, at the same time, be "possibly true." Consider

(C) Bill Buckner was Boston's hero in the 1986 World Series.

Since it was his error that everyone blames for Boston's loss, C is most decidedly not true but rather false. But still it is *possibly true*: he *could have* been the hero; there are conditions that *could have* obtained under which he would have been (had he not missed that ball, had he hit some key home runs, etc.). So all actually true propositions, and at least some actually false ones, are possibly true.

While no proposition can be both actually true and actually false (that would be a contradiction), many propositions are both *possibly true* and *possibly false*. We just noted that A is both actually true and possibly true, but again, things could have occurred that would have made A false (even though they didn't): so A is also possibly false.

A proposition that is actually true but possibly false we call *contingently true*; similarly, a proposition that is actually false but possibly true we call *contingently false*.

In contrast, we have propositions such as B, which are actually true but *not* contingently true: these are therefore *necessarily true*.

Similarly, now, we have propositions such as

(D) Fred created a round square.

D is not merely false but *necessarily false*: since "round" and "square" are contradictory terms, a "round square" would be a contradictory object, and thus no one could possibly create one.

Who knew that truth (and falsity) could be so complicated?

Modal Concepts Applied to Objects

But it is not merely propositions whose modality we are concerned with. We also apply these modal concepts to objects and their properties.

Start, for example, with the existence of various objects. You may exist, but we may ask whether you exist necessarily or merely contingently. (Answer, almost certainly, alas: contingently.) Unicorns (we assume) do not exist, but is their existence nevertheless possible, or is their nonexistence necessary? (Answer: not clear!) Similarly round squares don't exist, but in what mode? (Answer: they necessarily do not exist; i.e., they are impossible.)

Turning to the properties of objects, now: you may have brown hair, but do you *necessarily* have brown hair? Or could you possibly have had blond hair, or red hair, or no hair at all? You may be cheerful in disposition, but could you have possibly been grumpy? You are a woman (say), but are you necessarily one, or could you have been a man? And you are (I presume) a human being, but could you have been a chimpanzee? Or a butterfly? Or a stone?

These are fascinating questions, and deciding how to answer them would take us into a whole world of wonderfully strange ideas. But, unfortunately, our space is too limited *here* to go *there*.

Instead, we must restrict ourselves to asking something more basic: not which things have their properties necessarily, contingently, and so on, but rather what, exactly, we even mean—what are we committed to believing—when we say of something that it has its properties in these ways.

What, in other words, are these modal concepts really all about?

One More Modal Concept—the Big One

It's this: the idea of a *possible world.*

A possible world is just the way that the world could go or could have gone. More precisely, it's the complete history of a way that the world could go or could have gone from beginning to end, or at least to the moment at which you are considering the issue.

So consider the actual world, the way that the world has actually so far gone, from God's creating of it out of nothing or from the Big Bang (whichever you believe), all the way through the thousands or billions of years of all history, right up to this moment. The actual world—with its (say) Big Bang, evolution of life on Earth, *Homo sapiens,* French Revolution, Mets' 1986 World Series victory, and highly celebrated publication of *Uncommon Sense*—is one possible world, since its being the way that things in fact have gone proves it is a way that things *could* go.

But there are other ways things could go or could have gone.

First, there are many ways that the actual world *could* go from here, from this moment forward. One involves the earth ending rather quickly: human beings with their nuclear weapons may soon make some choices resulting in a large *ka-boom!* Another involves humans making different choices resulting in the *ka-boom!* only much later down the road. Another involves our pushing off those self-destructive choices long enough that we do ourselves in by global warming first. Or maybe we could make other choices, still, whereby we linger on this earth all the way until the sun itself finally explodes, some several billion years hence, taking us and our theories of modality with it.

Each of these, among many others, is a possible way that things could go from here, and so the history of our cosmos from its beginning to each of these alternative ends constitutes a distinct possible world.

And then there are other possible worlds looking backward.

Things went the way they did to get us here, to this moment, but they could easily have gone otherwise.

Had that first spark generating life on Earth not occurred, then perhaps there would never have been any life on Earth. Or had any one of the countless accidents of evolution not occurred, then the history of living things would have gone differently. Or, for the Bible believers, had Abraham brought the knife upon Isaac a little more quickly (before God intervened), had Moses decided the burning bush was a hallucination and not a message from God—just imagine the different course of subsequent human history.

Or, closer to home, chronologically: take any event in history and just imagine how things would have been had the people making the key decisions made different decisions—had George Washington decided not to join the rebel army, had Abraham Lincoln decided not to emancipate the slaves, had the pediatrician who took care of baby Hitler failed to treat him for that otherwise fatal childhood disease, and so on.

Or less obviously significant events: had that butterfly not flapped its wings just so over there on that island in Japan . . . had you not been ten seconds late to the bus stop that morning . . . had the sperm that fertilized the egg in the conception of you been beaten out by the next sperm . . .

Had any *one* of these things been different then, possibly, *everything else* afterward would have been, too. Every one of these completed collections of events is a possible world, and there are as many possible worlds as there are combinations of branching points.

That's a lot of different possible worlds.

The existence of such a bounty would cause an insufferable headache for any philosopher trying to think about them, were it not at least for the small consolation that using the concept of possible worlds sometimes simplifies other things that we philosophers get headaches about.

How so?

Possible Worlds, Propositions, and Objects

We've applied modal concepts so far to propositions, objects, and properties. Talk of possible worlds as a whole helps unify all of these ideas.

For we may now say the following.

To say that a proposition is "necessarily true" is to say that it is true in every possible world, that is, in every possible way that things could go or have gone.

To say a proposition is "possibly true" is to say that there is at least one possible world in which it *is* true. To say that it is "contingently true" is to say it is actually true, that is, true in the actual world, but that there is also at least one other possible world in which it is false. And to say that a proposition is impossibly true or necessarily false is to say that it is false in every possible world.

Similarly with respect to the existence of objects.

To say that an object exists necessarily is to say it exists in every possible world. (Some believe that God is such a being.) An impossible object is one that exists in no possible world. A contingent object exists in some possible worlds but not in others.

And we may say the same with respect to objects and their properties.

If you have brown hair only contingently, then you have brown hair in some possible worlds (such as the actual one), but there are also possible worlds in which you do not have brown hair. If it's true that though you are a woman, you could have been a man, then though you are a woman in the actual world, there are possible worlds in which you are a man. And if it is (presumably) impossible for you to have been a daisy, then there are no possible worlds in which you are one.

So all our earlier talk about modal concepts applied to propositions, objects, and properties can now be reduced to talk about possible worlds. You might not realize it, but for a philosopher that is a productive day's work.

Only one question remains: what the heck, exactly, is a possible world?

There *Are* Possible Worlds?

We're almost at Lewis. His strange idea is his answer to that question.

But first consider how strange the notion of a possible world itself really is (if you haven't already noticed!).

In ordinary conversation, the word "possible" typically indicates not how things are but how they might otherwise be or have been. When you talk about all the possible siblings of yours (sort of) who could have existed (had the sperm that fertilized the egg that became *you* been outraced by any of its competitors), you mean, partly, that such siblings are not in fact real or actual, although they could have been. And so talk of possible worlds, similarly, should refer to things that *are* not (but merely could have been).

But now look at that expression: "There are possible worlds in which . . . " "There *are* . . . "

In ordinary conversation (again), the phrases "there is" and "there are" are assertions of the actual existence of things. "Houston, there is a problem" informs Houston that there actually exists something that may lead to the destruction of the spacecraft. "There are humongous locusts entering the palace!" was some lackey's way of informing the Pharaoh that there actually exist some humongous reasons to let the Israelites go from ancient Egypt.

But "possible worlds" are the sorts of things that don't actually exist. They're merely "possible," not actual, in the typical case. So what could it mean to say that *there are* such things? That there exist these things that don't actually exist?

It sounds more than a little contradictory. Rather like asserting that there is a married bachelor over there or a round square. You can say it, but it's not at all clear what it means; what's more, it couldn't possibly be true.

But while not much is lost, for us, when we grant that there couldn't actually exist married bachelors, we lose an awful lot if we conclude that there couldn't actually exist any other possible worlds.

We lose the ability to understand (for example) the difference between propositions that *happen* to be true and which *have* to be true. We lose the idea that things might have (or could have had) different properties from the ones they do have. We may even lose free will, for to act freely (as we saw in chapter 2) may well require that in addition to doing what we actually do, we could at the same time possibly do otherwise.

To save all this requires, then, that we somehow make sense of the mysterious claim that "there are" possible worlds.

The Scylla and Charybdis of Strange Ideas

Two major options present themselves.

When we say, "There are possible worlds," on the first, we are treating possible worlds as being components of (yes) the actual world. Only the actual world is real, so everything "there is" or "there are" must be members of it.

But we must still recognize *some* distinction between "how things are" in the actual world and "how things could be or could have been." We'll spare the details here, but the way to do that, on this option, is to treat possible worlds as abstract beings of a sort: beings that exist in the actual world but not in any concrete way, within space and time. That idea might sound familiar, for it invokes Plato's strange idea (about Forms) from chapter 1 and therefore inherits all that idea's strangeness and problems.

That's our Scylla.

We also have David Lewis's Charybdis.

Lewis wants to take "There are possible worlds" seriously: there are (or there exist) possible worlds in exactly the same sense in which there exists the actual world and the things in the actual world. After all, he notes, our actual world is itself one such possible world: it is one of the ways that things could go. So if there exist other possible worlds, they must be precisely the same kind of thing that our actual world is: a concrete collection of concrete objects.

So there is our actual world, and there are other possible worlds just like it in nature but not in details, for they are worlds in which things have gone differently than they have in our world. These worlds are just as real as our world and its components—as your body and this computer and the still depressed members of the 1986 Red Sox.

They're just not *here.*

And not *now.*

Incredulous Stare, Anyone?

Your eyebrows are probably starting to twitch.

"The world," Lewis writes at the start of his book,

> is a very inclusive thing. Every stick and every stone you have ever seen is part of it. And so are you and I. And so are the planet Earth, the solar system, the entire Milky Way, the remote galaxies. . . . There is nothing so far away from us as not to be part of our world. Anything at any distance at all is to be included. (1)

But it's not just inclusive with respect to space:

> Likewise the world is inclusive in time. No long-gone ancient Romans, no long-gone pterodactyls, no long-gone primordial clouds of plasma are too far in the past, nor are the dead dark stars too far in the future, to be part of this same world. . . . Nothing is so alien . . . as not to be part of our world, provided only that it does exist at some distance and direction from here, or at some time before or after or simultaneous with now. (1)

Here Lewis expresses beautifully the earlier idea that the world, the actual world, is the "complete" way that things have gone and will go, from beginning to end. But we're now also stressing that the world is, here, a concrete object, consisting of concrete objects, all of which exist with spatial and temporal relations to everything else in the world.

But now where are those other possible worlds, representing the ways that things could go or have gone, whose existence we affirm when we say, "There are possible worlds in which . . . "? "Are there" really such other worlds?

Lewis answers:

> I say there are. I advocate a thesis of plurality of worlds, or *modal realism*, which holds that our world is but one world among many. There are countless other worlds, other very inclusive things. . . . The worlds are something like remote planets; except that most of them are much bigger than mere planets, and they are not remote. Neither are they nearby. They are not at any spatial distance whatever from here. They are not far in the past or future, nor for that matter near; they are not at any temporal distance whatever from now. They are isolated: there are no spatiotemporal relations at all between things that belong to different worlds. (2)

So there *are* other possible worlds, large inclusive concrete objects like our own actual world—except that they are nowhere and never. Since they enjoy no spatiotemporal relations to anything in our world, you will not find them no matter how far you travel nor how long you travel, nor would you find them if you could somehow travel backward in time. They are entirely spatiotemporally "isolated" from one another.

But they are perfectly real, nonetheless, and it is to these other worlds that we are ultimately referring whenever we use the modal concepts that we have been discussing. As Lewis puts it,

> there are so many other worlds, in fact, that absolutely *every* way that a world could possibly be is a way that some world *is*. (2)

So when you say that you could have been a contender (even though thanks to your rotten luck in life you weren't), what you are saying, what you are referring to, *what makes what you say true* (assuming it is), is that there is some other possible world, spatially and temporally isolated from ours, in which you *are in fact* a contender.

You may never have realized that this is what you were referring to, although of course in some other possible world, you saw this coming a mile away. Too bad there is no possible world in which they could have clued you in here.

Why on Earth—*This* Earth—Should You
Believe in a Plurality of Worlds?

"Because," Lewis writes, "the hypothesis is serviceable, and that is a reason to think that it is true" (3).

But Lewis is too modest here.

The hypothesis isn't merely "serviceable" but is capable of doing a lot of work—philosophical work, to be sure, which isn't quite the same thing as, you know, physical labor, but important work nonetheless.

Fortunately for us, the details are beyond our scope, but Lewis summarizes it quite concisely. If you admit the plurality of worlds, then you can go very far toward clarifying and resolving numerous complicated issues in many parts of the philosophy of logic, of mind, of language, and of science, not to mention in the philosophy of modality and in metaphysics themselves. The long first chapter of his book is devoted to doing just that.

But that isn't all.

Lewis then spends the bulk of his book raising and answering philosophical objections to the theory. These range all over, including claims that the theory is contradictory, that it wreaks havoc on morality, and so on, but what all the objections share (as Lewis shows) is that they each rely on various premises that ultimately turn out to be false. As far as he can see, he argues, no strong unanswerable objections may be raised to the theory.

But *that* isn't all.

He also explores whether various alternative theories could get the same philosophical benefits he outlined in his first chapter without the cost of the impressive strangeness of his own theory. The answer, he naturally argues, is no.

So he shows the benefits of his theory, shows that they are available no other way, and then answers every philosophical objection to the theory.

That is why you should believe it.

The Only Unanswered Objection

That irritating stare . . .

The arguments have been ventured, the objections met.

But what do you do with an incredulous stare?

What generates that stare, of course, is that Lewis's modal realism conflicts strongly with common sense, as he immediately acknowledges. But it is precisely here, at the conflict between philosophical theory and common sense, that the battle must be joined.

"Common sense," Lewis points out, "has no absolute authority in philosophy" (134). Of course not, I would add: nothing has any authority in philosophy (much less "absolute authority") which is not ultimately grounded in argument.

"It's not that the folk know in their blood," Lewis continues, "what the highfalutin' philosophers may forget" (134). Indeed, sometimes, I would add, philosophers can get so carried away with arguments that they *do* forget the most basic things. Recall the story from the introduction about the ancient philosopher Thales who fell into a well while contemplating the heavens above him. Well, this story no doubt reflects some insight about even today's philosophers. But then again, remember, if you want to get at a true understanding of the world, who *do* you want to talk to, exactly?

"And it's not that common sense," Lewis adds, "speaks with the voice of some infallible faculty of 'intuition'" (134). Indeed, I would add that common sense is what we believe about things when we haven't given them much thought. So why, exactly, should we automatically privilege its positions over those of a philosophically defended theory that conflicts with it?

In fact, we have but one way to proceed. We may, and rightfully so, be reluctant to accept theories that

> fly in the face of common sense. But it's a matter of balance and judgement. Some common sense opinions are firmer than others, so the cost of denying common sense opinion differs from one case to the next. And the costs must be set against the gains. Sometimes common sense may properly be corrected, when the earned credence that is gained by [the philosophical theory] more than makes up for the inherited credence that is lost. (134)

And that is the answer that Lewis provides in his defense of modal realism: numerous arguments in favor of it, demonstrations of all the useful work it can do in addressing philosophical problems, and responses to all the explicitly articulated objections.

This may not eliminate the incredulous stares, of course.

But it does dictate what we nevertheless ought to believe, even if, in the end, what we ought to believe is rather incredible.

Primary Source

Lewis, David. 1986. *On the Plurality of Worlds*. Oxford: Basil Blackwell.

Recommended Secondary Sources

Nolan, Daniel. 2005. *David Lewis*. Montreal, Canada: McGill-Queen's University Press.
Weatherson, Brian. 2010. "David Lewis." In *Stanford Encyclopedia of Philosophy*, edited by Edward N. Zalta. http://plato.stanford.edu/archives/sum2010/entries/david-lewis/.

18

Thomas Nagel, David Chalmers

MIND AND MATTER, TOGETHER AGAIN AT LAST (SORT OF)!

STRANGE IDEA

Conscious experience is associated with every physical process, all the way down to the subatomic level: mind is everywhere matter is, even *down there*.

MAJOR PROPONENTS

Thomas Nagel (b. 1937), David Chalmers (b. 1966)

BRIEF BIOGRAPHIES

Thomas Nagel graduated from Cornell University in 1958 and received a PhD in philosophy from Harvard University in 1963. After teaching at the University of California at Berkeley and at Princeton University, in 1980 he moved to New York University, where he has served as professor of philosophy, professor of philosophy and law, Fiorello LaGuardia Professor of Law, and (since 2002) as University Professor. He has written extensively on many areas of philosophy, although ethics, political and legal theory, and their applicability to contemporary issues have always been among his central concerns.

Australian philosopher David Chalmers studied mathematics and computer science at the University of Adelaide and carried on to PhD work in cognitive science at Indiana University in the United States. He taught at the University of Santa Cruz before moving to the University of Arizona to become professor of philosophy and then, in 2002, director of the Center for Consciousness Studies. Since 2004, he has been professor of philosophy, director of the Centre for Consciousness, and an ARC Federation Fellow at the Australian National University. His 1996 book *The Conscious Mind* was an instant and influential classic, and in addition to having published many papers and edited several other books, he has compiled the largest annotated bibliography of the philosophy of mind and related fields.

Full Circle

That's where, with this chapter, we have come.

We began in chapter 1 with Plato and his theory of Forms. On that theory there was an important distinction (or "dualism") between the ordinary physical world and some sort of nonphysical "other" world. A half-dozen chapters (and two thousand years) later came Descartes's theory that nonhuman animals lack minds, a claim grounded in his own *mind-body dualism* (the view that the physical is fundamentally different from the mental). Over the subsequent several chapters (and centuries) arrived some of the ideas that philosophers have supported within the framework of that dualism, concerning how the two domains are constituted and how they causally interact (or don't). And now we return, in our final chapter, to close the gap between the two domains, to an idea as strange as dualism and also deeply opposed to it: *panpsychism*.

The term "panpsychism," perhaps originally coined by the sixteenth-century Italian philosopher Francesco Patrizi, derives from the Greek words *pan* (meaning *all*) and psyche (meaning *soul* or *mind*). The doctrine thus may be understood as the claim that "all is mind." Of course, there are different versions of the claim, depending on what you mean precisely by the words "all," "is," and "mind." One rather dramatic version was that endorsed by George Berkeley (as we saw in chapter 11), according to which there is no physical world at all and all that exists are minds and their mental states.

But less dramatic, if no less strange, versions are available.

More common (and more contemporary) versions tend not to deny the existence of the physical world. Rather, they claim that in addition to the physical world, there is *also* the mental world, and that world is *fundamental*, that is, neither identifiable with nor reducible to the physical but a part of reality in its own right. To distinguish this position from dualism, note that the panpsychist must then go further: she denies both that the mental and physical are distinct substances, and that the mental somehow "emerges" from the physical on some higher level of organization.

For, first, to think of them as distinct substances, or "things," is already to exclude them from each other: it is to admit that each is capable in principle of existing independent of the other.

But to think of the mental as "emerging" from the physical, second, is also to exclude them from each other: it is to allow that at least the physical is capable of existing without the mental, on lower orders of complexity. For the *emergentist* typically will hold that the mental only comes into being at certain minimum levels of physical complexity, such as when matter gets organized into things like human (or perhaps animal) brains. Matter below that level would therefore be free of mental properties.

The panpsychist rejects both of these. The mind is not a kind of substance or thing: rather, there are only mental properties, states, or events. And these latter do not merely "emerge" at some higher level of organization, but, rather—and here's the most dramatic part—the mental is associated with the physical *at every and all levels of reality*: at the macroscopic brain level and at the level of the brain's neurons, as well as at higher levels (such as societies, ecosystems, planetary systems?) and at lower (such as the submicroscopic level of physical particles or waves).

Where there's matter, there's mind, and vice versa. Not to be identified with each other, exactly, but yet not exactly apart.

Twenty-five centuries after Plato, they're together again, at last.

Okay That Was a Little Dramatic

All right, so a little history reveals that panpsychism (or versions thereof) has actually been around for a while.

For example Thales, the star-gazing philosopher who fell into the well in this book's introduction, possibly held that all elements of reality were self-moving beings with minds. But still, while this theme was echoed by other early philosophers, the competing doctrine of emergentism (which denies the existence of the mental on the lower levels) came to dominate for the next two thousand years. (It helped that Christian philosophers—themselves dominating Western philosophy from the fourth century onward—far preferred the dualist and emergentist views since they wanted to restrict minds or souls to human beings.)

This only began to change in the sixteenth century, and particularly with the rise of the "mechanical philosophy" associated with thinkers such as Galileo and Descartes (as we saw in chapter 7). But while the mechanical philosophy endorsed dualism against panpsychism, its development, ironically, helped lead to the rise of panpsychism. For no sooner had the mechanical philosophy gotten under way than various thinkers began discovering some difficult problems for dualism, some of which led to the strange ideas we discussed in chapters 8 through 11—as well as to the resurrection of panpsychism.

For one example, the great Dutch thinker Baruch Spinoza (1632–1677) came to argue that Descartes's dualism was simply untenable. Rather, he thought, both mind and matter were merely aspects or attributes of the one eternal and infinite substance that he identified with God. As he puts it,

a circle existing in [physical] Nature and the [mental] idea of the existing circle, which is also in God, is one and the same thing . . . explained through different attributes. So whether we conceive Nature under the attribute of [physical] extension, or under the attribute of [mental] thought . . . we shall find one and the same order. (*Ethics* II.7, Scholium, 118)

This position is often called *monism*: the doctrine that there exists only one fundamental kind of thing. But Spinoza's monism is quite different from two competing monisms that we have already encountered: *materialism* ("there is only one kind of thing and it is physical") and *idealism* ("there is only one kind of thing and it is mental"). For Spinoza's monism holds that there is only one kind of thing but that it may be thought of *as* physical or *as* mental, as circumstances require. If this monism is correct, then the various difficulties confronting dualism go away, and you end up holding that everything that exists either is or can adequately be thought of as being mental: a panpsychism, in other words.

And while we treated Leibniz (in chapter 10) as a dualist, we should note here that more subtle interpretations of his philosophy suggest that he was actually a kind of idealist, holding that the fundamental constituents of reality were primitive minds that he called *monads* and that went through complex sequences of perceptual states out of which allegedly physical bodies were to be "constructed." We won't pursue the details here, other than to note that this idealism, in holding that reality is fundamentally mental, is also a version of panpsychism.

Nor, indeed, is it inaccurate to say that the nineteenth century was a sociable time for panpsychists, since there were so many of them. Many of these thinkers are not well known outside professional circles, but among the bigger names are the famous pessimist Arthur Schopenhauer (1788–1860) and Harvard philosopher and psychologist William James (1842–1910). And of course, the twentieth century was home to all-around genius Alfred North Whitehead (1861–1947), whose 1929 panpsychism-affirming book *Process and Reality* was shockingly innovative, at least insofar as people were able to make any sense of it.

But then things got quiet.

There were major developments in physical science, what with relativity and quantum theory and their remarkable implications; philosophers got busy with other matters and dropped metaphysics almost altogether. There was plenty of philosophical work in the middle of the last century, perhaps, but not a lot of it directly concerning panpsychism, dualism, emergentism, and materialism.

Then entered Thomas Nagel.

"What Is It Like to Be a Bat?"

Good question and, sadly, one that only a bat seems properly situated to answer; sadly for us, anyway, who seek a complete scientific understanding of things. Sadly, too, for materialism in particular, or at least so Nagel argued in his influential 1974 paper whose provocative title was that very question.

For Nagel argued there that the nature of conscious experience, its *subjective* nature, forever precludes the possibility of a scientific understanding, an *objective* understanding, of the nature of consciousness. What that meant, among other things, is that no "reductive" account of the mind, of consciousness, would ever be possible: that is, no account that explained the mental in purely physical terms. Since subjective, conscious experience seems to be an undeniable component of reality, the mental seems inescapably distinct from the physical. Nagel offered, then, an important new argument for a mind-body dualism of the sort we've been discussing.

But then, he realized a few years later, we also have more.

A Four-Premise Argument for Panpsychism

By "panpsychism," Nagel writes in his 1979 article of *that* name, "I mean the view that the basic physical constituents of the universe have mental properties" (181). Moreover, he claims, panpsychism seems to follow "from a few simple premises, each of which is more plausible than its denial"—to which he then adds, in a line that expresses the spirit of our entire book beautifully, "though not perhaps more plausible than the denial of panpsychism."

Indeed, the reasoning seems to be very persuasive even when the conclusion is almost impossible to believe: a perfect example of some uncommon sense!

So let's have a quick look at the premises, followed by some discussion of each.

Premise 1: Material Composition

All living organisms, including us, are complex material systems composed of material particles combined in special ways.

Premise 2: Nonreductionism

Ordinary mental states or processes (like thoughts, feelings, and the subjective quality of conscious experiences) are not physical properties, nor are they logically entailed by any physical properties. Or as we put it a moment ago, the mental cannot be "reduced" to the physical.

Premise 3: Realism

Mental states or processes are perfectly real, genuine properties of the organism, despite their nonreducibility to the physical.

Premise 4: Nonemergence

There are no truly emergent properties of complex systems. By an "emergent property," Nagel means a property that the system has on some higher level of organization but not on its lower levels. More precisely, a property is emergent if it neither exists on the lower level nor can be derived from the properties that do exist on the lower level. The claim here is, of course, that mental states or properties are no more emergent than any other.

But now an argument is only as persuasive as its premises. Before we spell out just how these premises lead to panpsychism, let's first examine them a little more carefully.

Why Should Anyone Believe These Premises?

Premise 1, that living organisms are complex material systems, is the least controversial. Few contemporary thinkers deny it, so we shall let it stand without further defense.

Premise 2, that mental states are nonreducible to physical, needs more defense. In fact, Nagel's earlier essay, the one about bats, constitutes the bulk of his own defense of this premise. To elaborate just a bit further on it, then, he argues there that no matter how much we come to know about the objective physical brain processes of bats, including how they navigate and hunt by means of sonar, we shall never have any grasp on just *what it's like*, what it *feels like*, to be a bat, to subjectively experience the world by means of their sonar, with their particular perceptual and conceptual apparatus. You may feel that you can get a sense of it, perhaps by imagining yourself hanging upside down in a cave, soaring through the dark, and chomping on some meaty insects, but when you imagine all that, you are in fact imagining what it would be like for *you* to *act* like a bat—not what it is like *for the bat* to *be* a bat. In being intrinsically subjective, in depending on the point of view of the conscious subject itself, these mental properties, the *what it's like*, are incapable of being explained or understood in purely objective terms, that is, in terms that don't depend on any being's point of view.

So subjective mental states cannot be identified with or reduced to any objective physical properties: thus, the nonreductionism of premise 2.

What about premise 3, that mental states are real? Well, some talented contemporary philosophers actually do deny this, and in a longer version of this book, there would be chapters devoted to the strange ideas of great thinkers such as Paul Churchland and Daniel Dennett. But since they are nearly alone in their denial and since most other people have no beef with premise 3, I shall say no more about it.

Finally, premise 4, that there are no truly "emergent" properties. That's all well and good, except for the fact that there really do seem to be some emergent properties. Take the property of being liquid. "Being liquid" clearly applies only to some reasonably large collections of molecules; it refers, ultimately, to the members of this collection not being too tightly stuck together (where they would constitute a solid) nor being too loosely attached (where they would constitute a gas). But that property of being a liquid does not apply to the individual molecules themselves: a single molecule of H_2O is not, cannot be, a liquid, or a solid, or a gas. But that is just to say that liquidity only applies on a higher level of organization, on the level of the collection, and thus seems to be an emergent property.

And indeed it is, at least by the first clause of our definition, as it "does not exist on the lower level." But there was a second clause: an emergent property must also *not* be derivable from lower-level properties. And while Nagel himself makes a rather sophisticated argument based on causality here, we can make a simpler, more intuitive one. Sure, "liquidity" does not apply to individual molecules, but it is fairly straightforward how its application to the collection of molecules does derive from lower-level properties: as noted, a collection is a liquid if the forces between its constituent molecules have just the right strength. But the "forces between molecules" just are lower-level properties, pertaining to the molecules. And so liquidity is not after all an emergent property.

Similar considerations apply to other candidates for emergent properties, particularly if we add Nagel's further comments about causality. And so we reach the conclusion that there are no emergent properties after all. If so, then mental properties cannot be emergent properties of material living organisms.

Now Why Should Anyone Believe in Panpsychism?

Because you should accept the preceding premises, as just suggested, and then because panpsychism follows from those premises.

For suppose we have a physical being that is also possessed of mental properties, such as various mental states (premise 1). These mental properties can neither be identified with nor derived from the physical properties of the organism (premise 2). Nevertheless, they are perfectly real (premise 3). And since there are no emergent properties (premise 4), they cannot just pop into existence on the level of the organism as a whole or its brain: they must in fact be present on all lower levels, such as the level of the molecules or particles of which the organism is composed.

But to say that mental properties are present at every level is to endorse panpsychism.

As simple as that.

Enter David Chalmers

Nagel's bat arguments for nonreductionism inspired numerous other philosophers to develop various lines of argument supporting the autonomy of the mental, as it were, from the physical. But the panpsychism conclusion rested not merely on the nonreductionism of premise 2 but also on the nonemergentism of premise 4, and that one did not quite win as many converts.

But then in 1996 David Chalmers published *The Conscious Mind: In Search of a Fundamental Theory.*

This book is, simply, amazing. It is rich, and thick, and thorough, addressing in detail just about every issue relevant to understanding the nature of conscious experience and its relationship to the physical world. This would include a particularly entertaining analysis of *zombies,* by which philosophers understand not the standard brain-eating monsters of horror stories (or at least not *just* these) but rather beings who might be very much like us who don't eat brains in all their behavior except that they completely lack consciousness "on the inside." You'd be surprised at how much you can learn about your conception of consciousness when you reflect on the idea of these zombies.

Along the way, Chalmers provides his own detailed and original defense of Nagel's premise 2 nonreductionism. Indeed, you cannot meaningfully insist that "the mind reduces to the brain" these days without first engaging with Chalmers's powerful arguments to the contrary. But, then, rather than just settle for some kind of mind-body dualism, as many other nonreductionists do, Chalmers expresses some sympathy for Nagel's premise 4, the "nonemergence" of the mental from the physical.

And although for some technical reasons, he himself does not quite endorse panpsychism, there's no question that his rejection of "emergence" has given panpsychism another extremely strong push.

"What Is It Like to Be a Thermostat?"

If you're going to open your mind to panpsychism, you might as well go all the way.

Conscious experience, the paradigm mental state or property, is going to be found everywhere: not just in complicated brains but even in simple mechanical systems such as thermostats. In fact, Chalmers suggests, it should ultimately be found wherever there is causation and, therefore, information— and that, pretty much, is everywhere.

Of course, it probably wouldn't be very *interesting* to be a thermostat. "The information processing," Chalmers writes, "is so simple that we should expect the corresponding [conscious] states to be equally simple" (293). Nor need we imagine that they have much in the way of a mental life, broadly construed. "A thermostat will not be *self*-conscious," Chalmers continues; "it will not be in the least intelligent; and I would not claim that a thermostat can *think*" (295). Indeed, it couldn't be "self-conscious" because it almost certainly would lack a "self": there would be nothing inside the thermostat "to serve as a subject" of its experiences. Nor, of course, reminding ourselves of Nagel, should we imagine that we would ever obtain a good grasp on just what it's like *be* a thermostat, any more than we could on what it's like to be a bat.

Nevertheless, there may well be *something* that it's like, and perhaps there must be if, in fact, mentality, consciousness, goes all the way down.

You might want to object to this idea because there just doesn't seem to be any room in a thermostat for consciousness: there's no place for it to be found within. But that, Chalmers replies, ignores the force of the nonreductionism, which ensures that "one will never find consciousness within a [physical] system on close examination" (296) precisely because consciousness is not itself physical. We don't find it "in the brain" in any literal sense either, after all!

You might object that we understand how thermostats work well enough to see that they simply do operate without consciousness, that we build them ourselves without putting any consciousness in. But again, Chalmers replies, there is no real difference here with respect to brains. Although we do not understand very completely how brains work, at this early stage of neuroscience, it is only that *lack* of understanding that allows the illusion that somehow consciousness derives from brain processes: the arguments for nonreductionism (such as Nagel's) are general in nature and suggest that no matter what objective, physical processes are eventually discovered in the brain, they could not explain the existence of subjective consciousness. Furthermore, there's no reason to doubt that scientists will one day be able to build brains, one way or the other. And when they do, we have full reason to expect that these functioning brains will possess consciousness despite the fact that we didn't explicitly "put it in" ourselves. But then why should we insist that thermostats lack experience merely because we didn't insert it when building them?

And then, finally, there is one more reason to reject the emergence of the mental from the physical—that emergence that would perhaps limit consciousness only to more complex physical systems (such as our brains) and correspondingly rule it out on lower levels.

The "Wink Out" Argument against Emergence

If you insist that consciousness "emerges" at a certain level of organization, the question will be what level precisely that is. Or put differently, you will be committed to holding that consciousness "winks out" at some lower level when, in fact, it is very difficult to imagine what that level precisely is.

For consider, Chalmers suggests, "what might happen to experience as we move down the scale of complexity" (294). Yes, humans have consciousness; easy enough. "Moving to less complex systems, there does not seem much reason to doubt that dogs are conscious, or even that mice are" (294) (Descartes's insistence to the contrary, from chapter 7, notwithstanding). Mice, anyway, "perceive their environment via patterns of information flow not unlike those in our own brains" (294), Chalmers continues, so the natural hypothesis is that they have a corresponding conscious experience of their environments, as we do.

Similar considerations then apply as we move down the scale "through lizards and fish to slugs" (294). There "does not seem to be much reason to suppose that [experience] should wink out while a reasonably complex perceptual psychology persists" (294), as it does in these animals. "If it does [wink out],"

> then either there is a radical discontinuity from complex experiences to none at all, or somewhere along the line [experience] begins to fall out of synchrony with perception. . . . The first hypothesis seems unlikely, and the second suggests that the intermediate systems would have inner lives strangely dissociated from their cognitive [perceptual] capacities. (294)

The alternative is at least as plausible: it may be less interesting to be a fish than to be a human, but still it seems that there is at least *something* there. But then,

> as we move along the scale from fish and slugs through simple neural networks all the way to thermostats, where should consciousness wink out? (295)

Wherever there is perceptual discrimination, on the higher levels, there is consciousness, but perceptual discrimination is merely a form of information processing, and that goes on at every level, all the way down to thermostats. And when we recognize that information processing is itself a matter of causal processes, and that these also go on at every level even below thermostats (including subatomic particles), we should also grant that conscious experience is to be found on those levels as well.

Again, once you strip away some of the more complex features of minds (the self-consciousness, the intelligence, the "thinking"), this conclusion might not perhaps seem so objectionable. It's not that an electron "is a mind" or "thinks": it's that some mode of conscious experience, extremely primitive no doubt, one that we are not capable of grasping any more than we can grasp that of bats, exists on all lower levels of reality.

Indeed, you must believe this if our own mental properties are real, are nonreducible to physical properties, and cannot suddenly emerge, or *wink in,* on the level of our brains.

Now go contemplate that—you, or your brain, or maybe just the molecules constituting the big toe on your left foot.

It's all good.

Primary Sources

Chalmers, David. 1996. *The Conscious Mind: In Search of a Fundamental Theory.* Oxford: Oxford University Press.

Nagel, Thomas. 1974. "What Is It Like to Be a Bat?" *Philosophical Review* 83, reprinted in Thomas Nagel, *Mortal Questions* (Cambridge: Cambridge University Press, 1979).

———. 1979. "Panpsychism." In *Mortal Questions* (Cambridge: Cambridge University Press).

Parkinson, G. H. R., ed., trans. 2000. *Spinoza: Ethics.* Oxford: Oxford University Press.

Recommended Secondary Sources

Seager, William, and Sean Allen-Hermanson. 2010. "Panpsychism." In *Stanford Encyclopedia of Philosophy*, edited by Edward N. Zalta. http://plato.stanford.edu/archives/fall2010/entries/panpsychism/.

Van Gulick, Robert. 2011. "Consciousness." In *Stanford Encyclopedia of Philosophy*, edited by Edward N. Zalta. http://plato.stanford.edu/archives/sum2011/entries/consciousness/.

Index

About the Author

Andrew Pessin is professor of philosophy at Connecticut College, with degrees from Yale and Columbia. He has spent two decades teaching liberal arts undergrads (at Columbia University, the College of William and Mary, Kenyon College, Wesleyan University, and Connecticut College) and has recorded an audio philosophy course, "The Philosophy of Mind," with The Modern Scholar. He has published many academic articles, two academic books, and two philosophy books aimed at a general audience (*The God Question: What Famous Thinkers from Plato to Dawkins Have Said about the Divine* and *The 60-Second Philosopher: Expand Your Mind on a Minute or so a Day!*), and is also known for his appearances as "The Genius" on the *Late Show with David Letterman*. Most recently, he has been putting the finishing touches on his first novel. You may find him on the web at www.andrewpessin.com.